When Equality Ends

When Equality Ends

Stories About Race and Resistance

Richard Delgado

Westview Press
A Member of the Perseus Books Group

Copyright © 1999 by Westview Press, A Member of the Perseus Books Group

Published in 1999 in the United States of America by Westview Press, 5500 Central Avenue, Boulder, Colorado 80301-2877, and in the United Kingdom by Westview Press, 12 Hid's Copse Road, Cumnor Hill, Oxford OX2 9JJ

Library of Congress Cataloging-in-Publication Data
Delgado, Richard.
    When equality ends : stories about race and resistance / Richard
Delgado.
        p.   cm.
    Includes bibliographical references.
    ISBN 0-8133-3578-7
    1. Afro-Americans—Civil rights.   2. Civil rights—United States.
    3. United States—Race relations.   4. Racism.   5. Afro-Americans—
    Legal status, laws, etc.   6. Race discrimination—United States.
    I. Title.
E185.615.D453   1999
305.8'00973—dc21   98-51659
                                                                                     CIP

The paper used in this publication meets the requirements of the American National Standard for Permanence of Paper for Printed Library Materials Z39.48-1984.

10   9   8   7   6   5   4   3   2   1

The power of a glance has been so abused in love stories, that it has come to be disbelieved in. Few people dare now to say that two beings have fallen in love because they have looked at each other. Yet, it is in this way that love begins, and in this way only. The rest is only the rest, and comes afterwards. Nothing is more real than these great shocks which two souls give each other in exchanging this spark.

—*Victor Hugo*, **Les Miserables**

"I think, Zorba—but I may be wrong—that there are three kinds of men: those who make it their aim, as they say, to live their lives, eat, drink, make love, grow rich and famous; then come those who make it their aim not to live their own lives but to concern themselves with the lives of all men—they feel that all men are one and they try to enlighten them, to love them as much as they can and do good to them; finally, there are those who aim at living the life of the entire universe—everything, men, animals, trees, stars, we are all one, we are all one substance involved in the same terrible struggle. . . ."

Zorba scratched his head.

"I've got a thick skull, boss, I just don't grasp these things easily. . . . Ah, if only you could dance all that you've just said, then I'd understand."

—*Nikos Kazantzakis*, **Zorba the Greek**

Contents

Acknowledgments

Thanks to Jean Stefancic and Niko Pfund for their continuing and steadfast support of my work. Ida Bostian and Gabriel Carter provided exceptional editorial advice and counsel. Diana Stahl, Cynthia Carter, Linda Spiegler, and Kay Wilkie prepared this manuscript with care and precision. This work was carried out, in part, with the assistance of the University of Colorado IMPART program and law school research funds.

I am grateful to the following journals for permission to adapt portions of essays that appeared in their pages: *Stanford Law Review*, for Chapter 1, "Rodrigo's Book Bag: Recent Conservative Thought and the End of Equality" (50 Stan. L. Rev. 1929 [1998]); *Northwestern Law Review*, for Chapter 2, "Rodrigo's Road Map: Is the Marketplace Theory for Eradicating Discrimination a Blind Alley?" (93 NWn L. Rev. 215 [1998]); *Georgetown Law Journal*, for Chapter 3, "What's Wrong with Neoliberalism: The Problem of the Shanty" (85 Geo. L.J. 667 [1997]); *Texas Law Review*, for Chapter 5, "Latinos and the Black-White Binary" (75 Tex. L. Rev. 1181 [1997]); *Minnesota Law Review*, for Chapter 6, "Conflict as Pathology: What's Wrong with Alternative Dispute Resolution" (81 Minn. L. Rev. 1391 [1997]); *Georgetown Law Journal*, for Chapter 7, "Rodrigo's Book of Manners: How to Conduct a Conversation on Race" (86 Geo. L.J. 1051 [1998]); and *Michigan Law Review*, for Chapter 9, "The Problem with Lawyers" (95 Mich. L. Rev. 1105 [1997]).

Richard Delgado

Introduction

Who is Rodrigo, and where does he come from? What about his narrator and straight man, the Professor? And what is a law professor doing writing fiction, anyway?

In many respects, the curious reader will find answers in the dialogs themselves. Readers of two previous volumes will recall that Rodrigo, my exuberant and talented alter ego, is both young and black. The son of an African American serviceman and an Italian mother, Rodrigo was born in the States but raised in Italy when his father, Lorenzo, was assigned to a U.S. outpost there. Rodrigo graduates from the base high school, then attends Italian universities and law school on government scholarships, graduating second in his class. When the series opens (with *The Rodrigo Chronicles*, 1995), the young man has returned to the United States at the suggestion of his half-sister, well known civil rights lawyer Geneva Crenshaw, to meet with "the Professor" for career advice: The young man wants to return to the United States, obtain a graduate law degree, and enter teaching.

Despite their age difference, the two become close friends, discussing affirmative action, the decline of Western culture, relations between men and women of color, black crime, and many other subjects in the years ahead. The reader meets Rodrigo's friend, Lazlo Kowalsky, and his wife and soulmate, Giannina, a playwright. He or she listens in as the two discuss inconsequential things like food and coffee, as well as quite consequential things like race and the government's role in fighting poverty. The reader learns how two typical intellectuals of color talk, what they talk about, and a bit about critical race theory (with as little jargon as possible). Even though the Professor, who is elderly and eminent, becomes to some extent Rodrigo's mentor, their relationship is not at all one-way. As it turns out, the Professor, a grizzled veteran of many civil rights struggles, needs Rodrigo's impetuous energy as much as Rodrigo needs his caution and counsel.

As this volume opens, Rodrigo has graduated from his LL.M. (master of law) program and entered upon a career as law professor at a school located in a neighboring state. The Professor, who had an unexpected brush with the immigration authorities at the end of the second volume (*The Coming Race War? And Other Apocalyptic Tales of America After Affirmative Action and Welfare,* 1996), is living in semiretirement in Mexico, tending his garden, adding to his art collection, giving an occasional address, and pondering publishing his memoirs. Now on a more equal plane, the two meet at conferences, airports, and at Rodrigo's law school during the Professor's return trips to the States, discussing hate speech, the conservative attack on affirmative action and civil rights, the plight of shantytown residents, and human reproduction and cloning. Rodrigo, who is of mixed race—his mother is Latin, while his father's family immigrated to the States via the Caribbean and speak perfect Spanish—discusses the situation of Latinos and their uneasy alliance with blacks in the search for civil rights. Running through all these chapters is the pair's sense that the country is approaching a crisis in race relations and that blacks, browns, and progressive whites must seriously consider the possibility of a strategy of resistance.

The events of this book, like those of the two preceding ones, form an integrated whole with characters, an unfolding plot, and intellectual discussions that build upon previous ones. Thus, the best way to read it is sequentially. Nevertheless, the reader interested only in certain subjects, or short on time, may wish to read certain chapters first. The reader interested in racial politics and the fortunes of nonwhite people should see Chapters 4, 7, and 10. One interested in understanding the recent right-wing surge and its impact on communities of color should not miss Chapters 1, 2, and 7. Readers interested in lawyers and legal thought should focus on Chapters 6, 8, and 9; if interested in practical, what-to-do prescriptions, see Chapters 6 and 10. The middle-aged reader, who may be just as interested in the Professor as in his youthful friend Rodrigo, should not miss Chapters 8 and 10. An example of narrative analysis or legal storytelling, the book combines stories and hard-edged, sometimes demanding social analysis. Readers intrigued by this form of writing, or by critical race theory itself, will have no difficulty finding more. Books by Derrick Bell, Patricia Williams, and the two predecessor volumes in this series would be good starts.

I hope the reader finds Rodrigo and his friends as engaging as I did in creating them. Rodrigo came into my life at a time when I was, personally, in transition, just as law—indeed, Western culture—are in transition today. As soon as I created him (first obtaining Derrick Bell's permission to give him a family tree that overlaps with Geneva's), I knew he would be foreign-raised (so as to see the United States with new eyes), multiracial (so as to take an interest in the fortunes of Latinos and other nonblack minority groups), young, and brilliant—like many students I have taught over the years. Writing in a fever, and aided by talented editors at various major law reviews, I created the series of chronicles that formed the first two books. They enjoyed a gratifying degree of success, yet I was not satisfied. This third, and probably final, volume attacks the hard question that every speaker or commentator on racial politics faces in the wake of a speech, op-ed column, or book. I mean, of course, the "so what?" or "what should we do?" problem.

Most academic writers and journalists content themselves with critique, with analysis of a racial or other issue, leaving it to others to work out the implications. As the reader will see, Rodrigo, now approaching vigorous midlife, will not rest content with that. As the book opens, imagine that the narrator, the aging but still alert Professor, has just gotten off a plane from Mexico. On leave from his institution, he has been contemplating permanent retirement. But the lure of a grandchild has brought him back to the States, to Rodrigo and Giannina's city, in fact. He hops a cab at the airport, and, a few minutes later. . .

When Equality Ends

1

Rodrigo's Book Bag

Recent Conservative Thought and the End of Equality

"Professor! You're back!" Rodrigo leaped to his feet, extended his lanky frame, and shook my hand fervently. "We heard you might be coming. What good news! Sit down. Did the authorities give you any trouble?"

"Not at all," I replied, setting down my travel bag and plopping down on one of the few uncluttered spots on my young friend's couch. "I breezed right across. They didn't even make me open my suitcase. I gather you didn't get my letter?"

"No, but Laz got a card and mentioned it to Giannina. So we knew you might be coming."

"You'll probably get it next week. The mails are glacially slow. It's one of the few things that take a little getting used to about my new place. I'm glad you're in town."

"It's been a while," Rodrigo said. "How's the grandchild?"

"She and her mother are both fine. They named the little one Gianna, after your Giannina, I think. I'll be seeing them later this evening, but thought I'd drop in on you since it's on the way."

"We were hoping the lure of grandchildren might bring you back. How long are you staying?"

"My visa's good for six months, but I won't stay that long. I'm helping my son-in-law lay tile for their new patio so my daughter and the baby can go out there when the weather's good. I hope this isn't a bad time. I tried calling from the airport, but your number was busy."

"Not at all. Giannina's at a wedding rehearsal, but I know she's dying to see you. Can you join us for dinner?"

"I'm not expected at my daughter's place until nine," I said, looking at my watch. "When will Giannina be free?"

"In about twenty minutes. We agreed to meet at a little place around the corner. If you've got time, I'd love to tell you about an incident that happened here just last week."

"What happened?" I asked, picking up my bag.

Rodrigo motioned me to follow him and locked his office door. As we rode the elevator down to ground level, he began: "It's really quite appalling. Someone defaced the lockers of some students of color, including my own research assistant's.[1] I know this kind of thing happens all the time, but what's unusual is that this time the perpetrators got caught. One of them had a qualm of conscience after a town meeting called by the dean. He came forward and named his three confederates."

"Sounds like it had a happy ending," I said as we stepped out onto the busy sidewalk in front of Rodrigo's law school. "Was any punishment imposed?"

"The hearing's next week. Three of them confessed and said they're sorry. I doubt they'll get more than a reprimand and some sort of community service. But the fourth—an undergraduate—is an interesting case. He refused to apologize, saying that he stands by what he wrote. He's citing *The Bell Curve* and Robert Bork's new book. Can I help you with that bag?"

I gestured that I was okay. "Now I've heard everything," I said. "A defense of truth! This new crop of conservatives is getting brazen. Even moderates like Dinesh D'Souza brag that it's now acceptable to say things—about the genetic inferiority of blacks, for example—that were unthinkable a few years ago."[2]

"This is the place," Rodrigo said, stopping to scan a menu posted on the window. "I hope you like Ethiopian."

"Sounds fine to me," I said. "Do they provide forks and knives, or will we be eating with our hands?"

"You have your choice," Rodrigo replied, peering through the glass. "And, it looks uncrowded."

We stepped inside. "Two for dinner?" The waiter asked.

"Three," Rodrigo replied. "One will be joining us soon."

Minutes later we were seated in a comfortable side booth in the homey restaurant. "I'll keep an eye out for Giannina," I said, indicating I could see the door. "And so, what do you think will happen to your unrepentant defacer?"

"It's anyone's guess," Rodrigo replied. "He's being represented by one of those conservative legal foundations.[3] They plan to make a test case out of it, arguing that if the student had written 'Malcolm Lives' or 'Workers of the World, Unite,' nothing would have happened. And they're prepared to argue that what the four did write on the lockers— 'Special Admit' and 'One Standard Deviation'—either was true or fell within the range of fair comment."[4]

"What do you know about the unrepentant one?"

"He's a writer for the campus conservative paper that just started up last year.[5] They've been publishing a series of exposés on the black professors at my university. It's been creating quite a stir. Now it looks like it's the law school's turn."

"I'm sorry to hear that," I sympathized.

"As bad as the whole incident has been, it's gotten me thinking about equality," Rodrigo said. "I've been reading those two books the defacer cited and have just picked up D'Souza's latest." Rodrigo pulled a thick red and black book from his book bag.

"Oh—*The End of Racism*," I said.[6] "I'm almost done with that one myself. The other two I've read. Bork, as you know, offers his usual dyspeptic assessment of multiculturalism, affirmative action, and pop culture, all of which he thinks herald the decline of civilization and the West.[7] In his view, our only hope is to revitalize the culture and ideas that made Europe and the West great—competition, liberty, and respect for the classics. The West has little to learn from other cultures, especially African ones, which he seems to believe have produced no great music, science, or technology—little except a good recipe or two," I concluded, wryly indicating the menu, which both of us had been scanning with interest.

"It's frightening to think he could have been appointed to the Supreme Court. He takes every cultural difference as an indication of inferiority"— Rodrigo gestured at the diners next to us who were eating with their hands—"ignoring that practices such as sitting on the floor, eating like that, or praying five times a day may be fully adaptive within some other society and that our versions are not necessarily better merely because they work for us."

"And you've been reading the Murray-Herrnstein book, as well?"[8] I coaxed.

"Re-reading it, actually," Rodrigo replied. "Now that the undergraduate defacer has made an issue of it, I thought I'd better have another look."

"It's a little subtler than Bork's," I offered. "But no less disparaging of other cultures."

"Indeed," Rodrigo said, raising a hand to let the waiter know we were ready to order. "Beginning with the premise that IQ is the prime determinant of success in a competitive society like ours, Herrnstein and Murray reason that the gap in resources, education, jobs, and lifestyle between the bright and the less bright will only widen as the job market changes. With elimination of many blue-collar jobs and the advent of an economy based on technology and information, the haves and the have-nots will move farther and farther apart. Since race and IQ are linked, according to Herrnstein and Murray, we are doomed to live in a society increasingly split along racial lines.[9] In their last chapter, they predict that America will soon have a seething, crime-ridden underclass, mostly of color, unable to find meaningful work; they speculate that we may have to wall off the inner city in what they call a 'high-tech and more lavish version of the Indian reservation.'"[10]

"Unbelievable," I replied. "It reminds me of Peter Brimelow's suggestion that we cordon off the entire Mexican border.·[11] Oh, here's our waiter."

Rodrigo ordered a savory-sounding lamb dish for himself and kabobs for Giannina. After some deliberation, I ordered my usual vegetable curry ("Doctor's orders—I'm supposed to cut down on meat"), and the waiter departed.

"And so, you're also reading D'Souza," I continued. "What do you make of him?"

"I'm nearly finished," Rodrigo replied. "Like Bork, he argues for a color-blind society, but with a twist. Reasoning that diversity, affirmative action, and multiculturalism are all forms of racism, he urges his readers to refrain from enshrining difference in government programs of any sort. Also like Bork, he believes other societies have little to offer the West. The best way to integrate nonwhite groups into society is to encourage them to give up attachment to 'inferior cultures' and fully embrace the Western version as earlier immigrant groups have done."[12]

"That also reminds me of Brimelow," I said. "Maybe they were members of the same study group."

Rodrigo laughed. "It *is* a little like him, although D'Souza focuses mainly on American blacks, not on immigrants from Mexico and Latin America. And he differs from Brimelow and the others in that he outlines the case against racism toward blacks—albeit only as a way of challenging preferences in any form. In the early part of his book, where he reviews the history of racism, he expounds some highly dubious premises of his own—such as that African society was backward and savage,[13] and that the slave trade may have done blacks a favor by forcibly bringing them here.[14] He's generally careful not to impute biological inferiority to

African Americans and other minority groups. In that sense, he's a little kinder than the others. But he leaves no doubt that he considers black culture inferior to the European kind and that programs that ignore this inferiority simply perpetuate it in a new kind of racism."[15]

"Oh, there she is!" I said, half-standing and waving to the dark-haired young woman who had entered the restaurant and was looking around. "Giannina—over here."

"Perfect timing," Rodrigo said, giving his wife a warm hug. "I was worried we had ordered too early. How was the rehearsal?"

"Fine. They liked my poem," Giannina replied. Then, giving me a warm smile and a hug, "Welcome back. We heard you were coming. How's the family?"

"All fine. I'll be seeing them later. I understand you're in law school now."

"I am. Not in Rodrigo's, but in the one across town. What have you two been talking about?"

"The controversy at his school. And also about three books he's been reading, all by conservative authors."

"Oh, Bork, Herrnstein, and, what's the other one?"

"D'Souza," I responded. "Have you read it?"

"No, he's been hogging it ever since we got it last week. He says he needs to read it before the hearing."

"I'm nearly finished," Rodrigo said, guiltily. "I promise I'll let you have it by this weekend. Brimelow, too, if you want it."

"Thanks, but I've already read him, and once was enough. Although hailed by conservatives when they first came out, all four books have proved controversial.[16] I kept thinking, 'Wait a minute,' after practically every sentence. They're tough going for someone of my persuasion. Mmmm—are those for us?" Giannina asked, as the waiter put a series of savory-smelling dishes before us. "Lamb kabobs, my favorite!" Rodrigo smiled.

After a few minutes in which we ate in silence, Rodrigo looked up. "This whole business—the incident at the law school and the flurry of conservative books—has got me thinking about the role of equality in our society."

"So you said. I, for one, am all ears."

"Me, too," said Giannina. "But before you start, I hope you don't mind ushering tomorrow. One of the wedding party came down with the flu."

Rodrigo took a big draught of his tea, commented good-naturedly that that was the least he could do since he couldn't write poetry, and began:

Rodrigo's First Theory: Surplus Equality—
The Case of African Americans

"The basic problem is that we're stuck with constitutional guarantees of equality that are becoming increasingly inconvenient, even embarrassing. You can already see beginnings of this retrenchment in the courts."

"I assume you mean all the recent changes in equal protection doctrine," I interjected. "Like new, tougher intent requirements, tighter proof of causation, and manipulation of standing and res judicata law, among others—all of which make it harder for minorities to sue for discrimination?"

"Yes, but the retrenchment reaches beyond the courts," Rodrigo said. "Decisions like the ones you mentioned are just the surface manifestations of something deeper."

"Namely?" Giannina asked, leaning forward.

"All the little, incremental cutbacks are only the tip of the iceberg. Conservatives in think tanks and foundations have begun to see the commitment to equality, enshrined in the Declaration of Independence and three constitutional amendments, as an inconvenience, an anachronism, a little bit like the Second Amendment.[17] Meanwhile, our system is in the process of forsaking that commitment."

"Forsaking it?" I exclaimed. "I certainly hope you have some documentation, Rodrigo! For someone like me, who has dedicated his entire life to working for civil rights and racial justice, that's a stunning indictment. If you're right, we all might as well pack up and go home."

"I wouldn't go that far," Rodrigo replied. "But we should know what we're fighting against. I don't mean to be dispiriting."

"Forget dispiriting. If it's true, it's true, and we'll just have to deal with it. Let's hear your evidence."

"My thesis breaks down into two parts, corresponding to separate mechanisms for attenuating the equality guarantees. The first shows how equality in our system is inherently and necessarily unstable. Without strenuous efforts, it fades over time. The second explains how we are shrinking the very notion of equal citizenship. The two mechanisms correspond, roughly, to blacks on the one hand, and Latinos on the other—although they overlap. Indeed, they work together in an unholy alliance. The latter even constricts equality of opportunity. Are you ready?"

Giannina and I both nodded emphatically. Rearranging his dishes slightly to give himself more room, Rodrigo began: "Have you two heard of the theory of surplus value?"

Giannina and I looked at each other. "Of course," she replied. "Attributed to Karl Marx, it holds, in one version at least, that in any closed system, such as a factory, capitalism is on a collision course with itself. Because the owner of a plant takes out a certain percentage as profit, believing himself entitled to it as a return on his investment, not enough money is paid out in wages for the workers to buy the products they make.[18] On a larger scale, this is true of countries, as well. That's why capitalism inevitably leads to disparities of wealth and, eventually, colonialism. According to Marx and Engels, capitalist societies must take over new countries to serve as markets and sources of raw materials and cheap labor.[19] Otherwise, everything collapses. Of course, capitalism proved more resilient than they thought. Still, Marx's theory, though discredited in some quarters, is widely regarded as one of the four or five most powerful ideas in all social science. It supplied the theoretical rationale for socialism and paved the way for the modern labor movement, as well as other important reforms of the social-welfare state."

Giannina paused, so I turned to Rodrigo: "What does this have to do with the host of recent books promoting theories of racial inferiority, such as *The Bell Curve*? I gather you think there's some connection."

"Have you ever considered that Marx's theory might have an analog?" Rodrigo asked.

"You mean a theory of some other kind of surplus?"

Before Rodrigo could answer, the waiter interrupted to ask how we were enjoying our meals. I noticed a slight accent in his English. We nodded—"Fine." As he departed, Giannina quipped, "Speaking of surpluses, I think we have a culinary one. These portions are huge. I'm afraid I'm going to have to take half of mine home."

The Relation of Liberty and Equality in Welfare Capitalism

"I can help you finish it later, if you like," Rodrigo volunteered. Giannina rolled her eyes at the famous appetite of her rail-thin husband, who shrugged and continued as follows:

"My theory has to do with the relationship between equality and liberty. Everyone knows we have a liberty-based system that, in the economic sphere at least, is committed to free-market capitalism.[20] Yet we are also committed to equality. The Declaration of Independence holds that all men are created equal. The Constitution requires equal treatment of citizens in voting, political representation, and other areas."

"Yes, and many people recognize that the two values interfere with each other, to some extent," Giannina interjected.

"True," Rodrigo acknowledged. "But what few realize is that each is *internally* inconsistent, in light of the other. As we mentioned earlier, Marx theorized that capitalism is on a collision course with itself. If he and his followers are right, profit cannot maximize itself without contradiction."

"That's the theory of surplus value," I said. "And I gather you think something similar checks promotion of equality?"

"Yes. I call it the theory of surplus equality."

"Surplus equality?" Giannina said, with a skeptical look. "I assume you mean something more than the idea that too much leveling—through taxation for example—is bad for free enterprise?"

"I do," Rodrigo replied evenly. "And that's where the books we were discussing come in. My theory is that our society must rationalize a larger and larger disparity—measured by the difference between equality of results and equality of opportunity. Because we want to believe that our country gives every person an equal chance to succeed, we must justify social stratification on other grounds. We turn to genetics since it allows us to explain why whites hold most of the wealth. People can then say that whites deserve to keep their wealth and power. People can claim that—after all—whites are *biologically* superior."

"Hmmm," I said. "I think I need to hear more. I read that the United States just overtook Great Britain as the most divided society in the Western world. Even Bork noted this. And we've certainly seen a great deal of blaming of the poor for their own condition, with tales of welfare abuse, Mexicans crossing the border to have babies, and, of course, the books you mentioned. But isn't this just a more or less inevitable consequence of deregulation and the more laissez-faire economy the public seems to want these days?"

"I think it's more basic than that, so that even if the Democrats took over, the situation would be difficult to reverse. Do you remember what we said about pro-rata equality—equality of results?"

"Yes, the notion that economic success and failure should be spread equally among all groups of people—that's the kind of equality conservatives love to hate," I said. "They much prefer the other kind, equality of opportunity, since it enables them to rationalize disparities in wealth and lay blame at the doorstep of poor people's work habits and family structures. But I still don't see why you think our national commitment to equality is on a collision course with itself. Isn't the deplorable state of the inner city only contingently, not necessarily, the case? It might right itself

if we all worked harder. We could resist what the conservatives are saying. We could create social supports for the poor to decrease disparities in
wealth and increase equality."

"I wish it were so," Rodrigo replied. "But my theory says it's unlikely.
Instead, the plight of the indigent will worsen over time, so long as our
system is committed to both equality and free-enterprise capitalism. Just
as the gap between workers and capital will continue to grow, our commitment to equality for nonwhite groups and the poor will, ironically, assure their continued degradation."

"Our commitment to *equality* will assure their continued degradation?"
Giannina replied. "I think you need to spell things out a little more."

How Our National Commitment to Equality
Necessitates Increasing Dehumanization of the Poor
and, Ultimately, Biological Theories of Inferiority

"Here's the idea," Rodrigo began. "Our society is supposed to be equal.
That is, everyone is supposed to have a decent level of comfort, not too
far below what others have. But that cannot happen: Free-market capitalism and the profit motive cause society to become more stratified over
time.[21] Industrialized nations must colonize; workers cannot purchase
what they make, and so on."

"Every system must have winners and losers," I pointed out.

"Must they?" Giannina queried. "Can't all systems, including capitalist
ones, try to combat stratification by adopting antitrust laws, welfare and
social security programs, and progressive tax rates? Haven't we, in effect,
done this?"

"To a degree," Rodrigo conceded. "But the disparity continues to grow,
flying in the face of our *other* great national ideal—equality. Looking around
us, we see cities full of gangs, deteriorating buildings, crack houses, and
schools so demoralized that teachers transfer out as soon as they get enough
seniority. How can this happen in a nation that prides itself on equal treatment? We can only explain it by blaming the poor. We coin physical or cultural theories of their inferiority, asserting that the poor must not want to
work or to take advantage of their opportunities. We assign an increasing
degree of inferiority to them precisely as our society becomes more and
more stratified. They do not deserve to be equal, we tell ourselves, because
they are not really like us. Something is wrong with them. There must be,
precisely because of our commitment to the second great ideal, equality."

"Are you saying the poor are worse off in a system like ours that believes in equality for all?" Giannina asked.

"Yes," said Rodrigo matter-of-factly, "considerably worse off than under a system that emphasizes just one or the other value. Capitalism requires an underclass. It requires colonies to exploit. Yet our commitment to equality makes us intensely anxious when these things happen—they imply that our ideology may be false—that maybe everyone really doesn't have an equal chance to advance and rise. But we refuse to confront this possibility, instead labeling those others as inherently inferior, as unable to rise, no matter what. That way we can still pretend to embrace both free markets and equality. Thus, my theory of surplus equality: More equality inheres in our national principles than can be accommodated at any time. Someone, usually blacks and Latinos, must end up constructed as unequal."

"And by virtue of their makeup," I added, shaking my head sadly.

"Right," Rodrigo replied. "If the group were merely contingently poor and miserable, that would stand as a contradiction to our commitment to equality. We would have deserving, energetic, ambitious, intelligent people—much like us—who were starving and desperate. This would be intolerable. We would have to tax ourselves radically to alleviate their plight, if we could not explain it away by dismissing them as inferior, lazy, undeserving, lascivious, not very intelligent, and so on."[22]

"Which we have done," Giannina added.

"Let me see if I understand you," I said. "You say that equality in the aspirational sense—equality of result—is the very source of inequality, that the very commitment to it injures minorities because our system is capitalist and expansionist, and whites got here first.[23] We can't mistreat our underclass without finding them innately, biologically inferior—not like us.[24] So they end up worse off than they would be if we had no such commitment."

"Nations without a commitment to radical egalitarianism have been much kinder to slaves and prisoners of war," Rodrigo pointed out. "Some of the great military societies of the ancient world made far better use of their captives for precisely this reason. They could assign them responsible jobs, such as tutoring the captors' children, because they did not need to deem them innately inferior. Having no commitment to equality, they could cheerfully exploit without having to disparage and demonize. But because free-market economics causes inequality to accelerate over time, we are compelled to assign more and more traits of hopeless inferiority to the losers in our midst. Just as early Industrial Revolution era societies required colonies, today's society requires books like *The Bell Curve* that tell us the poor are that way because of *who* they are. We get to hold on to our belief in democracy and sleep well nights, too," Rodrigo concluded.

"And the beauty of it," I added, "is that the Equal Protection Clause remains perfectly intact. We can continue to pay it homage even in the face of deepening social division, poverty, and racial animosity. And the reason is that we tell ourselves equality doesn't mean literally giving everyone the same amount—say, $30,000 a year. Rather, it means giving that other person what he or she is due."[25]

"Equality of opportunity," Giannina emphasized.

"Precisely," I continued. "We tell ourselves that equality only guarantees that people receive what they deserve because of their merit, intelligence, energy, and resourcefulness.[26] And then we arrange that this quantum decreases over time as distributive inequality increases because of capitalism—because of what is happening on the other side of the value divide."

"Two precisely counterpoised values, each with interlocking internal contradictions," Rodrigo mused.

"And the pair maintained nicely in balance through a system of popular imagery, books, novels, jokes, stories, and other narratives," Giannina observed. "In a more generous time, the public image of the minority was that of noble warrior, like Martin Luther King, Cesar Chavez, or Malcolm X."

"That was when the pie was expanding," Rodrigo continued. "Now there's not enough to go around, and so elite groups make sure that if anyone suffers, it won't be they. But because our system is geared toward equality, they can't straightforwardly pass laws and measures that hurt the poor and working classes. They have to demonize them first, show they are not deserving of what one might think a person should have in an advanced, affluent society like ours."

"But Rodrigo," I interjected, "I still can't see how having a political commitment to equality can be anything but good. Suppose you could live in either of two societies. Society A has a commitment to equality. Its constitution contains an equal protection clause. Society B has no such thing. As a person of color, where would you prefer to live?"

"In Society B, all other things being equal," Rodrigo replied. "This assumes that both societies are capitalist and have an economic system based on free-market principles, as opposed to, say, socialism."

"Okay," Giannina responded. "But even accepting those assumptions, aren't blacks and Mexicans better off in Society A because if they are discriminated against, they can go to court, invoke the national values, and gain redress?"

"In theory, yes," Rodrigo replied. "Although Mexicans will have difficulty winning such suits due to something I call the black-white binary. Mexicans in America occupy a sort of never-never land. Not really considered a minority, they are nevertheless subject to discrimination in housing, education, employment, and a host of other areas."[27]

"You're part Latino," I said to Rodrigo. "You once told me that even though you look black and identify as such, your father's family immigrated here via the Caribbean and still speaks perfect Spanish. Assuming you identify with your Latino roots as well, maybe you can give us your thoughts about equality and this group."

"I will," Rodrigo promised. "But if I could first return to your point, Giannina, about legal redress, consider the following: A black person comes to court trying to prove discrimination. He has a Ph.D., an M.D., and credentials exceeding those of Bill Cosby's fictional hero of TV fame. This paragon has been denied a position for which he is amply qualified, in favor of a white person. What happens?"

"I suppose you are going to say the black superstar loses," Giannina said. "But why? Is the judge biased?"

How the Dehumanization Is Effected

"He or she doesn't have to be, in any conscious sense," Rodrigo replied. "And the same goes for the jury, the attorneys, the witnesses, and all the other participants in the event. Each has been raised in our culture, which has ingrained in their psyches a host of images, pictures, and narratives that render the black superstar one-down. Maybe he is good—but too pushy. Maybe he got where he is by affirmative action. Maybe he applied for the position to make trouble—he wanted a lawsuit, not a job. Maybe the white candidate was actually superior, and the black one a spoiled affirmative action baby who can't take disappointment. And where do all these pernicious images come from?" Rodrigo cued, watching us expectantly.

"From the broader society?" I ventured. "From the system of free expression that enables moviemakers, utterers of hate speech, cartoonists, and others to trade at blacks' expense?"

"Yes. And this has been picking up lately, gaining in virulence and incessancy—"

"Because of your paradox," Giannina and I both said at the same time, then laughed. I motioned her to continue. She then elaborated, "Because our system produces increasingly greater gaps in wealth and comfort, with folks of color at the bottom, courtesy of racism. Then the theory of surplus equality kicks in. It's like Zeno's paradox, but in reverse. The distribution of goods and wealth becomes so different from what formal equality would dictate that we need to construct the losers as inherently inferior. That way they really aren't equal, cannot legitimately expect a fair share, and should be happy with what they have."

"Dinesh D'Souza says that the institution of slavery did the slaves a favor," I recalled.[28] "A few years ago, it would have been unthinkable to say something like this. Today, hardly anyone bats an eye."

"Not to mention the other books we were talking about, and yet others in the same vein," Rodrigo added. "Plus an increasing tide of hate speech on campuses and attacks by the right on programs like diversity, affirmative action, political redistricting, and school desegregation."

"Precisely what your theory would predict," I agreed, a little reluctantly.

We were all silent a moment, absorbing the bleak quandary Rodrigo had so remorselessly painted for us. The waiter arrived to clear our dinner plates. "Would you folks like some dessert?"

"I think we'd like to see the menu, right?" Rodrigo answered, raising his eyebrows at Giannina and me. The waiter placed three dessert menus in front of us and began to take away the dishes. "I think I'll have the lemon sorbet," Giannina said.

"The flan for me," Rodrigo added.

"The same," I said. Then, after a short pause, I asked, "You know, Rodrigo, you and I were talking about something similar once before. Do you recall our discussion of free speech and the First Amendment?"[29]

"I do."

"We agreed that our system of free expression has a powerfully apologetic, after-the-fact effect. Even though the poor and minorities have little access to it because they cannot afford microphones, TV access, press agents, and so on, First Amendment purists are fond of saying—in the hate-speech debate, for example—that this great amendment must remain unfettered. Supposedly, this will benefit minorities and the poor, even though hate speech is almost entirely directed against them and they are the ones asking for relief. Free speech actually turns out to be of greatest benefit to the powerful and wealthy. Conveniently for them, it contains exceptions—such as copyright, defamation, official secrets, and words of conspiracy—whenever speech threatens the interest of a privileged group. It also perpetuates conflict between, say, skinheads and minority groups, by leaving hate speech protected. Do you think your equality theory taps a similar insight?"

"In a way," Rodrigo replied. "Like all marketplace mechanisms, free speech enables life's winners to declare the race results fair and just. The winners' ideas must be better than the losers', since they competed and won. If members of other groups are poor and miserable while we are well-clothed, warm, and comfortable, well, that's how it must be in a competitive society."

"All this reminds me of something I've been thinking about recently," Giannina remarked. "I assume the two of you have heard of cognitive dissonance."

When we both nodded, she continued, "Although early Marxists thought egalitarian Western institutions, like the U.S. Constitution, would become increasingly criticized as the disparity between the wealthy and the poor worsened over time, this has not happened to any great extent. Jack Balkin pointed out that people will resist changing their beliefs in the face of inconsistent evidence, preserving, as long as possible, their ontological stake in the former belief.[30] This is especially so in connection with legal and political principles such as equality of opportunity. Not only is this principle central to a free-market economy, it absolves successful individuals of any responsibility for maldistribution of resources. That's why brazen statements like D'Souza's resonate well—they are part and parcel of a system of collective denial."

"So you're saying we construct the less fortunate as inferior beings, rather than face the hard fact that equality and free-market liberty are at odds, in order to reduce dissonance?" I added.

"Right, and don't forget that not only are equality and free-market liberty at odds with each other; they are also inconsistent with themselves, if you take things to their logical conclusion," Rodrigo said.

"And as you pointed out, speech is the main mechanism that holds everything together," Giannina observed. "Your theory requires an increasingly negative social construction of blacks to preserve the fiction that we are simultaneously a generous, egalitarian nation and a free-market one. Thus, we have books like *The Bell Curve*, movies depicting blacks as criminal, hapless, or lazy, and other similar scripts."

"It's the beauty of the marketplace," Rodrigo seconded. "It all fits together, the fulcrum being, ironically, our national commitment to equality."

The waiter arrived with our desserts.

Again we ate in silence for a few seconds, then I said, "Rodrigo, at first I thought your theory was paradoxical and off-the-wall. But now, I'm half-convinced. It explains much of what we've been seeing lately—the renewed ugliness, the spate of books that label black culture pathological. But earlier you mentioned you had some ideas about other minority groups, such as Chicanos and Puerto Ricans. What does your theory say about them?"

Rodrigo's Second Theory of Resurgent Inequality: Definitional Contraction and Second-Class Citizenship—The Case of Latinos

"Thanks for reminding me, Professor. It seems to me that the Latino situation is different from blacks', but in the end, not much better. Regarded by most people as a minority group, Latinos until recently were nevertheless held not to fall under the Equal Protection Clause or to receive the same degree of protection as others under federal civil rights statutes."[31]

Rodrigo's First Definitional Mechanism: Deployment of a Black-White Paradigm That Assigns Latinos a Subordinate and Often Invisible Position in the Racial Hierarchy

"And the reason is that the equality-protecting amendments were drafted with African Americans in mind," I replied. "Their purpose, like that of the early civil rights statutes, was to prohibit discrimination against former slaves. Only recently have legal protections been extended to non-black minority groups. Even today, when Latinos sue, say, for school desegregation, everyone is a little surprised. 'Oh, that's right. They are minorities, too,' we have to remind ourselves."

"In that respect, are not Latinos better off," Giannina asked—"not demonized as intensely as blacks?"

"True," Rodrigo replied. "But the problem is that even though Latino rates of poverty, infant mortality, unemployment, and school dropout rival those of blacks, most Americans don't think of them as occupying the bottom rung of the racial hierarchy. Latinos are seen as a little above blacks and below whites. The current image is of a slightly lackadaisical people who are content to work at menial jobs, speak their own language, have large families, and attend colorful fiestas."[32]

"And useful," I quipped. "Good gardeners, nannies, and restaurant workers."

"Also good overseers for those who occupy the real bottom rung, namely, African Americans," added Giannina. "Not too dark. Not too threatening. Obedient and hardworking. The radical inequality your theory predicts for blacks offers opportunities for Latinos who are willing to fit in and accept their role."

"Some Latinos seem happy to go right along," Rodrigo pointed out. "Some are conservatives and members of the Republican Party. Many adopt American ways, learn the language well, change their names. Some even have been known to join in scapegoating recent immigrants—something that is easier to do than face up to what Marxists and neo-Marxists consider the inevitably cyclical nature of capitalism."

"That's true," I conceded. "And unlike the vast majority of blacks, many Hispanics have the option to fit in. With light skins and European features, they can pass as white. Others who cannot nevertheless strive to assimilate. Uninterested in civil rights or confrontation, they rely on ingratiation. They try to be suave—or, at least, nonthreatening."

Giannina snorted. "I'm glad Rodrigo's not that way. Not that you lack charm, but it wouldn't be you. And I have the feeling that even those who try to assimilate pay a price."

"That they do," Rodrigo replied. "Assimilation is a double-edged sword. For blacks, society's on-the-book values at least open the door for some small number who meet the formal criteria of merit and excellence. I'm not saying this is an easy task. But every now and then one slips through. With Latinos, by being polite and quiet, one can hope to huddle a little below whites and above blacks. But, if you don't play along, you can be discriminated against virtually without recourse. Even formal equality isn't available."

"Except on the most minimal basis," I interjected.

"What you lawyers call minimal scrutiny," Giannina replied. "The kind that rarely results in courts' striking down state action."

"Since our system is both capitalistic and committed to formal equality," Rodrigo continued, "the misery of the Latino community must prove something is wrong with them. And because only blacks were enslaved, and because civil rights law presupposes a black-white paradigm, the public has few qualms about treating Latinos badly. One can tell an anti-Mexican joke, laugh at a cartoon of a character dozing under a sombrero in the shade of a cactus, much more freely than one of a black eating a watermelon. Our very commitment to equality—which admits that, as a nation, we made only one historic mistake—assures that Mexicans and other Latino Americans are given short shrift."

After a short pause for the waiter to clear our plates and offer refills of coffee, I continued, "To summarize, then, Rodrigo, you are saying that a mechanism—namely, the black-white binary—similar to the one you identified for blacks operates to suppress Latinos. Different—yet not afforded full legal protection or vigilant support from liberals—Latinos are consigned to an intermediate status as overseers and clerks. There's not enough equality to go around, so we give them half. Is that your theory?"

"Yes," Rodrigo said, "but don't forget the huge pressures toward conformity and assimilation that afflict the group. Society communicates to them in a multitude of ways that if they behave they can fit in."

Rodrigo's Second Mechanism: Inequality of Immigration

"The other author we mentioned earlier, Peter Brimclow, certainly thinks so," I added. "He's willing to tolerate older immigrant groups, especially those who do try to fit in. But the newer arrivals from Latin America are another matter.[33] They bring inferior cultural mores, including a propensity to go on welfare and commit crimes, poor health and hygiene, disregard for hard work and education, and a backward attachment to their language.[34] He's especially unhappy that immigrants from Latin America qualify for affirmative action at the expense of white males, like his son.[35] In his view, backward people who do not share our traditions and refuse to assimilate get ahead at the expense of real Americans—persons of northern European descent who work hard, save money, have small families, and live within their means."[36]

"According to Brimelow, Latino immigrants drain the infrastructure, contributing less in taxes and services than what they consume in health, education, and welfare costs," Giannina said. "America's core is white. Immigration threatens this, harming even blacks."[37]

"Rodrigo, I gather you think all of this is part of the general contraction of equality you outlined earlier in connection with blacks?" I asked.

"I do," Rodrigo replied. "Brimelow and others are contracting what I call equality of immigration. In 1965, Congress abolished the old, racist national origins immigration system that favored persons from northern and western Europe in favor of a more egalitarian version. Brimelow would like to go back to a system like the old one. Less desirable than ones from Europe, citizens from Africa and Latin America would find it more difficult to immigrate."

"They would be, in effect, less human," Giannina said. "At least in the eyes of U.S. immigration law."

Rodrigo added, "Brimelow's proposals include increased vigilance at the border and within the United States. Americans would have to show identification badges. Those who could not prove they were here legally would be denied social services or even deported."

"Some of this is already happening," I pointed out. "Referenda in California and other states, bills in Congress . . . and that close call I myself suffered."

"All placing the onus on the foreign-looking and -sounding to prove they're bona fide," Rodrigo said. "Inequality of immigration has consequences even for those, like Hispanics in New Mexico, whose families have been here for three hundred years."

"A little odd coming from conservatives, who tout equality of opportunity," Giannina mused.

Rodrigo's Third Mechanism: Inequality of Birthright Citizenship

Giannina and I were silent for a moment. Rodrigo sipped his coffee, looked up, then said, "But Brimelow and his crowd would also narrow equality in a third way. He proposes abolishing birthright citizenship so that the children of both legal and illegal aliens would no longer qualify automatically."[38]

"Would no longer be citizens?" Giannina asked.

"Exactly," Rodrigo replied, "he and others like him supported a resolution in California and a bill introduced in Congress that would have denied citizenship to children of aliens."[39]

"As well I remember," I commented wryly. "But to be legally effective, wouldn't that require a constitutional amendment?"

"It would," Giannina said, "because the Fourteenth Amendment guarantees citizenship to anyone born here. So it would require amending the Fourteenth Amendment for the first time in its history. A statute alone wouldn't do it."

"Yet Brimelow and others propose we do just that," Rodrigo continued. "The very amendment that guarantees equal treatment would no longer apply to a large group of people simply because of their parents' status at the time they were born."

"The carrot and the stick," Giannina said. "If they assimilate, Latinos can fit in. They can even naturalize, if they do it in a hurry. And that, in turn, requires that they assimilate. It's a closed circle. Yet if they don't crack it, they'll find that the Constitution affords them no equal protection. And if they live outside the United States and want to immigrate here, they had better forget it. Equality of immigration is on its way out."

"Sobering," I said. "No wonder Chicano activists are concerned."

We were silent for a moment. Then Rodrigo looked at his watch. "How much time do we have?"

"We need to be there in about twenty minutes," Giannina replied, looking at her watch. "But it's only a short walk."

"We're due at an alumni reception," Rodrigo explained. "Poor Giannina often ends up doing double duty. Not only is she the first-year class rep at her school, but she attends so many official functions at mine, she's sometimes mistaken as a faculty member."

"It wouldn't surprise me if she is one, one of these days," I said.

"Enough of that," Giannina replied with a smile. "I've a long way to go. And besides, I'm looking forward to my job next summer at a women's law clinic. You two can knock yourselves out trying to reform the legal academy. Now, where were we?"

"How our society relegates Mexicans and other Latinos to a low rung," I said. "The mechanism is similar to the one Rodrigo explained with blacks and, in a way, just as pernicious. Latinos, especially recent immigrants, end up unprotected by civil rights law and pressured to assimilate. Writers like Brimelow urge redefining equality so that they are not even included in the concept. Was there any more?"

Rodrigo's Fourth Mechanism:
Inequality of Language

"One more," Rodrigo said. "I call it inequality of language. The Official English movement is sending messages, both symbolic and real, to minority groups that their language is unofficial, devalued, even illegal in certain settings.[40] In certain states, you must speak English to vote, get certain jobs, or take a civil service examination."[41]

"Juan Perea describes one case where such laws contributed to a person's death," Giannina noted. "He called it 'Death by English.'"[42]

"Very appropriate. Like the other measures, English-only laws contract the circle of who is afforded full citizenship rights. If you are white, English-speaking, and your ancestors came from the right region of the world, all the equality amendments and civil rights statutes apply to you."

"The person who needs them least," I observed sardonically.

"And if you're of a different hue or origin or prefer to speak a different language, you can't insist on equal treatment. You can only be as obsequious as possible and try to convince the surrounding society you're worthy of their company. Defy assimilation, hold on to your language, and you'll have few defenders. All the laws will be arrayed against you."

"How do you suppose the English Only people rationalize that?" Giannina mused. "Some of them are college professors."

"I actually saw one of their ads just the other day," Rodrigo said. "It said that the president of the U.S. branch of English Only is a Hispanic."[43]

"Really?" Giannina asked. "He's actually a Hispanic?"

"I think so," Rodrigo replied. "It showed his picture, and he has a Latino name. The ad argued that forcing immigrants to learn English would further equality of opportunity."

"It sounds strange," I said. "But in a warped way it makes sense. If your only reference point is English speaking ability, forcing those who speak another language to conform to English-only laws will look like equality to you. You take persons who are outside that circle and move them inside. There, everyone's equal. Nice and neat. Outside, they're not full persons. Inside, they are. So you're really doing them a tremendous favor."

"One of the students whose locker was defaced at my school was a Chicano," Rodrigo mused. "The uproar from the student body was not nearly as loud as it was on behalf of the blacks."

"What do you think will happen?" I asked.

"The ones who apologized will be treated lightly," Rodrigo ventured, "even though their actions were clearly deliberate and hurtful. Two of them apologized only because they were caught. As for the one who refuses, I don't know. The school has no formal hate-speech code."

"So what is he being charged with?" Giannina asked.

"Violation of the honor code, which contains a general clause prohibiting conduct that interferes with the ability of other students to enjoy the benefits of their education. The defense is charging that the clause is void for vagueness and that punishing the student would violate his First Amendment rights."

"Sounds like a battle royal coming up," I commented. "In addition to a theory of surplus equality, I think we need one to explain surplus righteousness. These conservative litigation centers always seem to wind up on the wrong side, defending Nazis, cross-burners, and purveyors of hate speech."[44]

"Speaking of ending up on the wrong side," Giannina said, gesturing for the waiter to bring the check, "Rodrigo and I need to think about moving on. He agreed to give a few remarks to open the dean's reception. For my part, I promised I'd get him there on time."

"And on mine, I should get myself over to my daughter's by nine. Otherwise she'll worry, and the baby may be sound asleep." Then, after a pause for the waiter to arrive with the check, I asked, "Do you two know about the *científicos* movement in Mexican history?"

"You mean in the late nineteenth and early twentieth centuries?" Giannina asked.

"Yes," I said. "Even revolutionary Mexico was not free of supremacist impulses. Around the time eugenic theories were first being formulated here, a group of Mexican intellectuals and politicians calling themselves *los científicos* coined the theory that indigenous people were inferior and doomed to poverty.[45] Their theory rationalized the large inequalities in wealth and landholding that were developing in that country in the wake of industrialization."

"Depressing, isn't it?" asked Giannina. "The more things change, the more they stay the same."

The waiter arrived with the check, which Giannina quickly intercepted—"you paid last time." As she filled out the credit card slip, I noticed that the waiter, a light-skinned, lanky man with high cheekbones, could be either African—probably Ethiopian—or Latino. I wondered if he had overheard any of our conversation, and if so, what he had thought. Perhaps he had been a university professor or other professional back in his homeland. If so, what would he think of Rodrigo's bleak theory about the permanence of socioeconomic hierarchy in the United States? Perhaps he had immigrated to escape political repression and willingly endured his current privation as the price of physical security. I reflected on Rodrigo's paradox, in which equality, like the profit motive, is on a collision course with itself. Racial conditions in America were certainly worse than I remembered for some time. Would they deteriorate even further? Rodrigo's theory implied so—indeed, his friend Lazlo Kowalsky had recently warned of a coming race war.[46] What role would my talented young multiracial friends—indeed the left in general—play in warding that off, assuming it was even possible? For the first time, I felt a pang of regret over my own, partly self-imposed exile at a time when so much remained to be done in the States.

Just then, the waiter reappeared and took away the signed voucher. "Thank you, folks, and have a good evening," he said in the lightly accented English I had noticed earlier.

"Thank you," we said in unison.

As we waited for a taxi on the curb, Giannina said, "We hope we'll see you again soon."

"Let's make a point of it," I agreed. "Are you two going to be at the Michigan conference next month?"

"I think so. I will, at any rate," Rodrigo said, as two cabs pulled over to pick us up.

"Let's get together then," I said. "If not before. I want to talk to you about law and economics."

"I'm game," Rodrigo said, and Giannina nodded as well. "Maybe Laz will join us.[47] He'll be there, and as you know, it's his stock in trade."

Notes

1. For a description of other such incidents in law schools or universities, see RICHARD DELGADO & JEAN STEFANCIC, MUST WE DEFEND NAZIS? HATE SPEECH, PORNOGRAPHY, AND THE NEW FIRST AMENDMENT (NYU Press 1997).

2. *See* DINESH D'SOUZA, THE END OF RACISM: PRINCIPLES FOR A MULTIRACIAL SOCIETY 9–18 (1995).

3. On the role of conservative think tanks and foundations in the race, IQ, and eugenics movements, see JEAN STEFANCIC & RICHARD DELGADO, NO MERCY: HOW CONSERVATIVE THINK TANKS AND FOUNDATIONS CHANGED AMERICA'S SOCIAL AGENDA 33–44 (1996) (arguing that racial pseudoscience, like that popularized in *The Bell Curve*, can only be carried out with funding from elite conservative organizations).

4. One standard deviation refers to the supposed average difference in intelligence between whites and blacks. *See* RICHARD J. HERRNSTEIN & CHARLES MURRAY, THE BELL CURVE: INTELLIGENCE AND CLASS STRUCTURE IN AMERICAN LIFE 276 ("In discussing IQ tests, for example, the black mean is commonly given as 85, the white mean as 100, and the standard deviation as 15").

5. Conservative groups have poured substantial amounts of money into campus newspapers in an attempt to "bring conservative political thought to college campuses under the thrall of liberalism." *See* STEFANCIC & DELGADO, *supra* at 110.

6. D'Souza's second book, THE END OF RACISM: PRINCIPLES FOR A MULTIRACIAL SOCIETY (1995) traces the origin of racism against blacks and other groups of color. D'Souza argues that liberalism—characterized by cultural relativism (the belief that all cultures are equal) and equality of result (the belief that absent prejudice and racism, all groups should be approximately equally successful in most competitions)—today constitutes the main barrier to a just society.

7. *See, e.g.,* ROBERT BORK, SLOUCHING TOWARD GOMORRAH: MODERN LIBERALISM AND AMERICAN DECLINE (1996).

8. HERRNSTEIN & MURRAY, *supra.*

9. *Id.* at 25, 51–89, 269–315.

10. *Id.* at 523–26.

11. PETER BRIMELOW, ALIEN NATION: COMMON SENSE ABOUT AMERICA'S IMMIGRATION DISASTER (1995).

12. D'Souza, *supra* at 23, 118–20, 151–56, 206, 290–94, 337–86, 528–37, 551.

13. *See id.* at 51–56. For D'Souza, "It is impossible, even for scholars hostile to the West, to deny the civilization gap." D'Souza, at 54.

14. *Id.* at 88–91, 102, 112–13.

15. *Id.* at 23–24, 51–54, 290–91, 435–37, 454, 475–76, 484, 527–28, 537, 556.

16. *See, e.g.,* Richard B. Darlington, *On Race and Intelligence: A Commentary on Affirmative Action, the Evolution of Intelligence, the Regression Analyses in* The Bell Curve, *and Jensen's Two-Level Theory,* 2 PSYCHOL. PUB. POL'Y & L. 635 (1996) (taking issue with the tenets and reasoning of various authors attempting to demonstrate racial differences in intelligence); Garrett Epps, *Slouching Toward Gomorrah: Modern Liberalism and American Decline,* THE NATION, Jan. 27, 1997, at 25; Ronald P. Formisano, *The End of Racism,* 16 J. AM. ETHNIC HIST. 110 (1997) (criticizing D'Souza for overstatement and "sleight-of-hand prose"); Stephen Jay Gould, *Curveball,* NEW YORKER, Nov. 28, 1994, at 139 (criticizing the premises of *The Bell Curve*); Charles Lane, *The Tainted Sources of* The Bell Curve, N.Y. REV. BOOKS, Dec. 1, 1994, at 14.

17. The Second Amendment guarantees the people the right to bear arms and is "to put it mildly . . . not at the forefront of constitutional discussion." Sanford Levinson, *The Embarrassing Second Amendment,* 99 YALE L.J. 637, 639 (1989).

18. For general introductions to the theory of surplus value, see V.I. LENIN, INTRODUCTION TO MARX, ENGELS, MARXISM 43–44, 70–77 (Int'l Pub. ed. 1987); II ENCYCLOPEDIA OF ETHICS 766–67 (Lawrence C. Becker & Charlotte B. Becker eds., 1992); Donald F. Gordon, *Value, Labor Theory of,* 16 INT'L ENCY. SOC. SCI. 279–82 (David L. Sills ed. 1968). For Marx's original version, see KARL MARX, I CAPITAL 179–85, 207–30, 312–21, 508–18, 566–68, 591–98, 618–21 (Samuel Moore & Edward Aveling trans., Frederick Engels ed., 6th ed. 1974); II Capital, 177–98, 319–50 (on theory of surplus value and class struggle).

19. On capitalism and expansionism, see text *infra*; 2 Marx, *supra* at 177–98; KARL MARX, CAPITAL, THE COMMUNIST MANIFESTO, AND OTHER WRITINGS 324 (Max Eastman ed., 1932); 3 ENCY. OF SOC. 1203 (Edgar F. Borgatta & Marie L. Borgatta eds., 1992) (noting that modern capitalism walks a tightrope in an effort to allow capital accumulation while managing its negative effects).

20. *See, e.g.,* ADAM SMITH, AN INQUIRY INTO THE NATURE AND CAUSES OF THE WEALTH OF NATIONS (R.H. Campbell & A.S. Skinner eds., 1976) (providing Smith's theories on division of labor, capital production, and economic growth).

21. KEVIN PHILLIPS, THE POLITICS OF RICH AND POOR: WEALTH AND THE AMERICAN ELECTORATE IN THE REAGAN AFTERMATH (1990) (discussing the "triumph of upper America" during the Reagan administration).

22. *See* Richard Delgado & Jean Stefancic, *Images of the Outsider in American Law and Culture: Can Free Expression Remedy Systemic Social Ills?* 77 CORNELL L. REV. 1258, 1261–75 (1992) (describing the history of derogatory depictions of minorities

in America). *Compare* D'Souza, pp. 487–524 (arguing that insistence on the equality of all cultures—when one is so obviously dysfunctional—calls the struggle for civil rights into disrepute), *with* REGINALD HORSMAN, RACE AND MANIFEST DESTINY: THE ORIGINS OF AMERICAN RACIAL ANGLO-SAXONISM (1981) (arguing that the age-old use of racism as a rationalization for empire is at its most virulent in a system, like ours, that is committed to fairness and equality).

23. At least, whites conquered the Americas first, using Western legal thought to legitimate their dominance over the native people. *See, e.g.*, ROBERT A. WILLIAMS JR., THE AMERICAN INDIAN IN WESTERN LEGAL THOUGHT: THE DISCOURSES OF CONQUEST 6–8 (1990).

24. That is, we cannot do so without violating our commitment to rough equality and a decent level of comfort and wealth for all.

25. *Cf.* D'Souza, *supra* at 193 ("The Fourteenth Amendment was not intended to grant and does not grant an unrestricted right to equality").

26. *See* Bork, *supra* at 226–49; D'Souza, *supra* at 151–68, 528, 533; Herrnstein & Murray, *supra* at 25, 90–105; see also Richard H. Fallon Jr., *To Each According to His Ability, from None According to His Race: The Concept of Merit in the Law of Antidiscrimination*, 60 B.U. L. REV. 815 (1980) (discussing the role of merit as a principle of distributive justice).

27. *See* chapter 5 *infra*; Juan F. Perea, *Ethnicity and the Constitution: Beyond the Black and White Binary Constitution*, 36 WM. & MARY L. REV. 571, 573 (1995); *The Black/White Binary Paradigm of Race: The "Normal Science" of Racial Thought*, 85 CALIF. L. REV. 1213 (1997).

28. *See* D'Souza, *supra* at 112–13.

29. *See* RICHARD DELGADO, THE COMING RACE WAR? AND OTHER APOCALYPTIC TALES OF AMERICA AFTER AFFIRMATIVE ACTION AND WELFARE, chapter 3 (1996).

30. *See* J. M. Balkin, *Understanding Legal Understanding: The Legal Subject and the Problem of Legal Coherence*, 103 YALE L.J. 105, 146–48 (1993).

31. *See, e.g.*, Juan F. Perea, Los Olvidados: *On the Making of Invisible People*, 70 N.Y.U. L. REV. 965, 984 (1995) ("There is no meaningful legal protection against discrimination based on the ethnicity of Latinos").

32. *See* Delgado & Stefancic, *supra* at 1273–75 (describing popular stereotypes of Latinos).

33. *See* Brimelow, *supra* at 74 (describing how the recent rise in the Hispanic American population has led some Americans to feel that Hispanics "somehow started sprouting out of the earth like spring corn").

34. *See id.* at 108, 146 (recounting a propensity to go on welfare); 182–86 (citing as sources of crime); 35, 186–87 (citing as sources of disease); 267 (calling them "weird aliens with dubious habits"); 272–73 (admonishing them for refusing to assimilate).

35. *See id.* at 11, 29, 66, 218.

36. *Id.* at 56, 184.

37. *Id*. at 58–59, 62–65, 173–75.

38. *Id*. at 265 (asserting that birthright citizenship "must be ended, by amending the Constitution if necessary").

39. *Id*. at 265. For the text of the unsuccessful congressional bill, see H.R.J. 396, 103d Cong. (1994). *See also* Richard Delgado, *Citizenship*, in IMMIGRANTS OUT! *supra* at 319 (describing the California and congressional resolutions); RACE WAR? *supra* at 149–51 (1996) (referring to the various measures against birthright citizenship).

40. *See* STEFANCIC & DELGADO, *supra* at 9–19 (describing the Official English campaign); *cf.* Brimelow, pp. 88–89, 219, 273 (attacking bilingualism).

41. *See* Perea, OLVIDADOS, *supra* at 986–88.

42. *See id*. at 965 ("Bienvenida dies of English when she is confined to a nursing home where no one speaks Spanish, an environment in which she cannot communicate and in which no one cares about her language and culture. 'Death by English' is a death of the spirit").

43. *Why a Hispanic Heads an Organization Called U.S. English*, HEMISPHERES, Sept. 1994, at 42.

44. *See* STEFANCIC & DELGADO, *supra* at 27, 40, 47–51, 100, 128–31 (describing the role of conservative think tanks and litigation centers).

45. *See* RODNEY D. ANDERSON, OUTCASTS IN THEIR OWN LAND: MEXICAN INDUSTRIAL WORKERS, 1906–1911, at 34–37, 243–46 (1976).

46. *See* RACE WAR? *supra* chapter 4 (detailing Kowalsky's theory of an impending race war).

47. Lazlo Kowalsky, Rodrigo's best friend on his school's faculty, is a conservative and sponsor of the local Federalist Society. Poles apart politically, the two young friends nevertheless share the same love of ideas and respect for basic human values. One year senior to Rodrigo, Laz befriended Rodrigo and helped him adjust to his new profession. *See id*. at chapter 2.

2

Rodrigo's Road Map

Is the Marketplace Theory for Eradicating Discrimination a Blind Alley?

Soliloquy

It had been a glorious day in this quaint town in the great Northwoods. Sunshine filtered through massive hardwood trees, giving the underlying ground a dappled effect. Stately, flat-bottomed clouds punctuated the sky, keeping time with the hands of the great clock at campus center. The sudden peal of distant chimes reminded me that the final session of what had turned out to be a surprisingly stimulating conference on privatizing hydroelectric energy production was drawing to a close. I had decided to attend because, aside from visiting friends in the region, I was interested in environmental theory, having done a small amount of writing in this area earlier in my career. My hope that this midwestern location would draw some representatives of the famous Chicago School of "law and economics"[1] had been realized. In fact, the closing panel featured two individuals I had most hoped to see—Richard Posner and my friend Rodrigo's colleague, Lazlo Kowalsky, a young scholar with a growing reputation. As expected, they came out in favor of free-market solutions with minimal regulation of the hydroelectric industry.

My interest whetted by an earlier conversation with Rodrigo, I had been reading up on the law-and-economics movement, which has ascended to a position of great prominence in the legal academy over the last twenty years, and hoped to gain some additional insight from the speakers. Although I found the law-and-

economists' work elegant and even logically compelling, some of their underlying assumptions concerning human nature and motivation troubled me. If the premises from which these impressive thinkers derived their views of market efficiency were wrong, did this mean that their advocacy of free-market mechanisms at the expense of environmental and other forms of regulation was fatally flawed?

In particular, I was skeptical of the notion that "rational" actors would always, or even generally, act in a self-interested manner to maximize satisfaction—and that this would result in a greater social good.[2] If the hope that we would do better by doing less—that society would be better with less government—was wrong, then the implications were massive. Perhaps it was my romanticism for the civil rights spirit of the 1960s; perhaps I was simply set in my liberal ways. Nevertheless, I had great difficulty with the notion that eliminating governmental intervention would improve things for those already at the bottom of the social heap—women, gays, the poor, the homeless, racial and ethnic minorities, and new immigrants. I still felt in my bones that it was necessary to provide for government regulation of human nature, which I perceived as much more complex than the blithe prose of law-and-economics suggested.

It seemed to me that people act for a variety of reasons, some pecuniary, some emotional, some that can only be described as incomprehensible. Any attempt to assume human motive is perilous: We cannot, after all, look inside another's head.[3] To bypass this problem, the law-and-economists employ the market as the medium for communicating human preferences. Assuming that autonomy is not impaired by force or coercion, the market becomes a mechanism for inferring volition or motive on the part of individuals engaged in transactions. Further assuming that the parties have sufficient information to act upon, the motive for any free-market transaction is presumably that both sides will be bettered, or at least not rendered worse off. Moreover, encouraging a system of such exchanges is calculated to increase the wealth or utility of society as a whole.

I am not at all averse to economics or economic theory, which I regard as a powerful way of conceptualizing our lives under a capitalist system. What bothered me was its expanding application to apparently noneconomic phenomena, such as racial discrimination. Beginning with Gary Becker's groundbreaking work in 1957,[4] law-and-economics had come to dominate discussion in many areas that I, at least, felt were ill-suited to it. Like most humanists, I found something disturbing about applying cost-benefit treatment to phenomena like human emotions. If we haven't been able to make significant headway in unraveling many of the most intractable—some would say delicious—mysteries of life in more than two thousand years, why would one suppose that economic theory could succeed where the best minds had failed? Perhaps I was being merely romantic, but I rebelled against the thought of reducing human complexity to num-

bers and graphs. And I thought it dangerous to allow economics to dictate noneconomic social realities, like race relations—as a growing chorus of conservative voices in think tanks and Congress were beginning to urge—many going so far as to insist on the complete repeal of all our civil rights laws.

As the final afternoon discussion came to an end, the sun was just dipping below the stone façade of the clock tower. The hands read 5:35, and I was feeling weary. How tiring it can be to sit and listen to people talk for nine hours straight—or was it my advancing age? I made a mental note to go to bed early and get a fresh start in the morning. However, I first wanted to see if I could speak with Laz, who had just finished answering questions and was smiling as everyone enthusiastically clapped. As the crowd began to disperse, his tall, pale figure was surrounded by a small group of students, professors, and journalists, all wanting to speak with him personally.

Deciding to seek him out later, I headed out from the lecture room into the fading sunshine in the direction of my hotel. The sound of the school band, practicing off in the distance, made me smile briefly, remembering my own undergraduate days. My interest in the role of human nature in law-and-economics—and its possible mismatch in areas like racial discrimination—stemmed from a 1985 article by Robin West,[5] in which she argued that Richard Posner, in implicitly following the Kantian moral tradition of autonomy, justified the principle of wealth maximization *on the basis of consent. Because wealth-maximizing transactions promote autonomy, they are morally attractive; and because participants in a transaction—even the losers—have at least implicitly consented to the transfer in the hopes of maximizing their personal satisfaction, they are morally legitimate. Therefore, Posner argued, wealth maximization is a moral imperative with which the State should not interfere, except to correct injustices stemming from fraud, force, and other forms of interpersonal abuse that negate free choice.*

West's brilliant insight is that law-and-economics oversimplifies human nature by failing to account for masochistic, self-abasing tendencies. According to West, "We as a people are more authoritarian and submissive than the depictions of our nature relied upon by mainstream liberal theorists."[6] The "divergent phenomenological depictions of our inner lives" between mainstream law-and-economics liberals and more egalitarian social thinkers like myself, West points out, ultimately hinge upon the "ethical significance of choice."[7] If consent is a moral trump, as the law-and-economist asserts, then free-market transactions are morally appealing and insulated from critique—regardless of their inescapable tendency to produce winners and losers, haves and have-nots, rich and poor. West primarily focuses on the victimization side of the equation. Using the disturbing stories of Franz Kafka, she shows a "disjunction between a system that formally and outwardly insists upon the legitimating function of consent and a

*human personality that inwardly and persistently seeks the security of authority."[8]
Kafka's terrifying stories illuminate the resulting alienation—the disjunction between outward descriptions and inward experience—that typifies our modern
world and is "deeply familiar" to the contemporary individual at the existential
level. West criticizes Posner's vision of the social world as "unfamiliar" because his
hypothetical characters possess "welfare-maximizing inner worlds" required by the
overly simplified outer world of free-market economics.[9]*

*Just then, I passed a campus kiosk covered with flyers announcing a rich medley
of coming events, including a lecture by Dinesh D'Souza on hate-speech codes.
Knowing that he would undoubtedly speak out against regulation in this area, I
wondered idly what he proposed to replace it. Probably nothing, I mused. This reminded me that I wanted to explore another, implicit side of West's equation: authoritarian, cruel tendencies in human nature.[10] Authority and submission, sadism and
masochism are two sides of the same coin. If some individuals in the modern world
seek out submission to authority, then some must also seek out an authoritarian role.
It really is, as economists would put it, a matter of supply and demand. If modern
individuals desire submitting to authority, there must be authoritarian individuals
to whom one submits. If our social structure tolerates authoritarianism, then certain
individuals will be channeled into authoritarian roles while others will locate themselves on the other side, submitting to this authority. Indeed, a neo-Nietzchean like
Michel Foucault—a favorite of my friend Rodrigo—would probably argue that
modern institutions of authority, like penology or psychoanalysis, are designed to
produce and replicate authoritarian and submissive sets of individuals.[11]*

*West explicitly and compassionately focused on the victims in Kafka's stories—
and on their needs and desires to seek out and submit to authority—as a means of
criticizing Posner's "simplistic and false psychological theory of human motivation."[12] I wanted instead to focus on law-and-economics' failure to account for evil
as a major factor in human motivation. In allowing such a small role for state regulation of racism and other forms of cruelty, the law-and-economists were, I believe,
simply mistaken in holding that free markets would, by themselves, rectify such human shortcomings. I had the inescapable conviction that evil or moral wrong was
both socially constructed (e.g., racial prejudice) and biologically based (e.g., people
are naturally hostile and territorial toward outsiders) and that this residual, innate
hostility would not simply go away if the government retreated and let people function according to a free-market system. By rendering an inadequate account of human evil, the normative implications of free-market ideologies were thus danger-
ously conservative.*

I was shaken from my thoughts by voices. A small knot of conference-
goers was converging on the hotel. My walk had taken longer than antici-

pated and stirred a mighty appetite within me. Upon entering the hotel, I went straight to the restaurant, a homely, generic place with a menu, posted on an easel, that seemed to feature American cuisine. I would have preferred to go out and sample some of the local ethnic fare, but my hunger was overpowering. I sat down and ordered a hot turkey sandwich and a dinner salad. After the waiter left, I looked around the room and, to my delight, spotted none other than Lazlo Kowalsky. And who should be sitting next to him but Rodrigo! Seated in a booth on the opposite side of the restaurant, they were talking animatedly. I waited until a pause in their conversation, then half stood and waved in their direction. Laz spied me immediately, stood up, smiled, and waved for me to join them. Catching the waiter's eye to let him know I was moving, I picked up my table setting and water glass and joined my young friends.

"Professor!" Rodrigo exclaimed, shaking my hand warmly and gesturing me to sit down. "We wondered if you were here. It's great to see you!"

"As I might have mentioned, I'm visiting some friends in the region. I dropped by hoping to run into you two and maybe learn something about environmental law. Is Giannina along?"

"No. She's home, cramming for midterms. She said to give you her best."

"I didn't see you inside," I said to Rodrigo.

"It's a big auditorium," he answered. "And packed. I thought Laz did a great job, especially with the questions."

Laz grinned appreciatively, just as the waiter arrived to ask, "Are you gentlemen ready to order?"

My two young friends did, Laz a cold-cuts combo, Rodrigo a steak ("medium-rare, please"), after which we continued:

"So, what brought you here, Professor?" Laz asked, smiling to show that he was pleased I had shown up. "You're not switching sides, are you?"

"Not at my age, I'm afraid," I said. "Although I do have an amateur's interest in law-and-economics. Rodrigo and I had a long conversation once about its relation to racism and civil rights."

"He told me," Laz replied. "Too bad I wasn't there, but we didn't know each other then."

"It would have benefited from your contribution," I acknowledged. "But if the two of you have the time, I'd love to revisit the issue. A number of books have come out recently. . . ."

Rodrigo held up one hand to suggest a pause, while he rummaged for a moment in his book bag, which was resting on the floor at the foot of his chair.

"Including one I've just been reading in preparation for the conference," he said, holding up a slender black volume with Charles Murray's initials in familiar-looking silver printing on the cover.[13]

"That's one I had in mind," I said. "The other one's by Stephan and Abigail Thernstrom.[14] Both books advocate cutting back programs that assure equal opportunity for blacks and other minorities."

"I've read both," Laz said animatedly. "And I'd love to talk about them. Building on the framework laid down by early law-and-economists like Epstein,[15] Becker,[16] and Posner,[17] Charles Murray and the Thernstroms argue that the country's antidiscrimination laws—in the case of Murray— and commitment to affirmative action—in the case of the Thernstroms— ought to be jettisoned. And it may surprise you to know that I agree, with the Thernstroms, at least."

Rodrigo and I must have looked aghast, for Laz quickly continued: "Not because I oppose minorities' advances, for as you know I'm a well-wisher, being the son of immigrants myself. But conservative principles and ordinary common sense show that these programs really do people of color little good, while greatly increasing resistance by my side and by working-class whites. I think they also increase stigma for high-achieving blacks and Chicanos. I didn't think so before, but I do now."

"Well," I said, drawing a deep breath. "We do have a lot to talk about. Do the two of you have some time?"

In Which Rodrigo, Laz, and the Professor Ponder Arguments Against Our National Civil Rights Armamentarium, Beginning with a Brief Treatment of the Case of Women and Jobs

Laz and Rodrigo both smiled with anticipation, but before we could begin, the waiter arrived with our food. "Dig in, everybody," I said, and for the next few minutes we ate in tacit silence. Then Rodrigo looked up: "Giannina and I were discussing one aspect of this the other day. She had just read some news stories about the lack of women managers and executives. But her analysis has implications for minorities under a regime, like Laz's, of no civil rights enforcement."

"I didn't say *no* civil rights enforcement," Laz said pointedly. "As you know, I detest racism. I just don't think that governmental programs are the best way to combat it. I have some ideas that even the two of you might approve of. I can run them past you later, if you like. [Rodrigo and

I both nodded.] But first, I'd love to hear what your partner had to say about women in the job market."

"Okay," Rodrigo agreed. "But only on condition that you remember to tell us your ideas, Laz. You and I are so alike I sometimes forget you're a conservative. But, back to Giannina. We were talking about some of the same books the Professor just mentioned. She said that women's experiences cast doubt on the ability of the free market to redress sexism."

"Oh?" said Laz, looking up a little skeptically. "I just read that women are now slightly more than 50 percent of undergraduates at the nation's colleges. It seems to me only a matter of time before the job market sees them distributed, if not evenly, at least in large numbers, virtually everywhere."

"She wouldn't dispute that," Rodrigo replied. "In fact, she argued that changes in the job market, not kindness, were what prompted affirmative action programs in the first place. First, you'd concede, wouldn't you, Laz, that white women have been the main beneficiaries of affirmative action?"[18]

Laz smiled ironically and nodded yes.

"In that case, recall what was going on in the country right around the time affirmative action got rolling in the mid- and late 1960s."

"A civil rights revolution?" Laz replied. "Marchers in the streets? Two Democratic regimes in a row?"

"Those, too," Rodrigo said. "But Giannina was thinking of the job market. Transistors had just been invented. It must have been clear to elite groups that we were in the early stages of a technological revolution that would ultimately lead to an information-based society. And what kind of workers would that society need in large numbers?"

We were both silent for a moment. "Women?" Laz asked, finally.

"Exactly," Rodrigo replied. "The new data-processing industries would need millions of new workers. Clean, neat, and careful, to process data in, and process data out. The new workers would need to be conscientious and hardworking, but not very ambitious, because few of these jobs led anywhere. And who would be the perfect workers to fill these new jobs?"

"I see what you mean," Laz interjected. "But does Giannina's analysis, if true—and I'm not so sure that these jobs go nowhere—not just prove my point? The market worked. Women returned to the workforce, got jobs, lots of them, and without much governmental coercion, federal programs, or costly, inefficient, bureaucratic oversight and Big Brother looking over everybody's shoulder."

"That happened, but only to a point," Rodrigo agreed. "Two kinds of limitation set in."

"What kinds?"

"The first is the glass ceiling that a federal commission recently documented. That limitation, which sets in at some point in practically every woman's career, slows her advancement. And the reason we have glass ceilings is that some of the women the marketplace welcomed by the millions were not content with entry- and mid-level jobs. They began to compete with men, insisted on being considered for middle management positions, partnerships in accounting and law firms, and the like."

"So the point of affirmative action was to admit women, but in just the right numbers and for just the right low-level jobs. Not too competitive, not too highly paid. Ingenious," I said sadly, thinking of my own daughter and her dimmed professional prospects.

"The idea was to assure a supply of compliant, conscientious workers to operate computers, do legal research, and other forms of paper-pushing. It was not to revolutionize the workplace, much less to employ black men."

"Hmmm," Laz said. "I'll have to think about that. What's her second limiting principle?"

"Childbirth," Rodrigo replied. "Too few babies were being born—white ones, anyway. Recall that raft of books, most written by conservatives, lamenting the 'birth dearth?'[19] They warned that white women were having too few babies; minority women, too many.[20] The precious national gene pool was deteriorating. According to some, we were losing several IQ points per generation.[21] It was time to get white women out of the workplace and back in the bedrooms."

"It *is* interesting that the family-values movement sprang up when it did," I said.

"About five or ten years back, just as women's gains were cresting. Giannina pointed that out, too."

"Intriguing!" Laz commented. "I don't agree totally with what she says. But her theory of the market's unseen limitations, which click in when women's progress reaches a certain point, has the ring of truth. It reminds me of Derrick Bell's interest-convergence theory, which explains the twists and turns of blacks' fortunes in terms of the class interests of elite whites.[22] That I definitely agree with. But you mentioned that Giannina thought her theory might apply to people of color. What did she say about that?"

"Unfortunately, something else intervened. So, working that out is up to us."

"I'm game, if you are," I said, then paused for the waiter who had just materialized at our table to ask how we found our food. "Fine," we all said in unison, and he departed after filling our water glasses. As he left, Rodrigo resumed as follows: "I do have a theory that I can run past you, if you like. And, because it's a critique of law-and-economics, Laz, I'd love your comments. It'll also enable us to discuss those books we mentioned. In fact, they are what stimulated Giannina's and my discussion."

"Too bad she's not here, so we could benefit from her insights," I lamented. "Didn't you tell me once that she majored in economics?"

"She did," Rodrigo replied.

Will the Market Cure Racism? Rodrigo, Laz, and the Professor Consider the Neoconservative Argument That It Will

After a pause for the waiter to remove our plates and take dessert orders, I turned to Rodrigo. "I've had some thoughts on this myself, prompted by a marvelous article by Robin West. And Laz, I hope you'll jump in whenever you think we're wrong. We need you to keep us honest. Don't be silent just because you're outnumbered."

Laz smiled and said quietly, "Don't worry," so Rodrigo began: "My theory consists of four parts, all converging on the inadequacy of the account of evil in the work of classic liberals, as well as their modern counterparts. [I smiled inwardly as I realized my young protégé and I had been thinking along the same lines. But I decided to wait to voice my own thoughts and continued listening.] Both groups seem to think that racism and similar forms of power-tripping will go away if we simply let the free market function. But for four reasons, I think this is highly unlikely."

"Before you get into that," Laz spoke up, "I wonder if it doesn't make sense to lay out, if only briefly, the case that it will. That way, we'll all have a common understanding of the argument we're critiquing."

Rodrigo and I nodded agreement, a little abashed (in my case, at least) that we hadn't thought to do that first. "Laz, why don't you do the honors. Those two books we mentioned might be a good starting point."

Laz Summarizes Murray and the Thernstroms, Who Advocate Doing Away with Vital Programs for Racial Equality

After a pause to allow our waiter to refill our coffee cups, Laz began: "Agreed. In fact their books are complementary in some respects. The Murray volume, like earlier ones by Epstein, Posner, and Becker, proposes elimination of all employment discrimination laws as part of a gen-

eral program that would include deregulation of most industries, aboli-
tion of highway speed limits, vouchers for public education, and other familiar libertarian themes.[23] In this respect, Charles Murray, who as you
know is a scholar at the American Enterprise Institute and coauthor of the
best-selling *The Bell Curve*, goes much farther than other conservative reformers, such as Richard Epstein, who would eliminate workplace antidiscrimination laws but leave ones forbidding discrimination in housing, voting, or public accommodations intact."[24]

Laz looked up expectantly, with a slight smile. I took the bait: "Yes, yes.
We see your point. Conservatives exhibit variation, too. They are not
monolithic or all the same. Go on."

Laz smiled appreciatively, then continued. "Drawing on the early work
of Adam Smith, Murray begins by observing that human beings are social
animals who desire the approval of others. They are also self-regarding—
interested in pursuing their well-being and that of their friends and families. It follows that humans, if left alone and deprived of resort to force
and violence, will cooperate. They will also be generous and tolerant. 'To
satisfy my material needs,' Murray writes, 'I must persuade other people
to trade with me'."[25]

"Sounds good so far," Rodrigo conceded. "But suppose someone doesn't
behave that way. Then what?"

"You mean discriminates against others, by reason of their color, say?
[Rodrigo and I nodded.] Then, according to Murray, we must allow them
to do so. In a free society, he writes [Laz looked down at the slender volume lying open on the table], 'the freedom of association cannot be
abridged.' And this freedom entails, as well, the freedom not to associate
with someone, just as an employer does when, on a hunch, he or she decides to hire Worker A and not Worker B, or a landlord picks one tenant
over another, believing him likely to be quieter and to pay the rent more
promptly than the other. Citizens and private institutions—but not government—must have the freedom to discriminate and follow their tastes
and preferences in comrades, coworkers, and tenants."[26]

"But is not discrimination on the basis of race different from that which
is based on playing loud music in an apartment or absenteeism at work?"
I asked.

"Murray says you cannot separate the bad kinds of discrimination
from the good. 'They are of a piece.'[27] Moreover, he says, the effort to pur-
sue the one and not the other kind has done people of color little good.
The nation was already renouncing racism and discrimination before the
Civil Rights Act of 1964 was passed. The country did not make progress

against racism because Congress enacted that statute; rather, Congress enacted it because the old way of doing business was passing into history. And the act and subsequent edicts imposed a level of bureaucracy that suffocated business while sparking legitimate resistance among whites."[28]

Laz looked up to see our reaction. But just then the waiter arrived with our desserts. After we sampled them, Rodrigo observed: "That's more or less what I remember from my reading. And it will come as no surprise that I take issue with practically everything you recounted. But why don't we get the other book on the floor first."

"Fine," Laz replied, taking a deep breath. "The Thernstrom book is not nearly so negative about laws forbidding bias in housing, credit, voting, and jobs—although, interestingly, they take strenuous issue with the line of cases that penalize employment practices that have an adverse, or disproportionate, impact on minority workers.[29] But their main target is affirmative action."

"By which they mean preferences, based on race, for blacks, Chicanos, Asians, and Native Americans in hiring, promotion, and in higher education admissions," I chimed in.[30]

"Exactly," Laz agreed. "And although I don't agree with them entirely, they make perhaps the strongest case yet against that practice. I still think it is salvageable with a change here and there. They don't. For them, it's reverse racism, pure and simple. And, like Murray, they hold that it's entirely unnecessary since the country has repudiated racism for more than thirty years, and blacks have been making steady progress in every important area of life."

"What optimists," Rodrigo observed.

"A fair observation," Laz conceded. "They do appear to lay great emphasis on the offbeat statistic showing black or brown progress, passing lightly over all the evidence of stagnation and pain."[31]

"As I recall, they headline the growth of the middle class of color, ignoring frightening statistics about misery, crime, infant mortality, and school dropout on the other end," I said.

"What's more," Rodrigo seconded, "they draw a dubious conclusion from even those Panglossian statistics. The growth of the middle class is directly traceable to affirmative action policies in the nation's professional schools."

"Still, you must concede that things are better for minorities than they were in the days of Jim Crow. The Thernstroms who, like Murray, are longtime opponents of affirmative action, devote the first third of their book to showing how far we have come as a nation since those terrible days. Having shown how unimaginably bad conditions were in the South during the late 1800s and first part of this century, they then trace the start of improvement to World War II, when jobs opened up for blacks in industry and in the armed forces. It was the overall expansion of the U.S. economy, not civil rights legislation, that sparked black progress."

"I might agree," I said quietly. "But go on."

"When the Thernstroms come to the civil rights milestones of the modern era—*Brown v. Board of Education*, the Civil Rights Act of 1964, and the voting rights legislation of the following year, however, they change course. While hailing efforts to assure fundamental rights of citizenship, they criticize virtually every governmental program aimed at improving conditions for blacks.[32] Today, they write, few whites are out-and-out racists. Polls of white people supposedly show this. But programs that emphasize color and distribute benefits to blacks over seemingly more deserving whites inflame whites who would otherwise support black causes. They also induce dependency and reinforce a black leadership style that thrives on resentment, assuring that relations among the races remain tense."

"Do they have any solution?" Rodrigo asked. "I don't recall seeing one."

"Not really," Laz answered. "Conditions for blacks won't improve much more, they say, until they repair their family structure. Back in the era of rapid advances—the 1940s and 1950s—most blacks lived in intact families. Today many do not. That's why, according to the Thernstroms, despite two decades of civil rights and affirmative action, the situation is not better than it is. Affirmative action may even positively injure minorities. Without it, black entrepreneurship and ownership of small businesses would have flourished. Instead, too many blacks rely on government jobs and contracts."

"Which may be coming to an end—the contracts part, I mean," Rodrigo ventured.

"I'm sure the Thernstroms would say good riddance. But don't conclude that they're heartless. They do say that the early, color-blind civil rights laws were a good idea. Epstein and other libertarians do, too.[33] And they do leave a place for idealism, just as Murray argues for courtesy toward all."

"Maybe not heartless, but plain wrong," Rodrigo exclaimed. "Merely showing that improvement was under way before—or insisting, as they do, that people don't need affirmative action to trade with blacks[34]—does not mean social programs did no good. Black progress was stalling during the late 1950s and early sixties. Southern states mounted real resistance to integration and *Brown*. Everyone knows that white neighborhoods will accept a small number of black families, but then a tipping point sets in. So, the early gains might well not have continued. It's like arguing that society had no need for the federal government to build the system of interstate highways, because model-T drivers were learning to steer around the potholes. Are we ready to move on to my argument about the marketplace?"

I couldn't help but smile at the eagerness of my young protégé to parade his ideas before us. Laz, too, smiled and nodded assent. I thanked Laz for his comprehensive and evenhanded summary. We settled down, Rodrigo took a last swig of his coffee, looked up, and began:

In Which Rodrigo Puts Forward a Four-Part Argument
Why the Free Market of Social and Economic
Exchanges Will Not Eliminate Discrimination

"In a nation such as ours, with a long history of white-over-color subordination, racism will not wither away all by itself. I have a four-part argument. But let me start with a thought experiment or two."

"I love your thought experiments," Laz said. "Fire away."

"Imagine two black men, A and B. The first lives in a city with very little racism, say Seattle; the second in one where the white majority hates and despises blacks. Let's suppose both have similar credentials—they are engineers. Which will earn more money, A or B?"

I looked at Rodrigo and said, "A, of course. Experiencing fewer headwinds, he will rise to the top—or, at least, to the level his abilities allow. In fact, I was reading somewhere that Seattle has one of the lowest indices of prejudice in the country. Black workers earn more than 90 percent of what similarly qualified whites do."

Rodrigo replied, "I agree. But that's just the opposite of what law-and-economics would predict. The black living in the racist city ought to be at more of a premium than the one living in Seattle. Assuming that at least one firm would hire him, he ought to command top dollar. But this flies in the face of experience. Historically, blacks have always migrated from regions like the South with high prejudice to ones where it is low, rather than the other way around. And for good reason. Racism changes the market and depresses wages."

"But Murray and his colleagues say it's the reverse," I said. "If there's a market, it should depress racism. Your thought experiment does expose a possible flaw in the theory. But you mentioned another one."

"You and I were talking about this before.[35] It has to do with the unthinkable. Imagine a rural state, like Minnesota. The legislature is concerned about the high toll in deaths and accidents caused by teenage drivers. So, it decides to allow children to obtain driver's licenses at age eleven. Studies show that many children this age would make very good, careful drivers. With the new change, young Johnny can help Dad and Mom on the farm. He can drive the tractor a few miles along County Road 5 from the back twenty acres to the front fifty, which is a big help. At the age of sixteen, however, Johnny must surrender his license until age twenty-six, at which time he can get it back again."

"So the overall accident rate goes down with all those dangerous teenage drivers off the road. And Dad gets some help on the farm," Laz said.

"Exactly," Rodrigo said. "But would other states emulate Minnesota's example? No. The sight of little twelve-year-olds, hunched over the steering wheel, carefully and responsibly driving Mom to church, would fly in the face of society's conception of a child. Children are supposed to be dependent, small, in need of protection. That's part of their social construction. The notion that some of them might turn out to be safer drivers than older teenagers and young adults goes against the grain. No other state would follow Minnesota's lead. Even that state itself might repeal the law."

"And you think this shows something about the market and race?" Laz asked in reply.

"Yes," Rodrigo replied. "Minorities labor under similar stereotypes,[36] so that even if one firm prospered by hiring a brilliant black or Chicano chief executive officer, others would not rush to follow suit. They would be sure that something would go wrong with the other firm and its CEO—maybe he or she would be fired for graft. Or, if the black leader proceeded to double profits year after year, they would simply pronounce him or her an exception. The next black that applied would be ruled out for some reason."

Laz furrowed his brow. "I'm not so sure," he replied. "Profits that large should give even a racist competitor pause. But if you're right, why should that be?"

"It's because racism is so strongly supported by extramarket forces, including stereotyping and internalized, scarcely visible preconceptions. A thick web of culture, language, and institutional inertia discourages the competitive frenzy marketplace advocates place their faith in. If the market brings changes, they will come at best slowly and painfully. In the short run, minorities in the marketplace will confront a host of pseudo-economic stereotypes, including 'dull,' 'lazy,' and 'of bad character.'"

"But that's not because of any market failure, it's because of false information," Laz retorted. "As the market starts to work, businesses will gain exposure to more black and brown workers and learn that the stereotypes are false and the taste for discrimination costly."

"But there you are," Rodrigo replied, leaning forward excitedly. "You and your friends—nothing personal, Laz, you're my best buddy—are making what we might call a category mistake, like asking 'What color is the number seven?' To see racism as a matter of private taste is to mistake its very nature. It's a public harm, one that distorts the entire fabric of so cial and political life. Racism should be condemned socially, by all of society, and one means of doing so is by affirmative action and other forms of intervention in the free market."

"Well, are you saying that blacks and Chicanos somehow fall outside the free market?" Laz asked incredulously.

"Yes. Slaves were not parts of the free market, except as chattels. They could not buy their freedom, and the same is true to some extent today. A rich black or Latino is still subject to police harassment merely by reason of driving a nice car or walking the streets at night. No, Laz, racial equality is a public good that the market cannot easily by itself address. It demands a preallocative normative reckoning by society as a whole. Only once the difficult normative questions have been faced up to does the market become a viable means of effectuating those normative decisions, including the very basic one of who is an equal member of society."

"Political decisions have costs," Laz said. "And who is to say that society will make the right ones? We could decree fair treatment and hire an army of police to watch out for any show of racism. But blacks and Latinos would still, in most cases, be stuck in dead-end, private-sector jobs."

"We should make the effort, nevertheless," Rodrigo replied. "My thought experiments show that the market just won't drive out racism. Waiting around for it to catch up with our public ideals is not only morally unacceptable; it's a category mistake. If we believe in equality, we must condition the market and ourselves, to break down longstanding barriers to freedom for all."

Laz shook his head and smiled in spite of himself. "Interesting argument, Rodrigo. And your distinction between public and private commitments and category mistakes does give me pause. But before I'm convinced, I could use a little more analysis."

Rodrigo's First Argument: Cultural Texts
Show the Ubiquity of the Problem of Evil

"Okay," Rodrigo said. "Consider how four types of evidence converge on the necessity of confronting the problem of evil: cultural texts, social science studies of helping behavior, evolutionary science, and crosscultural studies."

"Hmmm," said Laz. "I'm curious to see where you're going. I've often thought you cheerful liberals lack an adequate account of human evil, visible in your treatment of crime and criminals, for example. But now it seems you are going to level this inadequacy against my side. This I want to hear."

"You'll have to decide for yourself which way the argument cuts," Rodrigo said. "The marketplace argument, which owes its origin to early utilitarians like Bentham, Mill, and Adam Smith, is almost entirely forward-looking. If one course of action doesn't work, try another. This may account for the cheerful, social-engineering character of liberal civil rights law that all of us have noted, as well as the short attention span of liberals who, once having put a plan or law in place, think the problem is solved and want to move on to another, such as saving the whales."

I wanted to move back to Rodrigo's evidence. "And by cultural texts, I assume you mean ones such as Shakespeare, Melville, and the Bible, which recognize the human impulse to harm enemies, distrust foreigners, and conquer and enslave other societies?" I asked.

"Those and more," Rodrigo answered. "They all show humans struggling with the impulse to war against and suppress others. Human nature, of course, also contains a generous and benevolent impulse, as even Adam Smith recognized. But unfortunately it's limited mainly to persons we know well."

"I think I can see where you're going," I interjected. "It's amazing—I was reflecting just this afternoon on Robin West's classic exchange with Richard Posner. Are you familiar with her Harvard article?"

When the two young scholars, who had entered teaching recently, nodded a little uncertainly, I elaborated as follows: "West, who teaches law at Georgetown, criticized Richard Posner, and implicitly the entire law-and-economics school, for rendering an imperfect view of human nature. Basing their theories on a view of mankind as interested in satisfying basic needs, Posner and his colleagues put forward a mechanism, namely, the market, and a medium, namely, economic exchanges, to enable that satisfaction to be maximized. In their view, exchanges and contracts, such as for labor, entered into freely by autonomous individuals ordinarily ought to be left alone, since they should be presumed to advance the interests and well-being of the parties who drew them up. Even if one of the parties turns out to be the loser in a transaction—an investment, say—allowing such exchanges benefits all of society and so should win the endorsement even of those who occasionally lose. They, too, benefit from the overall wealth and freedom a regime of free-market rules brings."

Laz asked, "And I suppose West took issue with that premise?"

"She did. Drawing on great literature, especially the stories of Franz Kafka, she shows that, in addition to a happiness-maximizing impulse, men and women have a darker side that causes us to surrender our autonomy and to allow ourselves to be dominated and made miserable."[37]

"That sounds like classical masochism," Laz said. "I agree that some people behave that way, although some of my fellow conservatives probably would quarrel over how much. Conservatives, as you know, tend not to be very interested in unconscious forces and motives. Richard Posner, in a reply to Professor West, said as much, if I recall.[38] But I gather you're emphasizing something different in human nature?"

"Yes," said Rodrigo. "The flip side of what she emphasized, in fact. Sadism—although that word may be a little more psychoanalytic than I would like. What I mean is that cultural texts, as well as the human record, show a recurring tendency on the part of individuals to want to dominate and mistreat others.[39] Early man limited his fellow-feeling to members of his family or clan.[40] Today, even though our sympathies are more universalistic, we still tolerate economic exploitation by ruthless capitalism in Latin America and Russia. And famines in Africa draw less attention than ones on our doorstep."

"Out of sight, out of mind, I suppose. But with respect to the law-and-economics school and their account of racism, your point is . . . ?" I coaxed.

"The cultural record shows that we are apt to be much less generous with people of other races. The English language alone boasts a rich vocabulary including *xenophobia*, *chauvinism*, and *racism*, as well as an extensive set of words that stereotype and demean others merely on account of their skin color. This implies that humans, left to their own devices, will not choose to deal with others they regard as different. They will not hire, trade with, or in general bring them into their circles of regard. They will engage in economic exchanges with them, such as renting hotel rooms or seeking them out as clients, only if others of their own kind are not available."

"This makes me think of your Minnesota thought experiment," Laz mused. "I think I have a reply, but why don't you go on. I'd like to hear your other arguments against marketplace theory first."

Rodrigo's Second Argument: Biology and the Study of Other Species Disclose That Many Adopt Strategies Similar to Those of Humans

"My second argument proceeds by induction," Rodrigo said. "Consider how other species engage in similar behavior. I hasten to add that I don't mean that biology is destiny, or that every species kills for pleasure—most don't. Moreover, I believe that racism and other forms of human aggression can be greatly reduced by teaching, religious appeals, and firm legal and moral pressure. Human beings, after all, have free will, or at least our political and legal institutions assume so. But seeing how other species, including ones closely related to us, adopt strategies that defend territory or exclude competitors from food, light, and other necessities of life adds to my argument. We can't safely rely on innate human goodness and impersonal forces like the market to curb such behavior among ourselves."

"I can think of works like Konrad Lorenz's 'On Aggression,'"[41] I added. "And Jane Goodall's work, which shows that the great apes not only cooperate but fight, and sometimes kill, to advance group interests in breeding, territory, and food. Sometimes they seemingly do it for what can only be described as the fun of it.[42] These and other works of animal and evolutionary science show how some species see to their own survival by attacking others, even ones closely related to them physically."

"But I hope you are not saying that these animal studies prove something about human behavior, are you?" Laz asked. "Because humans are different. We have souls. We have speech. We have an ideal, not just a material, nature. If parents indoctrinate children with a sense of right and wrong, certain realms *may* be left safely to the market, whereas a group of animals, say a flock of sheep or group of untrained dogs, might require constant watching—regulation, if you will."

"I don't want to make too much of the naturalistic argument," Rodrigo conceded. "It just puts us on notice not to assume too much. My next one addresses specifically human behavior. Ready to move on?"

It was late, and I was starting to flag. Rodrigo must have noticed, for he said, "I hope we're not wearing you out, Professor. You've been up longer than we and had to travel farther to get here. Want to postpone the rest until breakfast?"

"No, no," I insisted. "I'm going strong. I want to hear the last two prongs of your argument. But I could use a cup of tea."

Laz immediately looked around, attracted the waiter's attention, and seconds later we were placing our orders—more coffee for my two young friends (whose iron constitutions caused me, once again, to marvel—caffeine this late would have me tossing and turning all night) and a soothing chamomile tea for me. Then, Rodrigo continued:

Rodrigo's Third Argument: Studies of Helping Behavior in Crossrace Situations Cast Doubt on the Ability of Free Choice to Drive Out Racism

"Good idea, Professor. I'm a little bushed myself," Rodrigo admitted. "But I can go through my last two arguments quickly. I'm sure the two of you are familiar with the social science literature dealing with so-called helping behavior in crossrace situations, and also with the role of influence on cognition?"

"We were talking about the first group of studies before," I said,[43] "but I don't think the second. Why don't you summarize them for us."

Studies of Helping Behavior in Crossrace Situations.   The waiter set down our steaming beverages, and I motioned surreptitiously for the check. Rodrigo objected, but I waved him aside: "I'm on vacation. Please be my guests." The two exchanged glances, and I knew I would have a battle on my hands later, so I said, "We'll see. But why don't you go on." Rodrigo took the bait. As he did so, I stealthily removed my credit card from my wallet, which I had been holding in my lap.

"A host of social science studies explore what people do in crossrace situations. In a typical one, the scientist has a black female assistant stage an accident in which she spills a bag of groceries.[44] Later, a white assistant does the same thing, and they record what happens. Sometimes they do something similar with stranded motorists.[45] The studies show that people go to the aid of persons of their own race more readily than that of others. Some researchers explain the results in terms of 'norm theory.'[46] We respond to persons in need according to how normal or abnormal their plight seems to us. Famines in Biafra evoke little response, because we think they are normal in that part of the world. But if our middle-class neighbor shows up at our doorstep, not having eaten in two days because of losing his or her job, we immediately rush to his or her aid."

"I remember that line of experiments," I said, "and see how they fortify your argument. If an economic exchange is the kind that can also help the other person—a hiring decision, say—then one might well unconsciously look for people like oneself—freckle-faced blondes of European descent, if one is like that, rather than black men with afros, even if they have a Ph.D. This skews the marketplace in favor of any group who can exercise discretion not to deal. But what's the second line of experiments?"

"I was thinking of studies of authority and mind-set. Are you familiar with these?"

Laz said, "I know about Stanley Milgram and his studies of obedience. [47] In a series of articles and a book, he described experiments that show how people behave when commanded by authority figures. In one, he hooked up volunteers, who did not know the purpose of the experiment, to a fake console with a series of switches. A 'doctor,' wearing a white coat, explained that the purpose of the study was learning and reinforcement, and that they were to be the teacher, administering small electric shocks to a learner in another room. The doctor warned the volunteer, however, never to flip the switches beyond a certain point, because then he or she could administer a fatal dose of electricity. As the experiment proceeded, the doctor directed the teachers to administer higher and higher doses of electricity, each of which was followed by more and more heartrending groans from the other room. The shrieks were emitted, of course, by trained actors and were completely fake. Although the volunteers showed distress over what they were doing, fidgeting and sweating, most followed the directions of the doctor, even to the point of administering what they believed could be a lethal jolt of electricity to a fellow human being. Afterward, many confronted the realization that, like good Nazis, they had done what an authority figure commanded even though they might have killed another human being."

Studies of Belief and Group Influence. "And the other line of experiments," Rodrigo continued, "while not quite so graphic, is just as well known. Solomon Asch and his collaborators held up cards with lines drawn on them and asked a group of volunteers to identify which of two matched in length.[48] All except one were confederates of the experimenter and instructed to vote for the wrong line. The idea was to see if group pressure would cause the subject who was not in the know to go along."

"I read about those studies," I interjected. "In most cases, the subject did so. And afterward it turned out that many acquiesced, not to avoid trouble or just to get the experiment over with but because they actually believed the majority, despite their original conviction to the contrary. Group dynamics changed what they actually saw."

"I see why you cite these studies," Laz said. "As with your twelve-year-old driver example, they suggest that people won't trade with perfectly acceptable partners because racist stereotypes and narratives persuade them that they are not worthy. Again, I have some reservations, because I think people have more free will than that. But let's hear your fourth argument."

Rodrigo's Fourth Argument: Studies of Other Societies, and of Particular Institutions in Our Own, Show That Highly Formal Settings Elicit the Least Racism

"My final point also proceeds by induction—Oh, you tricky fellow!" I had just snatched the bill from the waiter, who had arrived bearing it on a small tray.

"You can say what you will about altruism in mixed-race settings," I replied with a smile. "In this one, I'm paying. My income's higher than yours, even in retirement, and my costs of living, lower. I've learned many a new wrinkle today. You young scholars don't realize how much we old-timers learn from upstarts like you. Especially when it comes to recent currents, like marketplace theory, that came along after we got our start. We can split breakfast if we're up that early. Want to eat together?"

Laz and Rodrigo glanced at each other. "We were going to go for a quick run, then grab a bite before we catch our flight back. Want to join us?"

"I did bring my running shoes," I said. "But I'm sure you two will want to set a faster pace than I can go comfortably—just as you do in intellectual conversation. Why don't we start out together, then you can go on ahead at some point. I'll finish my run and meet you back here at, say, eight-thirty?"

"Perfect," said Laz. "Let's meet outside the hotel at seven. The desk clerk said they have running maps for guests."

Having settled our morning plans, Laz and I sat back expectantly. After the waiter refilled our coffee and tea, Rodrigo looked up.

"My final argument draws on empirical and crosscultural studies. For example, in connection with hate speech, a specific form of racism, writers have been studying the effect of formal rules. Basing their conclusions both on the nature of prejudice and on the success of Canada and certain European societies in bridling it, these scholars have developed what they call the 'fairness and formality' hypothesis.[49] Are you familiar with it?"

"I've read about it," Laz said. "It holds that formal institutions are apt to diminish not just the amount of racism that is expressed in behavior but the very impulse itself. Formality, such as the robes, flags, and other paraphernalia of a court proceeding, remind all present that the higher values of the American creed are to predominate. Informal settings, such as those characterizing alternative dispute resolution, present fewer such reminders and so, all other things being equal, are apt to call up more prejudice. Scholars have used this to explain why racism is relatively absent in settings like the military and sports, which contain many formal rules and so afford less scope for discretion. They have also used it to compare the record of relatively laissez-faire societies such as the United States and ones such as Canada, Great Britain, Italy, and Germany that believe in freedom of expression but nevertheless forbid racist and anti-Semitic speech."[50]

"And so you agree that, all things being equal, formality offers better prospects for discouraging prejudice than its opposite?" Rodrigo asked.

"I would," Laz conceded. "Like most conservatives, I have no problem with formality. And although I don't draw quite the same conclusion you do from your four-part argument, I concede that you have shown a chink—maybe a large one—in the armor of the law-and-economics movement and some of my more complacent colleagues in the libertarian camp. Racism does present a unique challenge for free-market philosophy. Your thought experiments plant the seed of doubt, and your four sorts of evidence just drive it home: We cannot sit back complacently, rake in profits, and rationalize that the system that benefits us and our class is best for those at the bottom, too. Self-respecting conservatives must do better than that!"

"Can you do better, Laz?" I asked. I respected the young man's intelligence and candor. His befriending of Rodrigo, a year younger than he, junior on his faculty, and poles apart politically, spoke volumes for Laz's fair-mindedness and generosity. I hoped he would lay out his theory, and despite the late hour was delighted when he said:

In Which Laz Proposes a Cultural Synthesis: A Race-Neutral Program on Which Left and White Might Agree

"I've been giving this some thought. As you know, Professor, my own parents were immigrants. Raised to detest discrimination of any kind, I believe all men and women are entitled to rise according to their merits, without artificial barriers or preferences. At the same time, I agree with Rodrigo that merit is, to some degree, constructed, and is apt at any point to favor those activities that the empowered group do well. I also concede that with respect to race, neutral, process-oriented market strategies are not apt to pick out members of minority groups for advancement and beneficial trade. But the Thernstroms and Murray do make valid points. Formal governmental programs aimed exclusively at blacks and Latinos institutionalize bureaucracy, deprive people of the opportunity to act out of generosity by converting everything into an obligation, foster a hand-out mentality among the beneficiaries, stigmatize able minorities, and stir up hostility among working-class whites, like my family. The trick is to find something that minimizes these costs while allowing suffering popu-lations, until recently mired in slavery and Jim Crow laws, to move ahead."

Rodrigo looked up with an expression that I can only describe as a mix-ture of wariness and hope. "Please go ahead, Laz. You've listened care-fully to what we've said. I'm anxious to hear from you."

Glancing quickly over at me, Laz began. "The American public is tired of race-conscious remedies. Although one can quarrel over what the polls mean, it's only a matter of time before affirmative action and similar pro-grams targeted specifically at minorities come to an end. The question is what will replace them."

"Aren't they necessary to counter the effects of past discrimination, level the playing field, and provide professionals of color to serve as role models for others?" Rodrigo asked.

"All those things are important," Laz said, "and it's inexcusable that the Thernstroms offer no replacement for them. I think the answer is to put in place color-neutral programs to help *all* those who are poor and disadvantaged. These programs would include special consideration in college admissions for anyone who can show he or she was raised under impoverished circumstances. They would also include special outreach to inner-city schools and programs to create jobs and ameliorate urban blight. Many of the problems of the ghettos and barrios are not racial in nature but economic. Not only will universal programs be more palatable to the white middle class; they will help the truly poor and deserving. The son or daughter of the black or Chicano brain surgeon may not get special help, but why should they? At the same time, the child of Ukrain-ian immigrants who is the first in his or her family to attend college would get special consideration. Current affirmative action programs don't help desperately poor blacks, who can't get into college or win construction contracts even with a helping hand. My programs would."

Laz had been speaking quietly and urgently. Finally Rodrigo spoke. "Laz, your proposal reminds me of William Julius Wilson's recent book.[51] And much as I respect your humanism and commitment to equal rights, I doubt it will fill the bill. Even universal programs will end up giving blacks short shrift unless they have a race-conscious component or are monitored extremely carefully. Ellis Cose showed that even black executives and law partners suffer racism and slights every day.[52] It's true that we must deal with poverty, crime, drugs, and lack of services in the cities. But race will always remain a separate and independent subordinating factor. Blacks are not just white people who happen not to have any money right now. Pretending that race doesn't count is an evasion.

"Pretending that black people's problems are all due to race is also an evasion," Laz said evenly. "And programs based on race are social dynamite. They single out beneficiaries by an easily identified physical factor—one that already comes bearing much historical weight. If you could give aid directly to the black poor, which I admit are in great need of it, and could do it quietly and for a short time, without being discovered, I might favor it. But you can't do that in a society such as ours. And if you do it openly, you just foster resentment and make matters worse."

"You could try educating white folks to accept it," Rodrigo ventured. "Economic conditions are better than they have been for a time. The pie is expanding. Giving a job to A does not mean taking one from B."

"But programs that change the infrastructure are much better. They last forever," Laz replied. "And they have a cascading effect. Create more jobs in the inner city or the manufacturing sector, and you put more money into the pockets of the poor. Some will open small businesses, or send their children to community colleges, when before they couldn't afford it."

"Your approach is attractive," Rodrigo conceded. "And I, too, welcome the day when race doesn't matter. But, for now, it does. Perhaps there's no way out of the trap, and we just have to muddle through, using whatever degree of remedial race-consciousness that society will tolerate while hoping that broad, race-neutral programs aimed at the poor in general will provide some incidental relief. I just hope it doesn't all happen so slowly that the poor of color sink into an irreversible spiral."

"One last thing the two of you might want to consider, given your wary views on law and economics, is the difference between allowing free-market economics to rule and using market incentives to induce certain kinds of behavior. For example, in environmental law the first approach would correspond to allowing the national forests to be sold to whomever values them the most, environmentalists or timber companies; the second, to using 'pollution permits' that polluters must buy, but that they can sell if they become cleaner. This might work with affirmative action." Laz sat back with an expectant expression.

"You mean companies with good records of hiring blacks, say, could sell their surplus brownie points, so to speak, to firms who don't like them?"[53] I asked.

"Exactly," Laz said. "This should satisfy even Charles Murray, since his main objection to antidiscrimination laws is that they force people to refrain from what they may want to do, namely, satisfy their taste for discrimination. It also requires a lesser role for government—"

"Which should keep him happy," I interjected.

"Indeed," Laz said. "Government would not need to monitor and ride herd on every company and transaction, since the sales of these discrimination permits would go on privately."

"Perhaps the two broad sorts of programs—race-neutral and race-conscious—will work together," I said, sensing that our discussion was about to come to an end and hoping to set the stage for later. "As white folks begin to see that the new programs—job training, for example—benefit them and their struggling counterparts, their empathy and receptiveness to dealing with the special problems of racism may grow. The two plans, then, may work together, each being a necessary precondition of the other."

"An intriguing suggestion, Professor," Laz said, brightening and pushing his chair back from the table. "I'd love to know how your and Rodrigo's observations on human nature fit into it. Why don't we talk about it more tomorrow morning. Rodrigo and I have afternoon classes to teach back home tomorrow, so we might want to catch a few winks of sleep."

"I'm game," said Rodrigo. "It's almost ten. The Professor and I discussed something similar before. Maybe we can build on that."

As we stood up and started walking toward the elevator to our rooms, Laz turned to me and said, "If there's one thing I think we can all agree on, it's that the combination of the Thernstrom antiaffirmative action proposal and the Murray libertarian one to eliminate or water down all the civil rights laws is lethal. It would leave people of color with little protection, requiring them to pull themselves up by their bootstraps, something not even white immigrants managed to accomplish unaided. The market alone won't drive out racism or do much to alleviate the special problems of the underclass of color. Laws forbidding racial discrimination will remain necessary into the foreseeable future. Whether we can do more than that is open to debate. The two of you think we can. The Thernstroms say no. I say we can target poverty, of all kinds, black or white, and offer special help in college admissions and outreach to young people who have struggled with poverty and disadvantage. Will this improve conditions for your people quickly enough to turn things around? I wish I knew. I'm disappointed that the Thernstroms, whose intellect I admire, came up with no solution."

"It's a topic for another day," I said, standing up and yawning.

Rodrigo pressed the *up* button. "Or another night," he said smiling.

Notes

1. *See, e.g.*, RICHARD EPSTEIN, FORBIDDEN GROUNDS: THE CASE AGAINST EMPLOYMENT DISCRIMINATION LAWS (1992); SIMPLE RULES FOR A COMPLEX WORLD (1995); RICHARD POSNER, THE ECONOMICS OF JUSTICE (1981); ECONOMIC ANALYSIS OF LAW (3d ed. 1986).

2. *See, e.g.*, Posner, ECONOMIC ANALYSIS, *supra* at 3–13.

3. "Economics does not seek to depict states of mind; it is concerned with what people (even animals) do, not what they feel or think. To complain that economics does not paint a realistic picture of the conscious mind is to miss the point of economics." Richard A. Posner, *The Ethical Significance of Free Choice*, 99 HARV. L. REV. 1431, 1439 (1986).

4. *See generally* GARY S. BECKER, THE ECONOMICS OF DISCRIMINATION (2d ed. 1971). After exploring the economics of racial discrimination, Becker and his followers then pushed the application of economic theory to education, fertility, household labor, criminal behavior, prehistoric hunting, slavery, suicide, adultery, and even the behavioral responses of rats and pigeons. *See* POSNER, THE ECONOMICS OF JUSTICE *supra*. For example, law-and-economists employing the egoist behavioral model—that all individuals act in a strictly self-interested manner—have applied economic theory to altruism, love, marriage, and numerous other human emotions and actions. Even irrationality itself has been economically analyzed in this way. *See* Jeffrey L. Harrison, *Egoism, Altruism, and Market Illusions: The Limits of Law and Economics*, 33 UCLA L. REV. 1309, 1311 (1986).

5. *See generally* Robin West, *Authority, Autonomy, and Choice: The Role of Consent in the Moral and Political Visions of Franz Kafka and Richard Posner*, 99 HARV. L. REV. 384 (1985).

6. *See* Robin West, *Submission, Choice, and Ethics*, 99 HARV. L. REV. 1449, 1449 (1986).

7. *Id.*

8. *See* West, *Authority, supra* at 386.

9. *See id.* at 387–88.

10. In particular, racism, which entails deriving pleasure (and sometimes material advantage) from suppressing the chances of others.

11. *See* MICHEL FOUCAULT, MADNESS AND CIVILIZATION (1960).

12. West, AUTHORITY, *supra* at 385.

13. Charles Murray, WHAT IT MEANS TO BE A LIBERTARIAN: A PERSONAL INTERPRETATION (1997).

14. STEPHAN THERNSTROM & ABIGAIL THERNSTROM, AMERICA IN BLACK AND WHITE: ONE NATION INDIVISIBLE (1997).

15. *E.g.*, Epstein, FORBIDDEN GROUNDS; SIMPLE RULES, *supra*; *The Subtle Vices of the Employment Discrimination Laws*, JOHN MARSHALL L. REV. 575 (1996); *The Status Production Sideshow: Why the Antidiscrimination Laws Are Still a Mistake*, 108 HARV. L. REV. 1085 (1995).

16. GARY S. BECKER, THE ECONOMICS OF DISCRIMINATION (2d ed. 1971); THE ECONOMIC APPROACH TO HUMAN BEHAVIOR (1976).

17. ECONOMICS OF JUSTICE; ECONOMIC ANALYSIS OF LAW, *supra*; *The Ethical Significance of Free Choice: A Reply to Professor West*, 99 HARV. L. REV. 1431 (1986).

18. On the way white women have benefited from affirmative action, see Steven A. Holmes, *Defending Affirmative Action, Liberals Try to Place the Debate's Focus on Women*, N.Y. TIMES, Mar. 2, 1995, at B-7; Steven A. Holmes, *G.O.P. Leadership Backs Out on a Bill to End Preferences*, N.Y. TIMES, Jul. 13, 1996, at A-1.

19. *See, e.g.*, BEN WATTENBERG, THE BIRTH DEARTH (1987).

20. *See* JEAN STEFANCIC & RICHARD DELGADO, NO MERCY: HOW CONSERVATIVE THINK TANKS AND FOUNDATIONS CHANGED AMERICA'S SOCIAL AGENDA 33–44 (1996). On the history and politics of the eugenics movement, see STEPHEN JAY GOULD, THE MISMEASURE OF MAN (1974); STEFAN KUHL, THE NAZI CONNECTION (1994).

21. On this supposed deterioration, see RICHARD HERRNSTEIN & CHARLES MURRAY, THE BELL CURVE: INTELLIGENCE AND CLASS STRUCTURE IN AMERICAN LIFE (1994).

22. Derrick Bell, Brown v. Board of Education *and the Interest Convergence Dilemma*, 93 HARV. L. REV. 518 (1980), sets out and illustrates this famous axiom.

23. Murray, *supra* at 37–40, 52–54, 60–78, 93–97, 114–23.

24. *Cf.* FORBIDDEN GROUNDS, *supra* at xii; and *Subtle Vices*, *supra* at 575 ("principles applicable in private employment markets may not carry over to these other areas"), *with* CLINT BOLICK, THE AFFIRMATIVE ACTION FRAUD: CAN WE RESTORE THE AMERICAN CIVIL RIGHTS VISION? (1996) (proposing broad repeal of antidiscrimination laws in favor of letting the free market reign).

25. Murray, *supra* at 80–81.

26. *Id.* at 42–43, 81–84.

27. *Id.* at 86.

28. *Id.* at 24–27, 54–59, 87–88.

29. *Id.* at 422–92.

30. *Id.* at 171–77, 179–80, 312–461, 539.

31. *Id.* at 183–231, 232–54.

32. *Id.* at 16–17, 315–529.

33. *Id.* at 21–22, 122–48, 172–80, 532–33, 540; Epstein, *Subtle Vices, supra* at 575–76; *Standing Firm on Forbidden Grounds*, 31 S. DIEGO L. REV. 1, 26–32 (1994). See also FORBIDDEN GROUNDS, *supra* at 16–17 (only a "small, hardened minority" will disdain fairness and cooperation in favor of cruel, destructive behavior).

34. Thernstroms, *supra* at 450.

35. RICHARD DELGADO, THE RODRIGO CHRONICLES, chapter 2 (1995).

36. Richard Delgado & Jean Stefancic, *Images of the Outsider in American Law and Culture: Can Free Expression Remedy Systemic Social Ills?* 77 CORNELL L. REV. 1258, 1262–75 (1992); Margaret Russell, *Race and the Dominant Gaze: Narratives of Law and Inequality in Popular Film*, 15 LEGAL STUD. J. 243 (1991); Peggy Davis, *Law as Micro-Aggression*, 95 YALE L.J. 1559 (1989).

37. West, AUTHORITY, *supra*.

38. *Ethical Significance, supra* at 1439–40, 1444–45.

39. JOHN KEEGAN, A HISTORY OF WARFARE (1993).

40. Christopher Stone, *Should Trees Have Standing? Toward Legal Rights for Natural Objects*, 45 S. CAL. L. REV. 450, 450–56 (1972).

41. KONRAD LORENZ, ON AGGRESSION (1966).

42. JANE GOODALL, THE CHIMPANZEES OF GOMBE: PATTERNS OF BEHAVIOR 313–56, 488–534 (1986).

43. RICHARD DELGADO, THE COMING RACE WAR? AND OTHER APOCALYPTIC TALES OF AMERICA AFTER AFFIRMATIVE ACTION AND WELFARE, chapter 3 (1996).

44. *Id.* (describing this and similar experiments).

45. *Id.*

46. *Id.* (describing classic works in this vein of scholarship).

47. STANLEY MILGRAM, OBEDIENCE TO AUTHORITY (1969).

48. Solomon Asch, *Opinions and Social Pressure*, 193 SCI. AM. 31 (1955).

49. *See* Richard Delgado, *Fairness and Formality: Minimizing the Risk of Prejudice in Alternative Dispute Resolution*, 1985 WIS. L. REV. 1359, 1387–91, 1400–04; Trina Grillo, *The Mediation Alternative: Process Dangers for Women*, 100 YALE L.J. 1545 (1991).

50. *See, e.g.*, Richard Delgado & Jean Stefancic, *A Shifting Balance: Freedom of Expression and Hate-Speech Restriction* (book review), 78 IOWA L. REV. 737 (1993); Mayo Moran, *Talking About Hate Speech*, 1994 WIS. L. REV. 1925.

51. WILLIAM JULIUS WILSON, WHEN WORK DISAPPEARS: THE WORLD OF THE NEW URBAN POOR (1996); see also RICHARD D. KAHLENBERG, THE REMEDY: CLASS, RACE, AND AFFIRMATIVE ACTION (1996) (proposing that affirmative action on the basis of race be phased out in favor of a version based on class).

52. THE RAGE OF A PRIVILEGED CLASS (1994).

53. *See* DERRICK BELL, FACES AT THE BOTTOM OF THE WELL 47 (1992) (proposing a similar "Racial Preferences Licensing Act").

3

What's Wrong with Neoliberalism

The Problem of the Shanty

**Introduction: In Which I Take a Break from
Childcare Responsibilities to Discuss the
Problem of the Shanty with Rodrigo**

"Professor?" The familiar voice in the telephone receiver gave me quite a start.

"Rodrigo, I'm delighted to hear from you, especially so soon! What's up?"

"I know you're probably busy with your daughter and new grandchild, but something came up the other evening that we thought might interest you."

"Actually, I'm taking a break. The baby is asleep. Did I tell you I'm going back to teaching?"

"That's wonderful news. When?"

"This fall. My old school needed someone to cover my courses, so they asked me. I agreed to do it for a semester, on a trial basis."

"Any problems with the INS?"

"None at all. The dean checked, and they said I can work as long as I like. But, to what do I owe the pleasure of this call?"

"Do you remember when the three of us were talking not too long ago about the future of civil rights? Toward the end, we touched briefly on the situation of Latinos."

I recalled our conversation vividly, indeed had done little but play it over in my mind since I had parted company with my brilliant young colleague and protégé and his equally talented wife Giannina. "I remember well. We speculated about some of the complications likely to set in when the United States becomes a multiethnic society and Latinos begin to outnumber blacks.

"Exactly. And Giannina and I want to talk with you about race and Latinos. But the matter also has a class aspect."

"*That's* a coincidence," I said. "My old law school, from which I graduated nearly forty years ago, is thinking of changing its race-based affirmative action program for one based on class and socioeconomic disadvantage. The alumni magazine, which they still send me, featured the debate over it in the last issue."

"Giannina says they're talking about doing the same thing at her school. The students are up in arms. But that's not why I'm calling. When I got home from Michigan, I found a xerox of an article in my mailbox. Laz, who is out of town at a Federalist Society meeting, sent it with a note saying he thought we'd find it interesting. About the plight of poor Mexicans living in border settlements in Texas,[1] it's brilliant but also emblematic of what Giannina and I think is wrong with liberals, including the current administration."

"I'm glad to see you're an equal opportunity critic," I said. "The last two times we were together, you gave conservatives and libertarians a good going over. But speaking of poor Mexicans, I don't think I know that piece. Do you have the cite?"

"Better than that, Professor. Giannina's at her writing group this evening. She can drop off a copy for you on her way home. Then, if you have any free time later this week. . . "

"My daughter and son-in-law are taking the baby for her one-month checkup tomorrow. I have the afternoon off. How about if I treat the two of you to dinner?"

"Does six o'clock sound okay? We could drop by and pick you up."

In Which Rodrigo, Giannina, and I Discuss the
Problem of the Shanty

The next day, the three of us were seated in a corner booth in the homey, Italian restaurant that Giannina had selected. "They don't have a lot of glitz, but the food is good and the prices are right, now that I'm on a student budget again."

After placing our orders, broiled *pesce* for me, Neapolitan lasagna for my two young friends, Rodrigo began:

"Did you get a chance to look at the article, Professor?"

"I did. The baby was a little colicky after she returned from the doctor's office, so I couldn't go through it as carefully as I would have liked. But I can see why your friend Laz liked it. It's got more law and economics than your average article on race."

"Especially in the part about zoning," Rodrigo said.[2] "But he also was struck by the appalling conditions in the *colonias*. At the end of the first section, in which the author, Jane Larson, describes how the poor Mexican families live, Laz had attached a yellow stick-on with a dozen question marks and a note saying, 'This is terrible. Let's discuss this soon.'"

"I had the same reaction," I said. "I've never been to Texas, except when my wife was alive we would sometimes drive across on the way to see her family. Isn't Laz an immigrant, too?"

"His folks were," Rodrigo replied. "They came from an eastern European country. When he was growing up, they were very poor. Maybe that's why he identifies with the *colonia* residents."

"Any sensitive reader would!" I exclaimed. "The *colonistas* live in conditions like those of a Third World country—as bad as any inner-city ghetto."

"It's hard to believe these unincorporated, low-income settlements that have sprung up in the Texas border counties are home to more than 340,000 people living in 1,400 shantytowns, or *colonias*." Rodrigo looked down at some papers in his lap. "One large cluster is located in the southwest corner of the state near El Paso, a second in the southeast corner, and a third near Laredo. This author focused on the ones in El Paso County, where she did her fieldwork."

"Including conducting extensive interviews with the residents, most of whom are working poor people of Mexican descent, some legal, others not," I chimed in.

"Many of them are family units," Giannina added. "Although I find it hard to believe how anyone can raise families under those conditions. It's a testament to their courage and will to survive."[3]

"The *colonias* lack clean water," Rodrigo continued, "because they are located outside the city, and the county does not supply it. Grocery stores sell it, and a few businesses let their customers use their tap, if they have one. Many residents bring it in from elsewhere, storing it in abandoned industrial drums or uncovered containers where mosquitoes breed. Some *colonistas* improvise hand-dug, shallow wells, which often become contaminated by industrial or human wastes."

"That's because there are no sanitary sewers for disposing of human waste or carrying away storm drainage," I added, recalling a gruesome detail that had stuck in my mind even upon cursory reading. "Most families have outhouses, open pit cesspools in the backyard, or septic tanks. A study showed that ninety-eight out of one hundred wells contained water too contaminated to be safe for drinking. Both adults and children are at risk for diarrhea, dysentery, and hepatitis from living in unclean conditions. Everyone lives in fear of cholera outbreaks."[4]

"The buildings are equally poor," Giannina added, leaning over to peer at Rodrigo's papers, now sitting next to his water glass. "Oh, here's our dinner."

We were silent a moment while the waiter put down our plates. While he added grated cheese to my companions' lasagna, Giannina continued: "Some families live in dilapidated trailers, others in shacks made of wood slats, used tires, and pieces of tin or cardboard. Only half have indoor toilets. Roofs are often constructed of garage doors or planks covered with plastic sheeting. Many homes lack electricity or outlets; even more lack running water so that the people wash dishes and laundry outside the house in metal or plastic tubs. No building or housing codes apply, so that nonstandard and unsafe plumbing, wiring, and construction are rife. Families often live in these conditions for years, sometimes adding rooms or making improvements as they acquire the money to buy materials."[5]

Rodrigo looked up. "Deplorable," he said. "Unspeakable. And the strange thing is that the author writes with real passion and indignation.[6] She seems genuinely upset and angry that human beings should live in conditions like these, and disgusted with the shady realtors and land developers who defraud the *colonistas* with promises of running water and electricity 'within a few years,' and with the Texas legislature, which has so far refused to give the counties zoning and regulatory authority to impose minimum standards on housing in these areas."

"Why do you find it strange?" I asked. "She's a liberal who spent months talking with the *colonistas*. She wants things to be better for them."

What's Wrong with the Liberals' Approach to Poverty

"I mean that a puzzling gap separates the first half of the article and the second, in which the author puts forward her solutions for the problems of the *colonias*. The first part is full of passion; the second, bloodless and full of mild remedies. It reminds me of the Clinton administration."

"I noticed that, too," I said. "The first part is full of indignation. Then, she starts talking about interest convergence, what the factories want."

"Or will put up with," Giannina interjected.

"Precisely," I replied. "She urges regularizing land titles, which strikes me as not a bad idea, and providing credit at market rates to low-income households so they won't be prey for loan sharks. She urges extending the franchise in local elections to permanent resident aliens.[7] All of these are fine. But then she suggests enacting what she calls 'minimal but appropriate land use regulations' and encouraging the *colonistas* to build self-help housing under these relaxed standards."[8]

"That struck me as curious, too," Giannina interjected. "But I started out on her side. I gather the idea is not to price the poor people out of the *colonias* by driving up the cost of housing there."

"That's what I meant by bloodless," Rodrigo replied. "The author says any measures aimed at abetting the dreadful conditions in the *colonias* must"—he leafed through the article—"'strike the right balance between health, safety, welfare, and economics on the one hand, and affordability on the other.'[9] She seems stuck in a dilemma. Accepting the law-and-economists' neoliberal view, she sees only two options: regulation, which will increase the cost of housing so that the *colonistas* will have no place to live and have to move, or no regulation, in which case they will live in circumstances unfit for human beings."

"So she hedges," I said. "And opts for a little regulation."

"Mainly of water and sewage," Giannina added. "Which is better than nothing."

"As one who spent the past several days helping take care of a baby . . ." I began.

"Small children or not, no one should have to live like that," Rodrigo said emphatically.

"True, but how *do* you get her out of her dilemma?" Giannina asked. "The desperately poor have to live somewhere. If the *colonias* are the cheapest place, where will they go if the lawyers and regulators come in and make the developers clean things up? Isn't she right that increased vigilance can end up injuring the poor by causing landlords to allow housing to deteriorate, to walk away, or not to build it in the first place? My property professor mentioned that that had been the unintended effect of militant housing rights and tenant advocacy in certain cities."

"I hope you're going to address that gap between her descriptive first part and her second, or remedies, section," I reminded my young friend.

"Those are tall orders," Rodrigo said. "But I'll try. First, what lies in the gap is history. The author glides over the history of conquest, broken promises, and outright discrimination that minorities, especially Mexicans, have suffered in the state of Texas.[10] Second, to understand how to improve conditions in the *colonias*, one must look at how those problems came about."

"Rodrigo, we've not discussed your Latin side very much," I said. "Mostly we've talked about African Americans or people of color in general. I gather you're taking a greater interest in your roots these days?"

"I have. My dad's African American, as you know, and my mom was Italian. But some of my ancestors lived in the Caribbean and my dad still speaks fluent Spanish. Did I tell you that Giannina and I are thinking of applying for a Fulbright in Mexico sometime?"

"*You* keep talking about it," Giannina said. "You sometimes forget that I'm in the middle of a certain educational program. I'm not as free to pick up and leave as you professors, although it's something I'd love to do with you someday."

Rodrigo blushed. "I sometimes get carried away. Sorry, Giannina. Maybe we'll content ourselves with a quick trip down to see the Professor every now and then, at least until you graduate. Or maybe just a vacation. Where were we?"

"The situation in Texas," I said.

"Oh, yes. I've been talking to two of my Latino students from that state. It turns out that Texas is notorious in the Chicano community for treating Mexicans as inferior to whites during much of its history. Restaurants posted signs saying 'No dogs or Mexicans allowed.' Employers used a dual-wage system, paying Mexican workers less than Anglos. The Border Patrol hassled Mexican-looking people even if they were U.S. citizens, and school authorities sent Mexican kids to different, and worse, schools from the ones attended by Anglo children."

"And I gather you think that this has something to do with the dilemma the writer finds herself in?"

"It does. It explains why all three of us had the same sense that her section on remedies and the one detailing abuses don't match up. Do you recall our earlier discussion of norm theory, Professor?"

"I do," I said. Not knowing whether Giannina was versed in this new branch of social psychology, I said: "It holds, basically, that our response to someone in need is a function of what we believe is normal for that person. A white woman drops a bag of groceries and everyone stops to help. A black woman does the same, and fewer help out, and the same is true in experiments with stranded motorists. If we believe that the person in need is usually wretched—that that is his or her ordinary condition— we are less likely to intervene. Starving Biafrans evoke little sympathy because we think that famines are common in that part of the world. Our middle-class neighbor shows up at our door having lost his or her job and been evicted, and we are much more solicitous. Hunger is abnormal for such a person. Everyone rushes in to help."

"I wasn't familiar with the term," Giannina said. "But it stands to reason. And you think this is why mild remedies won't help society's desperately poor, Rodrigo? Namely, because we do not see their need as requiring acute intervention?"

"More than that," Rodrigo replied. "Mild remedies make matters worse, by virtually inviting the rest of us to conclude that the dirt, poverty, hunger, and despair in the *colonias* are normal and ordinary. No *colonias* mar Beverly Hills, no open sewers foul Marin County. We make sure that land-use and health regulations there are strictly enforced. We wouldn't consider arguments about the price of regulation or the trade-off between cost and code enforcement in those fancy communities."

"You're saying that no one argues, 'Let's drop all the codes—zoning, safety, housing, et cetera—in Marin County and disconnect all the sewers. They drive up the cost of housing; the people there should at least have the option,' right?" Giannina asked.

"Exactly," said Rodrigo.

"So it comes back to who lives there—to race—in the end," I said. "That's your gap, Rodrigo, right?"

"Yes. And that's why when liberals like the author or Bill Clinton reach for halfway measures, we must say no every time. Programs like that stand to do poor people great harm, maybe even more than the conservatives' because they seem to be on our side. But the harm they do is apt to last forever," Rodrigo concluded.

"Maybe half-measures are all that society will stand for," Giannina ventured.

"I hope not," said Rodrigo. "We must be careful not to do anything that reinforces someone's wretchedness, the sense that they deserve nothing better."

"Which a fatalistic approach does," I seconded. "It symbolically tells everyone that these are second-class citizens who ought to be satisfied with a little electrical wiring and a running tap or two per block. Even though one's intentions are entirely laudable, as the author's clearly are, her solutions would deepen the predicament of those she is trying to help."

"Like *Brown's* 'all deliberate speed,' "[11] Giannina mused.

"Or the current administration's waffling on welfare, retreat on affirmative action, and compromises with the Republicans on aid to the cities.

But half-measures like these lead society to believe that misery is accept-able in certain quarters because squalor is normal there. This creates a slavelike class that can be hired for less—a positive advantage for the fac-tories. Eventually, no nonracist white firm will hire a Mexican at full salary, even if he or she has a Ph.D. No school board will consider a pupil-assignment scheme that mixes Mexican and white kids. The idea simply won't come to mind," Rodrigo concluded.

"This agrees with something I've long thought," I added. "Low status tends to worsen over time, even as society becomes better educated. Stigma deepens, even as polls show Americans are less racist. The gap be-tween the rich and poor widens every decade. The mechanism you point out may be part of the reason."

Giannina put her fork down. "I'm starting to agree with you. In fact, I thought of another reason why we should move decisively to aid the *colo-nias*. Their existence adds to racial and social segregation of the rapidly growing Mexican population by encouraging border populations to re-main outside the city, away from such things as public education and high-quality health care. I would bet children grow up in the *colonias* without knowing any Anglo, or at any rate non-Hispanic, kids and with-out first-rate teachers, books, or schools."

"I wouldn't be surprised," Rodrigo said. "Do you remember those studies of teacher expectations?"[12]

"I do," Giannina replied. "Researchers told teachers that certain stu-dents had been identified as likely to show a learning spurt during the coming year. This was a sheer hoax—the idea was to see if the announce-ment by a respected authority would change the teachers' and the chil-drens' behavior."

"And it did," I interjected. "The students predicted to be late bloomers earned higher grades and standardized test scores.[13] It stands to reason that the opposite effect may set in as well. If teachers look around them and see only dilapidated schools in rundown neighborhoods, they will assume that society expects little from the children who grow up there. And with lower expectations, lower performance will come as well."

Toughlove Economics

We fell silent as the waiter cleared the empty dishes. Then Giannina con-tinued: "Well, if the author's first approach, namely, half-hearted regula-tion, won't work, what about the alternative—leaving the *colonias* essen-tially alone? At the author's law school, half her colleagues would do this. They're classical law-and-economists like the one we were discussing before. She discusses this avenue briefly at the beginning of her article, but then more or less discards it."

"Not entirely. Elements of it appear in her minimalist regulatory strategy," Rodrigo clarified. "Remember that she wants government to come in only to bring water and sewers. It should stay away when it comes to housing standards and land use zoning. A battery factory or filling station might go up right next to a family's residence."

Giannina grimaced. "But why *not*—for the sake of argument—go the whole way?"

Rodrigo looked dubious, so I said, "For the sake of argument, let me spell it out. Deregulation ought to drive the cost of housing down, and does. The *colonias* boast some of the cheapest housing in the state; that's why the poorest people live there. They couldn't afford to live in the cities where the schooling, shopping, utilities, and cultural opportunities are better. So, they go to live in the *colonias*, putting together a shanty of some sort on a shoestring—maybe a few thousand dollars, intending to add to it, build new bedrooms when more babies come. So they start out ahead compared, say, to newlyweds setting out in the suburbs or the city. With this extra money, the Mexicans should be able to bounce back. They start out poor, but the boost they get in housing—at a cost, to be sure, since the houses are substandard—enables them to enter other markets. They can educate their kids, maybe sending them to a parish school, or open a small business like an auto repair shop. They can move right up the ladder, like those early immigrants from the eastern or southern parts of Europe who huddled together in tenement districts before learning English, getting jobs, and moving out."

"And you want to know why that won't work?" Rodrigo asked.

I nodded, so he went on: "For many of the reasons you and I discussed earlier. In theory, the Mexican family should be able to move up and enter those other markets on an equal footing with Anglos. But the same forces that produce the *colonias* will plague them there as well. They'll apply for a job, a mortgage, a better school for their kid, and be turned down. Racism is woven into the warp and woof of society. They'll confront it everywhere. Popular culture constructs them as lazy, siesta-loving, good-natured singers and dancers—or else as vicious shoot-you-in-the-back gunslingers and desperadoes. Countless tales, scripts, songs, and TV programs depict them this way. How can a modest set of housing regulations begin to compensate for that?"

"A thoroughgoing law-and-economics approach would have forced the nearby factories to internalize the costs of their own pollution," Giannina interjected, "would have made them pay to filter the poison out of the water table and haul away their effluents and toxic wastes. They're the cheapest cost-avoider."

"Yet our author missed that," I said. "You can bet nobody would if the chemicals were being pumped into Beverly Hills."

"So, there's no quick fix," Rodrigo summarized. "Not regulation, of either the heavy- or the light-handed variety. The one, because it will drive up the cost of housing to levels poor people cannot afford, the other because it merely reinforces their otherness. And not laissez-faire economics, for the reason we just mentioned. Racism is endemic and inhibits the willingness of members of all those markets to deal with us."

"She misses the tragic meaning of her own article," declared Giannina gloomily. "She glanced at the abysmal conditions prevailing in the *colonias*, then backed away from their implications. Like many liberals, she overlooks that racism is the ordinary state of affairs in our society. It's the norm, not the one-time-only, easily-fixed aberration. To her credit, she *does* see the squalor, which is good. But her reaction is liberal, not 'double' enough."

"She overlooks that the wretched conditions in the *colonias* are becoming normal and ordinary in the eyes of Texans," Rodrigo seconded. "In fact, all this is functional, not dysfunctional, for the larger society, which benefits from cheap labor in the factories and fields while avoiding the expense of providing utilities and zoning enforcement for the families and workers."

"In other words, she doesn't ask the 'Who benefits?' question," I interjected.

"Exactly," Rodrigo continued. "She misses the ubiquity of the shanty, the way they appear over and over in East Los Angeles, Watts, the Bronx, and dozens of other bombed-out slums and shantytowns scattered around this wealthy country. To her credit, she chooses the less-popular remedy—self-help plus minimal regulation, realizing that something other than the ordinary quick-fix must be done."

"Would you folks like some dessert?" the waiter, who had been waiting patiently at the side of our table, notebook in hand, asked. "Could we see the menu?" Rodrigo asked, looking around at the rest of us.

I mumbled my usual excuse about doctor's orders but Giannina looked up with an interested expression. The waiter put down menus in front of my two young friends and departed saying he would be back. He looked Latino; I wondered if he had caught a whiff of our conversation.

As he walked away, I looked up. "He might be Mexican. Anyway, what's the solution? If neither of the time-honored approaches will work, what will?"

Rodrigo's Solution

"Neither regulation nor the free market will work. Both approaches lack an adequate account of evil—specifically, racism—treating it as a case of market failure or ignorance. As we discussed before, it's neither, but a ubiquitous, deeply entrenched system that confers class advantage. Like other deeply engrained social problems, such as Garrett Hardin's tragedy of the commons,[14] it will yield only to a combined program that embraces both love and hardheaded political theory."

"Your solution, Rodrigo," Giannina urged. I sat back and listened.

In Which Rodrigo Sketches the First Part of His Solution—Government's Role

"There are no white *colonias*," Rodrigo began.[15] "We wouldn't tolerate them. It would seem abnormal. We are accustomed to poverty's having a black or brown face. Seeing pictures of starving Biafrans on TV doesn't move us, because we believe famines are common in that part of the world. But seeing our nice suburban neighbor evicted or deported causes everyone to feel concerned."

"That's your norm theory idea," I commented.

"Blacks are not just white people who happen not to have any money right now. A black lawyer still is the object of discrimination on the bus or when he or she shows up at work early and confronts people who don't know him or her."

"Are you folks ready to order?" the waiter asked.

"We haven't even looked at the menu," Giannina replied with a start. "Give us a second." My two young friends made their selections—a tiramisu for my lanky young colleague, a mango gelato for Giannina and me ("I've relented. That sounds good, and it won't violate my diet too much"), and the waiter departed.

"The answer breaks down into two parts," Rodrigo continued. "The first deals with what government must do, the second with the role of private citizens."

"Well, what should government do?" I asked. "Surely you don't mean massive programs and giveaways. Those will never go over today."

"No, I don't," Rodrigo replied firmly. "But government must be activist. Nothing requires that the state let counties get away with lack of provision of such basic amenities as water and sanitation. If the state won't enforce a minimal level of these services in the *colonias*, the federal government should. Services such as these are part of what it means to be a member of the human community.

"The author of the article says we must be flexible about our demands. Are you saying the *colonias* should have the same high level of services as Beverly Hills, where everyone holds high-paying, straight jobs, the average level of education is one of the highest in the world, and the residents pay for a high level of services out of property taxes?"

"No." Rodrigo replied, frowning slightly. "But not as disgracefully low as now. Written standards should govern such commodities. Beverly Hills will choose to be far above basic standards. But we should make sure every community has water that meets a minimum level of cleanliness and sufficiency. Sewers, too."

"No trade-offs or exceptions, in other words," Giannina asked. "Of the kind our author is willing to tolerate as a matter of pragmatic realism."

"No," Rodrigo replied, "because we would inevitably see a ratcheting-down in which we tolerate worse and worse conditions for those we see as different from ourselves. And these conditions, in turn, will simply confirm to us that the residents are indeed a different order of humanity, in a self-reinforcing spiral. In time, ghetto, barrio, or *colonia* conditions will seem natural and just, 'the way things are.'"

"Like famines in Biafra," Giannina interjected.

"That's why we need governmental enforcement, formally administered, under universal standards," Rodrigo concluded.

"You and I discussed the fairness-and-formality critique of alternative dispute resolution,"[16] I said. "It was in Michigan, I think. It sounds like you're drawing on something similar."

"I am," Rodrigo replied. "And the same reasons that argue against relegating the poor and disempowered to mediation, arbitration, and other deformalized dispute resolution forums, instead of to court, argue against Larson's approach. In fact, I heard her speak at a conference recently. She expressly likened her approach to ADR."[17]

"I was reading about that critique for my civil procedure class," Giannina interjected. "It holds that informality increases power differentials, so that if one is, for example, a high-school graduate woman divorcing a highly educated professional-class man, one is likely to do better in formal court than in a mediated divorce.[18] And the same is true for minorities, children, consumers, and others coming up against more powerful disputants, such as General Motors or a union."

"Did the author you were reading give the reason why?" I asked.

"He did," said Giannina. "It's not simply because of the greater discretion the decisionmaker wields, although this does open the door for prejudice even wider than it is in court. Rather, it's because all the hallmarks of formality you find in the courtroom—the flags, the robes, the judge sitting on high, the codes of evidence and procedure—remind everyone present that the values that are to prevail are those of the American Creed: fairness, equal treatment, a day in court for everyone.[19] Americans subscribe to two sets of values—the noble ones we apply during occasions of state, such as on the Fourth of July when all the flags are flying. During these times, the same person who might at other times—say, in a bar or private club—tell an ethnic joke or do something hurtful to a woman or minority will behave in truly egalitarian fashion. Formality triggers the former values and tends to assure a better result, all other things being equal."

"I can think of lots of exceptions," I said. "But you may be right as a general proposition. And so, the two of you think this has something to do with Larson's thesis?"

"I do," Rodrigo said with conviction. "In relegating the people of the *colonias* to self-help and weakened regulation, she forfeits the powerful advantage of formality. Government, which could and should side with the underdogs, looks the other way."

"The fairness-and-formality critique has a social science dimension," Giannina said. "I'm sure the two of you remember how during the sixties institutional integration was a principal objective of the civil rights movement."

"Of course," I replied. "It remains a mainstay of liberalism even today."

"Then, I'm sure you recall how it was premised on what social scientists would call the 'social contact hypothesis.'"[20]

"I assume you mean the idea that racism and other forms of bigotry are simple mistakes," I ventured. "The bigot mistakenly believes that blacks, for example, are stupid and base. Arranging that a prejudiced worker or student interact with a member of the other group in the workplace or school will correct this error. Over time, the prejudiced individual will learn that members of the other group are just like his own—some good and nice, others not. Prejudice will end."

"You don't hear that thesis as much today," Rodrigo interjected.

"No," Giannina added, "because social scientists now realize things are more complex than that. For social contact to alleviate prejudice, the contact must take place between equals and relate to a common objective or goal."

"Like sports," I said.

"Or the military," Rodrigo added.

"Exactly," Giannina said. "And those conditions are found relatively rarely in our society. For that reason, social scientists today subscribe to a different approach to combating racism."

"Namely?" I asked.

Giannina took a bite of her gelato, looked up, and said, "The so-called confrontation theory. It holds that the best way to combat discrimination is to arrange that its every outward manifestation is noticed, remarked, and sanctioned. It rests on the premise that most people know that prejudice is wrong and violates the American Creed. They act on it because it brings advantage or satisfies a psychological need. If they realize that doing so not only is wrong but likely to bring swift censure, they'll refrain."[21]

Rodrigo gave his wife an admiring look. "You've stated my case better than I could have myself."

"All this ties in to what we were mentioning earlier," Giannina added. "Larson underestimates the role of racism both in creating the conditions in the *colonias* and in dooming the strategies she puts forward for relieving them. She is shocked at the terrible conditions in the *colonias*, but her passion tapers off in the cool, pragmatic second part. She treats the residents' predicament as though it were simply lack of money, giving little more than lip service to the racism, conquest, and exploitation that produced the *colonias* in the first place , making them profitable for the developers and factory owners today."

"Her remedies don't go far enough," I summarized. "They forfeit the advantages of formality. And they overlook the proper role of government in redressing historical wrongs."

"Would you folks like some coffee?" The waiter asked politely.

"Decaf for me. It's rather late," I said.

"The same," said Giannina.

"Do you have cappuccino?" my young colleague asked. When the waiter nodded, he said, "Make it a double."

"He sleeps like a baby," Giannina said, looking at me wonderingly. "If I did that, I'd be up all night."

As the waiter departed, I reminded Rodrigo, "But you promised to tell us of a second strategy—one for private actors."

In Which Rodrigo Sketches What Private Individuals Should Do About the Problem of the Shanty—A Program of Resistance

Moments later, the waiter returned with our beverages. Rodrigo took a deep sip of his high-octane brew, then continued:

"Private individuals, both inside and outside the *colonias*, ought to devote themselves to a program of outright resistance."

"Do you mean like in the sixties—with civil disobedience, sit-ins, mass marches, that sort of thing?"

"That and more. Are you two familiar with the tenants' union movement?" Rodrigo asked.

I nodded. Giannina did so as well, adding, "How would rent strikes and enactment of repair-and-deduct laws, for example, help the people who live in the *colonias*? Most of them are owners, not renters. Their problem is that they have been sold overpriced lots, with shaky titles and no utilities. The developers skip town—or go limp—so there's no recourse."

"True," Rodrigo acknowledged. "But resistance could take the form of demonstrations outside the offices of the county and the utility companies that are not supplying water, gas, and sewers. Some highly imaginative tactics come to mind.[22] Another possibility would be for the *colonistas* to stop paying on their land-deed contracts. The money could go into an escrow account held, for example, by a regional office of the Mexican-American Legal Defense and Educational Fund. The Fund would disburse the payments only as they saw the developers carrying through on their promises to put in electricity, water, and sewers."

"What about pollution from the nearby factories?" Giannina asked. "It sounds worse than Love Canal, yet nothing is done."

"The *colonistas* should link up with the environmental justice movement,"[23] Rodrigo said. "That movement challenges the placement of toxic dumps, freeways, water treatment plants, and other undesirable things right in the middle of minority communities."

"Of course, the *colonias* are so bad off residents might welcome a water treatment plant right in the middle of town if need be," I added. "But I love the idea of turning lawyers like Luke Cole loose on them."[24]

The waiter arrived to ask if we would like refills. "Not for me," I said, placing my hand over my cup. "I'll have another if it's decaf," Giannina said. Rodrigo motioned eagerly for more, which the waiter obligingly supplied.

"And so that's your program," Giannina summarized. "Vigilance and formal equality from the public sector, resistance from the private. But what about the cost of all this? Won't it just price the *colonistas* out of the only place they can afford to live?"

"No," Rodrigo replied. "The idea is to force the developers to carry through on what they promised to deliver, at the same time one presses government to supply what every human being needs. The relatively small cost would be borne by all of society. The Texas economy benefits from the low-cost labor of the *colonias'* workers. It's only fair that the state should bear the cost of better schools and sanitation for their families."

"That which the developers cannot be made to shoulder," I added.

"Right," Rodrigo replied. "They should be made to pay for the basic hookup, since that's what developers are expected to do and what the people who bought the lots expect. After that, the state takes over."

"What about housing and zoning ordinances?" Giannina asked. "You said you wanted formal fairness. Would you condemn two-thirds of the houses because they are made of pieces of tin and plywood and don't meet the housing code? The people would be out in the street. And what about land-use zoning? If you prohibited people from operating businesses out of their homes, you'd have to close down all the auto repair, laundries, and sewing piecework that go on now in the homes. Half the income of the *colonias* would dry up. You'd start out doing the people a favor but end up harming them."

"I'd grandfather in existing businesses," Rodrigo answered, "so that no one would be thrown out of work. As for newcomers, I'd make them toe the line but offer loans and job assistance to enable them to set up legitimate businesses."

"What about the author's voting solution?" I asked. "She would bolster voters' registration and permit noncitizens to vote in local elections, as a number of communities outside Texas have done. That way, adults who are permanent aliens could vote for local officials—sheriff, for example, or county tax board member. Wouldn't this make government more accountable?"

Before Rodrigo could answer, Giannina interjected: "I, for one, doubt it. The counties are a very large unit. In most cases the *colonias* are satellites of large cities. Her proposals are likely to end up as mere windowdressing. Everyone will feel much better because the Mexican families now are able to vote. But studies show that poor people don't vote, even when they can. Sometimes they do vote when a candidate or issue of importance to them appears on the ballot. But this is unlikely to be the case, since they will be so outnumbered."

"Her solution—I hate to say it—is typically liberal," Rodrigo added. "The idea is that democracy can cure all ills. But racism is a classic failure of democracy. Unless one deals with that, the majority will continue oppressing the minority into the future."

"What about the possibility that Mexicans living in the *colonias* will form a bloc with those living in the cities?" I asked.

"This could happen," Rodrigo conceded. "And the two groups might find issues in common. But it is essentialist to suppose that an urban Chicano family with a mother working as a library aide and a father driving a city bus will find common cause with the poverty-level Mexican families scratching out a living in the *colonias*."

"And do you think the author commits that mistake?" Giannina asked.

"Her article contains overtones of essentialism," I interjected, reaching over for Rodrigo's copy. "Let me see. Here's one. She says, for example, that she favors a self-help housing 'movement as a whole.'[25] Right here on page 246. She urges that political pressure be brought to broaden self-help housing beyond the *colonias* to other areas where housing is scarce.[26] To be sure, she wants to do this while respecting cultural difference. But housing is an intensely personal matter. Everyone needs certain basic amenities. But beyond that, one community's or person's approach to shelter might be completely unsatisfactory to another. Larson elsewhere commits the sin of treating the poor in lump fashion, generalizing about them as though they were all the same. She reasons that those in control of the local labor market of the border economy have an interest in supporting minimal regulation in order to guarantee the availability of durable, affordable housing for the low-wage workers of the El Paso region.[27] And again—yes, here it is—she argues that the economic reality of 'falling wages and declining support for housing programs' implies that 'it can be predicted that working poor households in the United States increasingly will turn to self-help housing to survive'—not just *colonia* residents."[28]

"Hmm," said Giannina. "I'd missed that part. But I agree that her focus on the plight of the *colonias* foreshadows a larger sociopolitical agenda with essentialist aspirations."

"Not just essentialist," said Rodrigo, "but accommodationist as well. She seeks to impose a single story line on people living in the *colonias*. It is commendable that she takes their plight seriously, wholly laudable that she attempts to incorporate the practical realities of a disenfranchised people through empirical research in coming up with policy recommendations. Hers is a valiant response to the criticism that too much legal research is empty, self-referential, normative, and otherworldly. But the use to which she puts her research is troublesome. She is trying to adjust the people to their situation rather than the other way around."

"The pathos of her article is entirely separate from the logos," added Giannina. "The empirical portion elicits genuine empathy for the plight of *colonistas*. Yet the theoretical portion is cold and calculating, containing little of the prior compassion. In this way, she makes it appear that her theoretical perspective is an outgrowth of the communal and emotional solidarity of *colonistas*. But it ends up marginalizing them, essentializing their problems in the service of an unstated political agenda that I, for one, find frightening."

"I didn't find it frightening," I replied mildly. "But I agree with you about its essentializing thrust. It takes the multifaceted and probably often conflicting feelings of *colonistas* about their situation and merges them all together into a solution that just happens to be good for the nearby factories."

"It also gets government off the hook," Rodrigo added. "And come to think of it, I have some nagging doubts about the author's self-help program. Did either of you?"

"It does tend to foster a conservative, property-owner ethic that could undermine potential bases of political activism," Giannina replied. "In encouraging people to look to themselves, she overlooks the possibility of solidarity and communal, cooperative group action. The *colonias* residents are not a large enough bloc to accomplish much through voting. But if even a few dozen or a hundred of them form a rent-strike union or march to city hall to protest insects and fecal matter in the water, they may get government's attention in a way that a few hundred votes won't."

Rodrigo said, "You've put your finger on something that had been bothering me. Larson highlights the sense of pride that some *colonistas* feel about having their own houses. But this justifiable dignity should not count against the fundamental realization that these impoverished Latinos have been forced into the *colonias* and their on-the-edge lifestyle because of dire economic circumstances and racism. For example, she argues [Rodrigo looked down] that 'home ownership represents something more than a shelter choice. Rather, it is a powerful symbol of self-reliance, personal dignity, and family advancement.'[29] All true. But her minimal regulation coupled with self-help housing merely treat the symptoms as a much larger problem: The historical and social reasons for poor Latino people being racially, economically, and finally spatially marginalized to the fringes of the greater El Paso area."

"Treating wounds with Band-Aids, in other words," Giannina commented.

"More than that. Her approach has a blame-shifting aspect. Suppose the *colonistas* fail at self-help. They run out of money or become discouraged. Society can then write them off. 'See?' we can say, 'they had a chance to help themselves and didn't.' We can wash our hands of the whole thing, ignoring that their predicament is the product of conquest and centuries of racism and neglect."

"They are already living in dismal circumstances. In many respects, they are in the least advantageous position to shoulder any additional burdens," Giannina said. "What they need is help."

"Which my program promises," Rodrigo replied. "We stand shoulder-to-shoulder with them, offering help and resistance at the same time that we insist government do its duty."

"Will your program work?" I queried. "These are conservative times."

"It has a chance," Rodrigo replied. "Resistance, sit-ins, and various forms of civil disobedience will get the attention of the developers, factory owners, and lazy bureaucrats who benefit from the current arrangement. It's hard to ignore a hundred mothers carrying babies in *rebozos*, sitting in the lobby of the water department building carrying signs saying, '*Agua pura para los bebes*.' And lawsuits and direct action aimed at shaming government also have a chance. All these petitions can tap narratives such as 'All men are brothers,' and 'As ye do to the least of us. . . ,' ones that resonate with our religious and political traditions. At some point, government will come around."

"The author says there is a—here it is—'Direct tradeoff between higher standards and affordability,'"[30] I said. "Your approach sounds good, Rodrigo. But doesn't she have a point? To the extent you succeed, the more housing will cost. At some point, the people now living in the barrios and *colonias* will have to pick up and go. And where else can they settle? They live in the *colonias* because they can't afford a house in a city or suburb."

"It's not A or B," Rodrigo replied. "Let me see that quote. Here: she says there's a direct trade-off between 'higher standards and affordability *for lower income residents*.'[31] I'm sure she didn't intend this, but her theory is explicitly predicated on a legal acceptance of otherness, difference, and perhaps inferiority. She justifies this pragmatically, but can it ever be justified as a matter of social principle?"

"Reminds me of *Plessy v. Ferguson*,"[32] Giannina commented quietly.

"Agreed," Rodrigo said. "It's too crabbed an approach. We can enlarge the pie for the poor people of the *colonias* by standing with them in a program of resistance and activism."

"I'm not sure her program is even pragmatically justified," I said. "In a book I was just rereading, *American Apartheid: Segregation and the Making of the Underclass*,[33] Massey and Denton argue against a color line in housing. Are you familiar with their thesis?"

My two interlocutors nodded a little uncertainly, so I went on. "Racialized spatial inequalities create and perpetuate an impoverished underclass that exists separate and apart from the rest of the cities and society. Larson's laissez-faire approach seeks tacitly to translate the already highly racialized spatial inequalities that exist into an official program. But seeking to integrate *colonias* into a broader scheme with the goal of giving them what Larson calls 'decent, affordable, and long-lasting housing' will simply duplicate what we now see in cities, namely, all-black ghettos, except in reverse. In her plan, a spatial inversion will take place, similar to the inner-city, black ghetto that Massey and Denton describe: an outer-city, Latino ghetto."

"Another form of residential color line," Giannina added.

"Exactly," Rodrigo added. "Translating the *colonistas*' lifestyle, already a spatialized result of the culture and history of racism in southern Texas, into a legal codification of this dynamic of social hierarchy."

"What about her credit program?" I asked.

"Not a bad idea," Rodrigo replied. "But she notes that many of the residents work in the informal economy, at home, 'off the books.' This implies that *colonistas* already have little long-term financial stability. Credit programs might end up merely another form of subordination in light of their preexisting economic inadequacies."

"Speaking of credit programs," I said, "I hope you two will let me put this on my bill. I'm on vacation, and you two are working. This is my treat." I handed my credit card to the waiter a split second before Rodrigo, who had been fumbling in his pocket, could intercept it.

"But I'm on a payroll and you're not," Rodrigo protested, putting away his wallet. "Well, we're hoping to visit you down there during spring break. You'll have to let us take you out to one of your favorite restaurants."

"It will be my pleasure," I responded. "This conversation has proven as stimulating to me as to you. For a law student, Giannina, you certainly keep up a good reading program."

"Don't thank me. Thank our reading group. We try to read at least one background article or paper in connection with each new line of cases. That's how I knew about tenants' repair-and-deduct strategies. Now, when do we get to meet that baby?"

"Let me check with my daughter," I said. "Maybe all of us can get together for a picnic before I head back home. The new patio is nearly finished. It almost did in my back."

"You're not as old as you keep saying," Rodrigo said. "You keep up a pretty good pace in conversation, and I bet at laying tiles, too."

The waiter returned with the credit card bill, which I signed.

"Would you like to share a cab?" Rodrigo and Giannina shook their heads, indicating they wanted to walk. "Then I'll call if a picnic seems feasible."

"Great," said Rodrigo and Giannina. We waved good-bye to our waiter, who smiled and said *Buenas noches*.

"I *thought* he looked Latino," Rodrigo remarked.

Seconds later, a cab pulled up and I was on my way. My parting sight of my two young friends was of them striding along the sidewalk, hand in hand, lost in conversation, too busy to wave. As the taxi drove down the dark streets to my daughter and son-in-law's neat suburb, I reflected on what we had discussed. I agreed with Rodrigo that norm theory argued powerfully against liberal half-measures. I also agreed that deregulation and free-market economics would do little good. The market is unlikely to drive out racism because the incessant but low-visibility demonization that society inflicts on people of color inhibits their chances everywhere.

But were his two proposals any more promising? As the taxi droned down the near-deserted streets, I wondered how many would join the Mexicans in resistance and civil disobedience. Society is different now, I pondered. Would Rodrigo's suggestion work in today's libertarian age? And what of his notion that we insist on equal enforcement of all housing, zoning, and sanitation codes? I saw the force of Giannina's fairness-and-formality critique and agreed that confrontation theory called for strong, official responses to racism and neglect. But our age abhors governmental programs. Would the *colonias* and their advocates really be able to call upon a host of state agents to remedy the dangerous and filthy conditions prevailing there?

My reverie was interrupted as the cabbie, who had just entered the street on which my daughter lived, turned around and spoke to me, I thought a little sharply. "You sure you have the right address, buddy?" he asked.

I assured him I did, once again reminded that despite my neat suit, briefcase, and gray hair, a minority-looking man like myself will always strike others as out of place in certain settings. As I got my wallet out I wondered, Are we all, in some sense, *colonistas*? If so, resistance and remonstrance may be all we have left. As I fumbled for the key I resolved, rather sleepily, to write Professor Larson, who I knew slightly, and ask what she thought.

Notes

1. Jane E. Larson, *Free Markets Deep in the Heart of Texas*, 84 GEO. L.J. 179 (1995).

2. *Id.* at 179–83, 232–38.

3. *Id.* at 183–87, 192, 205, 259–60.

4. *Id.* at 186–90.

5. *Id.* at 184, 191–93, 198–201, 203.

6. *E.g., id.* at 182 (conditions "deplorable"); 183 (*colonias* lack the basics others take for granted; "Main Street America" oblivious to these problems); 191 ("If . . . statistics are dry and distancing, the human body has its own language"); 235 (noting "human degradation by dirt, danger, and disease").

7. *Id.* at 238–44.

8. *Id.* at 244–51.

9. *Id.* at 250.

10. *See* text and notes, *infra*; RODOLFO ACUÑA, OCCUPIED AMERICA (3d ed. 1988). To be fair, Larson does take note of the historical experience of Mexicans and their mistreatment at the hands of the Texan citizenry. But she considers it mainly a matter of bad attitude ("dirt and disregard," see *Free Markets, supra* at 220), and only "part of the explanation for the long-standing neglect of the *colonias'* problems," *id.*—as though racism and a culture of white supremacy played little part in the creation of the problems themselves.

11. 349 U.S. 297 (1955) (implementation decision: *Brown II*).

12. *E.g.*, ROBERT ROSENTHAL & LENORE JACKSON, PYGMALION IN THE CLASSROOM (1968).

13. *Id.* at 121–45 (on "blooming"—growth spurts in the students singled out); 174–82 (summarizing results).

14. *See* Garrett Hardin, *The Tragedy of the Commons*, 162 SCIENCE 1243 (1968).

15. I thought immediately of exceptions: Appalachia, white southern poverty, homeless and hobo communities, and communities based on barter or voluntary simplicity. Still, I realized Rodrigo was right on a relative basis and decided not to interrupt him in order to see where his argument would lead.

16. *See* Richard Delgado et al., *Fairness and Formality: Minimizing the Risk of Prejudice in Alternative Dispute Resolution*, 1985 WIS. L. REV. 1359; Trina Grillo, *The Mediation Alternative: Process Dangers for Women*, 100 YALE L.J. 1545 (1991).

17. Section on Remedies, Association of American Law Schools Annual Meeting, San Antonio, TX, Jan. 1996.

18. *Risk of Prejudice, supra* at 1387–91, 1402–04.

19. *Id.* at 1383–84.

20. *Id.* at 1385.

21. *Id.* at 1386–91.

22. *See* the demonstration described immediately *infra*. Consider also a phalanx of disgusted homeowners bearing containers of polluted water, dead insects, and plastic bags of animal waste and marching on city hall.

23. *See, e.g.*, Luke Cole, *Remedies for Environmental Racism: A View from the Field*, 90 MICH. L. REV. 1991 (1992); *Empowerment as the Key to Environmental Protection*, 19 ECOLOGY L.Q. 619 (1992); *Environmental Justice Litigation: Another Stone in David's Sling*, 21 FORDHAM URBAN L.J. 523 (1994).

24. An attorney with California Rural Legal Assistance, Cole also writes, teaches, and is considered a founding figure in the environmental justice movement.

25. *Free Markets, supra* at 246.

26. *Id.* at 246–47.

27. *Id.* at 220.

28. *Id.* at 246.

29. *Free Markets, supra* at 206–07.

30. *Id.* at 249.

31. *Id.* (emphasis added).

32. 163 U.S. 537 (1896) (separate-but-equal case).

33. DOUGLAS S. MASSEY & NANCY A. DENTON, AMERICAN APARTHEID: SEGREGATION AND THE MAKING OF THE UNDERCLASS (1993).

4

Rodrigo's Chromosomes

Race, Biology, and the Replication of Elites

Introduction: In Which I Receive an Old-Fashioned Scare

"Rodrigo!" I exclaimed, looking up at the tall, smiling young man standing in my office doorway, hand in hand with another youth wearing dark glasses and a wide grin. "And Laz," I sputtered, abandoning any pretense of equanimity. "My favorite—uh—couple. What are you doing here?"

"We're in town for the ABA meeting. Laz is chairing the section on sexual minorities, while I'm here to see my grandmother, who's in the hospital for a minor operation. We tried calling, but your recorder must have been switched off. Do you have a minute?"

"Of course. What a surprise! Please sit down."

My two visitors unclasped their hands, and Rodrigo guided Laz to a seat on my couch, then sat down next to him. As they did so, I was filled with alarm. Were Laz and Rodrigo gay? And if so, what about Giannina? I cautioned myself not to overreact—the younger generation takes these things much more casually than us old-timers. Say nothing to show surprise or condemnation, I cautioned myself.

Rodrigo must have sensed my confusion, for he laughed and explained: "Laz is gay. He wanted to tell you himself. He just came out."

A glowing Laz took off his glasses, then explained how he had sensed his own differentness for years but had just recently ventured to explore his homosexuality on a physical level with another man. He said he was very

79

happy with his decision and that he planned to make gay rights his life's work, considering it a form of civil rights scholarship, like Rodrigo's and mine on behalf of people of color. He hoped the news was not coming as too great of a shock, for he understood I was raised in a different era.

"Well, er, congratulations," I replied, a little lamely. "Et tu, Rodrigo?"

"Oh, no," Rodrigo replied with a smile. "Giannina and I are still together, and Laz's still my best friend. He just had his eyes dilated at his old optometrist's. That's why I'm guiding him around."

"Your old . . ." I said with a mixture of relief and confusion. "Oh, yes, your family used to live in this city, Laz, right?"

"That's right," Laz replied. "My parents have always sworn by this guy, so I'm almost afraid to go anywhere else for my eyes." He laughed slightly, and I sensed an easiness about him I'd never seen. *This must be a great relief for him*, I thought.

"Speaking about parents," I said, "have you told them, and, if so, how are they taking it?"

"I plan to tell them next week," Laz replied, a flicker of anxiety showing on his handsome face. "My mom's birthday is coming up. I'm waiting until it's over so as not to spoil things for her."

"Laz's parents have been after him for years to marry and have children," Rodrigo explained. "He's afraid it'll come as a shock."

"Although my sister, Nadia, who does know, just told me she might be pregnant. If so, that'll do a lot to cushion Mom and Dad's disappointment."

"Don't count on it," I said. "The older generation doesn't take these things as lightly as you young folks do. When I was growing up, homosexuality was a serious stigma, particularly in the black community. When James Baldwin, for example, proclaimed his gayness, it made the front pages.[1] I hope you'll break the news gently. Waiting until after the birthday is not a bad idea."

"Thanks for the advice," Laz said. "I was kind of hoping you'd give me your blessing for holding off a little while."

"Well, I'm happy to have served as a sort of dress rehearsal, if it helped."

"There's something else," Laz said. "It concerns children and reproduction. Rodrigo and I were talking about it after my talk and on the way over. Do you have a minute?"

"Of course," I said. "I was just about to head out for a bite to eat. Would you care to join me?" The two nodded eagerly, so I stood up, turned off my desk lamp, and said, "A nice little place opened up just last week, right down the block from the school. Is Moroccan okay?"

Both my young friends said sure, so I motioned them to follow me out. "I'm well past reproductive years myself, but I remember when my own children were young and facing similar dilemmas."

"You're our best sounding board, Professor," Rodrigo said. "Laz and I are really looking forward to your thoughts."

Minutes later, we were seated in a comfortable booth in the small ethnic restaurant, low candles on the tables and bric-a-brac everywhere. The waiter brought our menus, and after we examined them, Rodrigo said, "I forgot to ask—how's your return to teaching going?"

"Fine. The students seem happy to see me back. And the dean was nice enough to give me my old office. And, best of all, she's put me on only one committee."

"I'm glad. Let me know if I can do anything to help." Then, closing his menu, Rodrigo said, "I already know what I'm having the chicken cous-cous. Are you ready for my latest thesis?"

I smiled at Rodrigo's impatience. "Rodrigo, I think you would rather talk than eat, not that I've noticed anything wrong with your appetite for food." I closed my own menu. "I think I'll have the couscous with vegetables. How about you, Laz?"

"The lamb and apricots, I think," Laz replied. Then, looking over at Rodrigo, "Why don't you start?"

In Which Rodrigo and Laz Point Out the Opposite Role Sexuality and Reproduction Play in the Social Construction of Two Outgroups

Just then the waiter arrived for our orders. After he wrote them down and departed, Rodrigo began.

"Laz and I were talking about this on the way over. Have you ever noticed, Professor, what a large part reproduction plays in the social construction both of minorities of color and of gays?"

"You mean the way the religious right condemns homosexuality as unnatural because gays cannot have children?" I asked.

When Rodrigo nodded, Laz interjected: "That's part of the reason I'm dreading telling my parents. They're devout Catholics."

Rodrigo gave his friend a sympathetic look, then went on. "It's not just the religious right that malign gays and lesbians. Many cultural conservatives who are not especially religious do as well, on the grounds that your orientation is against nature."[2]

"I'm not sure the two impulses are easily separated," I said. "But let that go. What do you draw from it?"

"First, that it's really unfair. Heterosexual couples who are childless for medical reasons or because they want to preserve a yuppie lifestyle don't come in for nearly so severe condemnation. But Laz and I were discussing what will happen when increasing numbers of gay men and women start having children artificially. Will their detractors let up, or become even more outraged?"

"Interesting question," I conceded. "I've read of gays and lesbians who try to adopt children. Agencies give them a devil of a time, if I recall."

"My partner Enrique and I know a lesbian couple who have been try-ing for years and getting nowhere," Laz agreed. "And we couldn't think of a single gay couple who succeeded in adopting a child, at least if the child was not the natural offspring of one of them and the mother a total misfit while the two men had sterling characters, Ph.D.'s, and several mil-itary medals of honor."

I laughed at Laz's story. Then: "Rodrigo mentioned the possibility of gay men having children by technological means. I take it you meant arti-ficial insemination?"[3]

"That way and others," Laz replied. "Including one I want to discuss later. But for now, notice how reproduction works exactly the other way with minorities of color. Society stereotypes them as *excess* breeders.[4] They have too many children. Rodrigo pointed this out."

I shook my head admiringly. "It is an amazing reversal, when you think about it. One group blamed for too much breeding, the other for too little. How did this occur to you two?"

"Oh, on the bus ride over here Rodrigo and I were talking about the problem of parents. Almost every gay friend I know had to deal with fa-milial disappointment over the prospect of no grandchildren. Just then, a young black teenage couple, the boy-girl type, obviously very much in love, got on the bus carrying college science textbooks. Even though they were just holding hands, laughing, and looking deeply into each other's eyes, half the passengers looked away. The other half looked disapprov-ing. You could just read their thoughts."

The waiter arrived with our food. "That looks good," I said, examining my couscous and vegetables, which the cook had arranged in an attrac-tive symmetrical design on my plate. Then I asked, "So, what *do* you make of the different role reproduction plays in the social construction of gays and minorities?"

"Outgroups always seem to be defined, at least partially, in terms of their sexuality," Laz replied. "The hapless, effeminate Asian male, the oversexed Latin lover, the ever-breeding black woman, and so on. We agreed that they should challenge those roles, mix things up. Then the bus got crowded so we had to put our conversation on hold."

"Well, let's continue now," I replied, very interested. "But before we start, how's your food?"

"Great," my young friends said simultaneously. Then Laz continued: "We hoped to get your input. With sexual minorities, the course is clear. We have to try to break down the barriers, formal and informal, that stand in the way of access to reproductive technologies, like the one you mentioned."

"Artificial insemination?" I asked.

"Yes," Laz replied, "for lesbians, that is. The technique most gay men would use is surrogate motherhood.[5] Gay males like me have semen. So we can supply the sperm. What we need are eggs and someone to gestate the fetus for nine months."

"I see," I said. "But don't many states barely tolerate surrogate motherhood even in the more normal case—I mean, the common case—in which a couple with infertility lying on the wife's side enters into a contract with another woman to bear their child? This woman, called the surrogate, agrees to be inseminated with the husband's semen, then to carry the child to term. After it's born, she releases the infant to the couple, who adopt and raise it for life, just like an ordinary baby. The surrogate receives her medical expenses and a payment of $20,000 or so."

"But with gays, certain barriers get in the way," Laz said.

I hesitated for a second. "You mean the distasteful overtones of economic exploitation and commodification of sex?"

"Yes," Laz said. "But even if one can get past that, one has to find a surrogate who will agree to perform the service for us in the first place. Since many surrogates are apt to be somewhat traditional, blue-collar women, that will often not be easy. But even if the couple can find one, when they try to adopt the child nine months later, state authorities may not cooperate—even though the child is genetically 50 percent related to one of the men in the couple."

"What about arranging a trade with a lesbian couple," I asked, "in which the men provide semen for two pregnancies, both of which the lesbians agree to gestate. At birth, the gay couple takes one child, the lesbian couple the other. This eliminates the troublesome power imbalance that afflicts most cases of surrogacy, as well as the risk that the surrogate, faced with turning a child over to someone with an alien lifestyle, may change her mind."

"Hmmm. That actually might work," Laz said. "Although the need for two couples might cut down the number of people who could do it, and it might be hard to decide which child goes with which couple." Then after a pause: "I wonder if you've heard of a second technique called in vitro fertilization?"[6]

"I think so," I said. "If I recall, the physician gives a woman donor hormone therapy so that she produces several eggs in one ovulation. The doctor then removes the eggs by aspiration and mixes them in a laboratory dish with semen from a male. After fertilization, the doctor implants one or more ova in a woman—who might or might not be the same one who donated them—and the fetus develops until it's born. The baby is then transferred to the couple who arranged for the procedure."

"That's right," Laz said. "In that sense, it's the female-side equivalent of artificial insemination. And it's a promising avenue for gays and lesbians—if they can find a clinic willing to perform it—because it separates the functions of insemination, conception, gestation, and child-rearing. Ordinarily, these all occur within a single, married couple consisting of a man and a woman who engage in heterosexual sex. With in vitro fertilization, this dyad broadens. It may be a triad, consisting of a man who donates sperm, a woman who donates an egg, and a third woman, who gestates the child to term. The original contracting couple need not be a heterosexual pair, just one that wants a child and is willing to pay for it. And you don't need the same woman to donate both eggs and womb."

"It occurs to me that the triad could expand to four," Rodrigo added.

"It could," Laz agreed. "The contracting couple, say a gay pair like me and Enrique, may not want to use their own semen. They may fear genetic disease running in their families. Or they may have worked in an environment that exposed them to chemicals and radiation. So they obtain semen elsewhere, say from a commercial sperm bank.[7] That way four parties would participate in the creation of the child. The sperm and egg donors, the surrogate mother, and the custodial couple who pay for the whole thing and adopt and raise the child after it's born."

"Kind of mind-boggling," I said, "for an old-timer like me. Things were much simpler in my day. We only knew the old-fashioned way. But speaking of sperm banks, haven't I heard of ones for Nobel Prize winners only?"[8]

"At least one actually exists," Laz replied. "William Shockley, the eccentric scientist who won a Nobel Prize for inventing the transistor and then went on to espouse eugenic theories and sterilization of the poor, suggested the idea, even donating his own sperm."

"If you and Enrique would like an eccentric child good at fixing electrical appliances around the house . . ." Rodrigo began.

"Very funny," Laz said with a wry grin. "But when we're ready, we'll donate our own sperm. Either that or adopt, if we can find an agency willing to help us."

"If you're prepared to adopt a child of color or one with a developmental disability, your chances will be much higher," I pointed out.

"We are. And I don't know if I told you this, but Enrique's Puerto Rican and from New York. He says the agencies there are much more liberal than around here."

"But you mentioned another technique," I said. "What was it?"

In Which Rodrigo, Laz, and I Discuss the Next Step in Artificial Reproduction—Human Cloning—and Scientific Momentum

"It's human cloning," Laz said, "and it has a special application to people of color that Rodrigo said we should hold off discussing until we were with you."[9]

"I've been reading about it," I said. "But remind me how it works."

Laz looked over at Rodrigo: "Why don't you start?"

"Okay," Rodrigo agreed. "Cloning, or asexual reproduction, is already advancing more rapidly than anyone thought. Well past the experimental stage, it has already enabled scientists to produce genetic carbon copies of sheep, frogs, cows, mice, and monkeys,[10] and human beings cannot be far behind.[11] A few years ago, a famous experimental embryologist let slip that he had started a few human clones in his laboratory, just to make sure his technique wasn't slipping.[12] Recently, a physicist, Richard Seed, announced his willingness to clone the offspring of anyone who can afford his services."

"Although he might have to leave the United States to do it," Laz interjected.

"Right," Rodrigo acknowledged. "The FDA commissioner asked him not to do so in the United States, at least for now. Otherwise, it's perfectly legal."

"Didn't the cloning of Dolly the sheep take a lot of tries?" I asked.

"Two hundred seventy-seven, to be exact. And that gave pause to human fertility experts, who feared genetic damage to children produced this way. But recent developments are improving the odds, as well as lowering the cost. A technique announced by two University of Massachusetts scientists created clones of adult cows with a success rate, 5 to 10 percent, close to that which clinics achieve in certain standard fertility treatments, and higher than that for in vitro fertilization in women older than thirty-nine."

"Eye-opening," I said.

"And another technique, pioneered by a Wisconsin-Oregon team, promises greatly to simplify the procedure," Laz added. "They insert genetic material from animals of different species into cow eggs whose nuclei have been removed. The eggs start dividing, raising the possibility that animal eggs could be used to create human clones."[13]

"And this simplifies the procedure?" I asked a little dubiously.

"Yes," Rodrigo said. "Women would not have to undergo the risk and expense of donating human eggs. You would take a few cells from a human donor, say from the inside of a cheek, and insert them into a cow egg. Those, of course, are very inexpensive. The Wisconsin scientist got his from a local slaughterhouse."

"I wonder about the mitochondria," I said. "But let that pass. See if I've got this straight. My science is not quite as up to date as that of you two youngsters. Cloning requires human genetic material. . . "

"That's right, DNA," Laz added encouragingly.

"From an adult human being."

"Right," Laz interjected. "From any somatic cell. One from your cheek or the inside of your wrist will do."[14]

"Then it goes inside the egg of some animal, whose own nucleus—"

"Which was haploid," Laz added, "that is, containing half the complement of chromosomes necessary to produce a baby. In ordinary sexual reproduction, the sperm of a man is necessary to complete the complement of genetic material and fertilize the egg. With cloning, you take some diploid material—the nucleus of an adult body cell—and insert it into the hollowed-out nucleus of an egg. If you do this cleverly enough, you trick the egg into thinking that it is fertilized, which it is: now diploid, with a full complement of chromosomes, it is ready to be implanted in a uterus. Nine months later you have a baby."

"Just like surrogate motherhood or in vitro fertilization," I said. "But if I may ask a naive question," I said, "what prevents the fertilized egg from developing into a cheek, if the donated material comes from there?"

"That's the problem of differentiation," Laz explained. "Early in the embryological development of any higher animal, differentiation sets in. Although a lung or nose cell contains the genetic blueprint of the entire animal, the part that contains the code for the whole creature shuts down. The cell grows to be tissue from that one part of the animal only, over and over again until it dies. The Scottish team that cloned Dolly the sheep used one technique to overcome differentiation. Others are in development."

"Although sometimes scientists don't want to overcome it. Rather, they want to clone a particular organ or body part for medical use or transplant,"[15] Rodrigo interjected. "Indeed, some worry that bills to stop human cloning might unintentionally block the cloning of skin, blood, or individual organs for transplantation."[16]

"Which brings us to the idea of momentum. I've heard some legislatures want to block human cloning.[17] What do scientists think of that?" I asked.

"Lori Andrews points out that fertility scientists, by and large, are impatient with ethicists, theologians, and legislators who are raising objections to it," Laz said. "She also points out that Clinton's order forbidding the use of federal funds will have little effect, because almost all fertility clinics are private. The feds have refused for twenty years to provide money for in vitro fertilization, but that hasn't stopped the more than one hundred privately funded clinics around the country that perform it. They just pass the cost on to the patients, who are desperate to have children. She points out that cloning is unlikely to be either more dangerous or costly than many techniques now routinely employed.[18] The American Society of Reproductive Medicine, for example, opposes bans on the production of human clones from a technique called embryo splitting.[19] Many scientists are said to be chafing to go ahead. They believe the First Amendment guarantees a right of scientific inquiry[20] and that infertile patients have a right to reproduce free of unreasonable restraints."[21]

Qualms About Cloning: Autonomy and the Psychological Well-Being of the Cloned Child

"Safety issues aside, don't some worry that the clone will be psychologically unfree since it's created in the image of a parent?" I asked.

"Yes," Rodrigo replied. "They point out that when the clone grows up, he or she will realize he or she was created to be the genetic carbon copy of someone else. This realization could damage the psyche of the growing child, who will lack what some call a 'genetically open future.'[22] Other critics worry that the parents of a clone might try to overdetermine the clone's personal and professional choices."[23]

"So that the clone of a talented musician, say Arthur Rubinstein, will be sent to the piano several hours a day instead of being allowed to play baseball," I said.[24]

"Exactly. One might even accuse the parents of a clone produced with a genetic gift of some sort of parental malpractice if they do *not* steer the child to discover its talent," Laz pointed out. "Musicians, chess players, mathematical geniuses, and ballet dancers must start young. Suppose the Rubinstein family, out of concern for their child's freedom, remove all the pianos from the house so that Arthur senior has to go to a studio to rehearse. The child, who might be quite ordinary in other aspects, could grow up to be a clerk in a shoe store who only discovers late in life that he has an extraordinary musical talent."

"That seems kind of unlikely," Rodrigo said. "With all the music around us, music classes in the public schools, and so on. But what about a child cloned to have a particular defect or limitation?"[25]

"Is that really likely?" I said.

"Consider a bookbinder who is blind and deaf," Rodrigo replied.[26] "Nevertheless he makes a good living binding books. Needing someone to help him in the shop, he clones himself so that his son grows up to be a blind, deaf bookbinder, too."

"I hadn't heard that example," Laz replied. "But one scholar argues that cloning carried out even with ordinary motivations—for example, overcoming infertility—might violate the Thirteenth Amendment, since it creates a child whose genetic destiny is determined in advance.[27] Cases like the one you just described would seem even more troublesome—and more plausible than the hackneyed Hitlerian army scenario."

"I think I remember that analysis," I interjected. "Didn't the same author also argue that cloning for special gifts might run afoul of a different constitutional provision?"

Even Worse Qualms: A Racially and
Economically Stratified Society

"Yes," Laz said. "The antinobility clause. The idea is that tinkering with human germ tissue to produce in perpetuity a line of gifted offspring runs afoul of the underlying values of that clause, which prohibits the establishment of permanent dynasties of special individuals."[28]

"At least, if it's the state bestowing the benefit," I countered.

"Right," Laz answered. "If Donald Trump chooses to clone himself for whatever combination of inheritable traits he thinks contribute to his business success, rather than play the genetic lottery and risk having a perfectly ordinary son or daughter, nothing in the Constitution would seem to prevent it."

When my two interlocutors were silent for a moment, I said, "This is all quite sobering. I want to hear more, especially about the angle you mentioned, Laz. But if you two are almost finished with your meals, I wonder if you would like to stretch your legs for a bit."

My two young friends looked at each other. "Laz and I were hoping to take you out to a second place for dessert later," Rodrigo said. "A college friend of Laz opened an ice cream parlor uptown. He says the food and prices are good, but it's a thirty-minute walk."

When Rodrigo mentioned the address, I said, "I'd be happy to hoof it, if you two don't mind. I missed my morning run, for no good reason other than feeling lazy, so this will make up for it. In fact, we could stop in at University Hospital's neonatology clinic. It's on the way, and I know the chief of staff. We can look in at the babies through the window, then continue on with our walk."

Both friends nodded a little dubiously, but Rodrigo said, "That makes sense to me for a reason I'll tell you later. Let's go."

As we set out along a side street I chose because it would have little traffic, I asked the question that had been on my mind.

"So, Laz, you think all this has implications for race and civil rights?"

We waited for a late driver to speed through the intersection even after the light turned green in our direction. Then Laz said, "Maybe we all should clone and freeze ourselves to guard against drivers like that. But to answer your question, consider something Rodrigo and I were talking about on the way over. When cloning services are perfected, as they will be soon, they are likely to be distributed on the basis of ability to pay. Fairly expensive, probably in the $100,000 to $500,000 range; only the wealthy will be able to afford them.[29] Egg transfer and in vitro fertilization are expensive, so you see this to some extent now. Few people of color and almost none from the lower and working classes can afford these procedures; if infertile, they stay that way."

"The same must be true of surrogate motherhood," I added.

"Indeed, though the cost is a little lower. But Rodrigo pointed out that cloning will go far beyond these technologies in reinforcing racial and class hierarchies."

"And not just because of the greater initial cost," Rodrigo added. "Consider how cloning will allow persons with good looks, talent, and genius—or simply the luck to have rich parents—to reproduce themselves.

When it becomes available, we will begin to see hereditary dynasties of a sharply delineated sort.[30] Other reproductive technologies such as surrogate motherhood and embryo transfer have the same potential, but cloning, which produces an offspring with the same genotype as the clonor and a very similar phenotype, presents all these risks in much heightened form."

"You mean that talent will reproduce itself?" I asked. "The Arthur Rubinstein scenario?"

"That and many others," Rodrigo replied. "Already, members of minority communities have begun to wonder whether cloning will end up being the exclusive preserve of moneyed whites. A friend pointed out to me how recent statistics show that heroic, lifesaving operations such as open-heart surgery or kidney transplants are distributed differently by race, with whites the more frequent beneficiaries. Even for a minor operation like hers, my grandmother had to insist on treatment. At first, they weren't going to give it to her."

"And it just occurred to me," Laz added, "that in the United States blacks and Latinos very rarely are the recipients of organ transplants, yet very often the donors."

"Recently, a colleague of color mentioned how curious it seemed to him that just as the U.S. population is poised to change from one in which whites are the majority race to one in which Asians, blacks, and Latinos together will outnumber them, cloning comes along. He meant, of course, that the cloning of elites, even in a majority-rule democracy such as ours, could greatly skew the distribution of political power," Rodrigo said.

"One of my law-and-economics–minded friends pointed out how human traits like beauty, good health, athletic ability, and, of course, intelligence, are *resource attractors*, enabling their possessors to accumulate wealth—which, in turn, enables them to purchase medical, educational, and procreative services that confer additional increments of those very resource attractors.[31] Cloning, if distributed in accordance with market forces and ability to pay, will utterly transform the distribution of wealth and merit in society," Laz concluded.

"Hmmm," I said. "Society so far has done little to guard against that. With surrogate motherhood, for example, teams of doctors and lawyers arrange private, three-way contracts in which the contracting couple, generally two yuppified professionals earning high salaries, locate a willing third party, typically a lower-income woman who agrees to be impregnated with the husband's semen and carry the fetus to term for a fee. When born, the fetus is adopted by the contracting couple who raise it, send it to prep school and Harvard, and help it get a job in Dad's company. The contracting woman doesn't have to miss a beat or take a day off work from her law firm or advertising agency."

"Cultures that value male birth, perhaps because of the higher earning potential of males, use sex selection," Laz added. "Some of that goes on in the United States as well, because of the transplanted values of immigrants. The couple achieves pregnancy, then the woman submits to a test that indicates the fetus's sex. If it turns out to be the wrong one, they obtain an abortion and start over. The procedure is common in India and China, where the skewing of the ratio of male to female births can be very great—in some areas as high as 60 to 40.[32] In Italy, a third technology, ovum transfer, has been used to produce pregnancy in postmenopausal women as old as 60.[33] This technique, too, can enhance the procreative options of social and economic elites at the expense of the rest of society, which must stop reproducing at age forty-two or so, for most women."

"But isn't this just another case of the rich getting richer?" I asked. "In free-market economies, economic classes tend to rigidify over time even without technologies such as these. Ordinary market forces—interest, leverage, and the ability of a large farm or factory to achieve economies of scale—guarantee this. You're pointing out that the rich also get healthier and have children more intentionally. Is this really new?"

"I think so," Laz said, furrowing his brow slightly. "Let me try to explain. In any society, social and economic advantage tends to be self-perpetuating, as the wealthy use part of their income to purchase additional increments of education, health care, reproductive services, and other forms of social capital. Movie stars extend their careers—and become even more beautiful—by buying cosmetic surgery and treatments. Highly educated people send their children to the best schools. Top athletes can afford special diets and training facilities that ones who start out with lesser talent cannot. But this stratification will accelerate exponentially when biological technologies enable those who own resource attractors and socially constructed 'merit' to pass these qualities on to their descendants directly, as with cloning—or, somewhat less perfectly, with other reproductive technologies."

"I see what you mean," I said. "Currently, some children of wealthy parents turn out to be slackers and good for nothing. Or simply not as smart or industrious as Mom and Dad. Over time, what scientists call the tendency toward the mean assures that most families—"

"Outside the royal family of England," Rodrigo cracked.

"Right," I said. "Outside special situations like that, most families don't become dynasties. The sons and daughters of some rich parents dissipate their fortunes and end up poor. The offspring of some working-class people, by dint of hard work and talent, rise to become wealthy and influential. So, there's a degree of social mobility between classes."

"And you see how cloning puts this in question?" Laz asked.

"I do," I said. "The cloned child of a very beautiful parent, given adequate nutrition and health care, will grow up looking very much like the clonor—that is, very beautiful. Beauty in our society correlates with success and fortune. Similarly, an athlete whose superb coordination and reflexes bring him or her a huge income can have a child just as physically gifted. And to the extent that intelligence, temperament, musical ability, and other talents have a biological basis, cloning will enable parents to reproduce them in their progeny.[34] The edge that surrogate parenting confers on the couple of busy professionals who don't want to take time out for ordinary pregnancy will be multiplied many times over. I can see why you find this troublesome."

"Right," Laz said. "Although this goes somewhat against my own interest, since as a gay man these technologies are my lifeline. But if we want to assure equal access to social resources across racial and ethnic lines, we must consider how new procreative technologies are distributed. If we don't, the wealthy will be able to consolidate their position, securing advantages for their progeny, and so on indefinitely, while everyone else is left hoping that Junior will turn out to be bright enough to help out in the family auto shop. All technology exacerbates the gap between the haves and the have-nots."[35]

"The haves make sure it comes out that way," Rodrigo interjected.

"True," Laz said. "But reproductive technologies, and especially cloning, do this in a way that increases class separation rapidly and permanently."

In Which We Take Time Off to Look at Some Babies and Discuss Certain Quarters That Would Like Fewer of Them—of Color, at Any Rate

"Here we are," I said, pointing out the entrance to the shining office tower housing the famous teaching hospital. "If you two are ready for a break, we could go upstairs and see some babies. If my friend Rufus is in, that is."

The two young men looked at each other a little quizzically, then said, "Why not?" Minutes later, we were standing with my doctor friend, who was wearing a white coat and stethoscope, next to a window beyond which we could see rows of newborns sleeping, waving their fists, wiggling, or crying. One, next to the window, looked up at me with a cross-eyed grin that reminded me of one of my own daughters, more than forty years ago. With a twinge, I envied Rodrigo and Giannina their prospect of enjoying parenthood, yet at the same time I felt sorry for Laz and his parents, who would not. At least without resort to one of the technologies we had been discussing, I reminded myself. Laz, at least, seemed to have no inhibition against resorting to them. Maybe the next generation would benefit from one or more children with his undeniable brilliance, warmth, and intellect. I hoped so.

I was brought out of my infant-induced reverie by the low, booming voice of my friend Rufus, who asked how we came to be interested in babies. Laz blushed slightly (something I had never seen in him) and said something noncommittal, while Rodrigo, noticing his friend's discomfiture, quickly piped up with, "My wife, Giannina, and I are thinking of starting a family soon, so I thought I'd come see what's in store for me."

Rufus chuckled and said, "You and your wife come right over here when you're ready. We'll take care of you when the time comes for a little Rodrigo or Rodriga."

"Thanks," Rodrigo said. "We'll keep that in mind. We don't live here, but we do visit often, so who knows?"

"Looks like you've got a full house," I said, nodding toward the row upon row of babies on the other side of the partition.

"Yes," Rufus said. "It's a good line of work these days, even if I didn't enjoy delivering them, which I do." Then after a pause: "Our friends and neighbors, Professor, are truly following the biblical mandate, 'Go forth and multiply.' I'm on call practically around the clock. Yesterday I delivered seven babies."

"Seven babies!" I exclaimed. "Sounds like giving a bar review course. When do you rest?"

"Oh, I let the interns and residents handle some of the routine tasks, while I catch a break here and there," Rufus replied. "It's not as bad as it sounds. I stop in and supervise. This is a teaching hospital, you remember."

"Oops," we all said in unison as Rufus's beeper went off suddenly.

"Duty calls," Rufus said. "Good meeting you gentlemen. I assume you don't want to witness the miracle of birth. We do have extra gowns and masks."

Laz and Rodrigo hastily demurred, and Rufus strode off with a wave.

Minutes later we were outside on the sidewalk, striding in the direction of Laz's friend's ice cream parlor. "That was quite something, wasn't it?" I asked.

"It was," Laz agreed. "Did you notice that most of the babies were black or Latino-looking?"

"Come to think of it, yes," Rodrigo replied.

"I bet it's the same in most big-city hospitals," I said.

"An illustration of what we were talking about before," Laz said. "And why some of my conservative friends are running scared.[36] Oh, here we are."

"Is this your friend's place?"

"I think so," Laz said, looking around. And to the clerk behind the counter, "Is Herb in today?"

"He's taking the day off. Can I offer you gentlemen something? We have takeout and tables."

We indicated we'd like a table, so the clerk said, "Sit anywhere you like. I'll be over to take your orders in a minute."

Minutes later, we were diving into our concoctions, banana splits for my young friends, whose endless appetites never ceased to amaze me, mango sherbet for me. After a short pause, I asked: "And so, Laz, where do you come out on this? I mean, do you see any way of reconciling the tension in which gays and lesbians need access to procreative commodities in order to replicate themselves and challenge their own social stigma, while if society develops those technologies, especially cloning, people of color and the poor will almost surely be shut out? People of means will spend some of their wealth to reproduce their talents in their offspring, which will get richer and richer, generation after generation."

"While the poor get poorer and poorer," Rodrigo interjected, "as competition with the taller, healthier, more beautiful rich—most of whom will be whites—gets stiffer and stiffer."

"It would get stiffer for poor whites, too," I pointed out. "Anyone not wealthy enough to afford technologically enhanced reproduction will have to take a chance on ordinary childbirth. But still, a few geniuses will be born to poor parents per generation, and maybe a superb athlete or two will slip in."

"Some of those babies back in the hospital looked pretty formidable," Laz interjected.

"And no doubt they'll be steered by teachers, coaches, and counselors into sports and physical work,"[37] I said ironically. "But on the whole, the preexisting gap between the rich and the poor, white and black, will widen greatly."

"The perfect solution to John Tanton's problem," Rodrigo mused. "You remember him, don't you?"

"Isn't he the guy who got into trouble with his statements about Latino breeding?" Laz asked with a grimace.

"The very one," Rodrigo replied. "Active in various causes and think tanks, Tanton also was one of the leading figures in the fight to limit immigration and establish official-English laws. No friend of blacks, he seemed to have a special fixation on the Latino threat. In his 'Witan IV' memo written for a sort of think tank, he warned that unless whites took action they would be swamped by the faster-breeding races of color. 'Perhaps this is the first instance,' he warned, 'in which those with their pants up are going to get caught by those with their pants down.'"[38]

"Did you two read about the California group that rewards welfare mothers who agree to be sterilized?"[39] I asked.

"I did," Laz said. "A conservative group in Orange County pays women who have taken crack cocaine to undergo permanent sterilization. Some have already taken the bribe."

"That's appalling," said Rodrigo. "Why don't they sterilize savings and loan executives who bilk taxpayers of millions of dollars, or cigarette and automobile executives who market known dangerous products that kill millions?"

"No one thinks of that," I said. "But as you and I discussed once, they should. White-collar crime, carried out almost exclusively by upper-class whites, costs more money and lives than all street crime combined."[40]

"Do you remember William Shockley, who proposed the Nobel Prize sperm bank?" Rodrigo asked.[41]

I nodded.

"That California group reminds me of another scheme of his—the bonus sterilization plan. Widely thought to be aimed at blacks, his proposal would have paid $1,000 per point to every person with an IQ under 100 who agreed to be sterilized. A person with an IQ of 90 would receive $10,000 and so on."[42]

"It didn't catch on, except in a few totalitarian countries," I mused. "Maybe that California group will get quantitative and offer a sliding scale of reward money. They could appoint Shockley scorekeeper."

"He is a prime exponent of race-IQ theory, according to which blacks and Latinos have IQs about one standard deviation below those of whites," I said.[43]

"Then that job is exactly the one for him," Laz said with a smile. "He could test candidates for sterilization. If they really scored one standard deviation below the mean, the bonus would have to be $15,000. More if they tested lower. Holding to his convictions would be costly."

"We'd see the rapid development of a culture-free test. For the first time, the difference between whites and blacks would come out to be very small," Rodrigo cracked.

"Maybe one point," I added, smiling. "Just enough to support the program, but not cost too much in bonus money. Law-and-economics in action!"

The waiter materialized to ask if we wanted coffee. Laz ordered a cup of regular American; Rodrigo, his trademark double espresso; me, "A decaf cappuccino, please." The waiter disappeared with our orders.

In Which We Discuss Solutions for Outgroups of Color

As the counter clerk drew the steam for the espresso and my cappuccino, Laz said: "Deplorable as this all sounds, I think the solution lies with your friend Rufus."

When he looked at us inquiringly, I said, "Do you mean that liberal and black doctors should help gays, lesbians, and people of color with their reproduction problems?"

"I don't mean to come across like a free-market fanatic," Laz said, "but that's the only solution I see. Gays and lesbians do tend to have very high combined household incomes, especially gay couples, while for various reasons most people of color don't. So we'd have to find some way to get around that."

"But how?" I countered. "The gay and lesbian community may contain enough doctors to satisfy demand. But the black and brown communities are radically underserved, and the number of those physicians of color is even smaller."

"And I bet that those who specialize in experimental reproductive medicine can be counted on the fingers of one hand," Rodrigo added glumly.

"What about all those medical schools on offshore islands?" Laz asked. "And don't a lot of American doctors go to medical school in Guadalajara and Bologna?"

"Some do," Rodrigo replied. "I met several when I was a college student in Italy. But only one or two were nonwhite."

"I'm afraid we need a different solution for people of color," I concluded. "The free market just won't work for us. If we want to clone poor but brilliant black or Latino intellectuals or poets, we'll have to find another means."

"Remember when the three of us were discussing whether the free market would eliminate discrimination all by itself?[44] We concluded it wouldn't," Rodrigo said.

"And I guess you're suggesting that just as it won't stop the imposition of *bads*—evils, discrimination—it won't see to the equitable distribution, across race, of *goods*, in this case scarce procreative technologies," Laz said, a little reluctantly.

"I know you hate to concede that," Rodrigo said, smiling at his friend. "As an advocate of the free market, your instincts always run toward laissez-faire solutions. But our analysis seems to lead ineluctably to a different conclusion."

"Namely, governmental action of some sort," Laz said a little glumly.

"A civil rights act of 2001, guaranteeing equity in access to procreative services that portend radical shifts in the distribution of merit, health, talent, and happiness. It's kind of mind-boggling," I mused.

"But essential," Rodrigo said, "if we are to avoid society's rapid transformation into a system of near-feudal castes, with the superior breeding the superior, who in turn use their superiority to assure it for themselves and their progeny."

Laz nodded, a little dubiously, in spite of himself.

Laz's Argument: The Decision to Clone Is Not a Private but a Reconstitutive One

"While the rest of us struggle to keep up," I said, suddenly struck by the full impact of the Huxleyesque scenario my two young friends had painted and that was beginning to seem more and more plausible.

"A wholly new type of civil right," Laz mentioned. "Unlike anything we have seen before. My libertarian friends will be shocked, but frankly I don't see any way around it. Unless society intervenes to bestow biologically based talents and possibilities equitably, we'll end up a caste-bound society like South Africa or India in the old days."

"Maybe you could use economics and rational choice theory to explain it to your friends," Rodrigo said.

"One way to do that occurs to me," Laz said. "Have you two heard of the notion of a *reconstitutive decision*?"

Both of us must have looked a little blank, because Laz went on as follows. "Put forward by Laurence Tribe in recent times,[45] but foreshadowed in Continental philosophy, the basic idea is that certain major decisions, such as one to proceed with building a giant hydroelectric dam, or to develop a line of scientific research that can change the very concept of what it means to be human, have a reconstitutive dimension."

"Is this any different from ordinary risk-benefit analysis that technology assessors do all the time?" I asked.

"It is," Laz replied. "Ordinary decisions, such as to build a supersonic transport, present a standard and predictable range of costs and advantages. Travel gets faster and easier. But the world has to deal with the problem of sonic booms and jet trails. And so on."

"But cloning or your giant hydroelectric dam are different?" I asked. I wanted to see where the conservative wunderkind was going.

"Yes. In cases like these, the impacts are not out there, as with the SST or a decision to open a new shipping channel. With them, the decision-maker merely tries his or her best to forecast the future and figure out the respects in which society will be better or worse off."

"And I gather that in your hydroelectric example, or in cloning, the impacts are somewhere else?" I asked.

"Yes," Laz said. "They are in here. The decision whether to go ahead or not changes the society's very self-concept, its very definition of itself as a community. And it does so instantaneously, in the very act of decision. That's why it's called a reconstitutive decision."

"Why would a decision about a hydroelectric dam present that aspect, but one to fix the potholes on the south side of town first, not?" Rodrigo asked.

"It's all a matter of degree," Laz replied. "Imagine a region of the country that contains a beautiful mountain valley. Bluebirds and other wildlife live there. The people go there to enjoy nature and receive spiritual refreshment. They've maintained it pristine for generations. Now, a utility company proposes to build a giant hydroelectric plant. The valley will be under tons of concrete and millions of gallons of water. The people have to vote on whether to go ahead or not."

"And the vote, however it comes out, affirms one self-definition or another," I said.

"Exactly," Laz replied. "Suppose they opt for the dam. In doing so, they commit themselves, as a region, to values of jobs and cheap electrification. If they vote the other way, they reaffirm a different set of values, declare themselves a different kind of people: one who prizes natural, spiritual, and recreational values above those other ones."[46]

"So the vote has a reconstitutive dimension," Rodrigo said, "however it goes."

"Even if the dam is never built, the people who voted will have redefined themselves a certain way. They are a different people from that day forward. They voted for jobs. Or consider when the Wright brothers flew the first airplane at Kitty Hawk. Until then, for all of history mankind had been earthbound. Confined to two dimensions, people could only admire birds, the only creatures who could fly. After news of the first flight spread, humanity's self-concept changed. The human race could now fly. We would never be the same."

"I think I see where you are going," I said with rising excitement. "A societal decision to allow human cloning, and maybe other forms of technologically induced procreation, has that very same reconstitutive dimension. We would now be a people who can control genetic destiny, create carbon copies of ourselves, and guide the course of evolution."

"Shutting some out and enabling others to see themselves in the next generation," Rodrigo said. "Do you think this is a good enough reason for a new civil rights act, Laz?"

"It might be," Laz replied. "The argument is straightforward. Before scientists or other private actors go about reconstituting society, they have an obligation to inform the rest of us and get our consent. For the impact of their work is potentially irreversible and widely felt. Before you radically redefine me, or the conditions in which I live and learn what it is like to be human, you must ask me. Or rather, all of society."[47]

"And not just the lucky few who will be able to pay for your invention," I said. "It's a straight-out application of informed consent, with connections to the political theory of the social compact. But would courts enforce it?"

"I don't know," Laz said slowly. "But if the reconstitutive impact is clear, frightening, undeniable, and touches a fundamental human liberty, such as procreation. . . "

"And, if those who would be injured or shut out are discrete and insular minorities . . ." I added.

"Courts could analogize to informed consent cases to require that cloning scientists hold town hall meetings and get the consent of the citizenry. But I think that a better decisionmaker is the legislature."

"Didn't certain city governments in fact pass resolutions banning recombinant DNA when it was first developed in university labs?" I asked.

"They did," Laz replied.[48] "That could serve as a precedent. After it happened in Cambridge and a few other places, the scientific community quickly met at Asilomar, California, and voted for a moratorium and period of public comment."[49]

"Hmmm," I said. "That argument might make points with conservatives. You would be a better judge of that, Laz. But you also mentioned something about irreversibility. What are your thoughts on that?"

"I'm glad you reminded me, since conservatives are by and large cautious people who don't easily rush into things, especially ones that depart radically from tradition and from which there might be no turning back. So if a decision to go ahead with cloning could change society in a way unlikely to be undone, they might well oppose it."

"Except if the change in question benefits them," I added wryly. "Maybe it's unkind, but I was thinking of certain corporate decisions, like cutting down the rain forests, that are probably irreversible but bring hefty profits. Conservatives seem to have little trouble joining in with this sort of measure."

"And, of course, the aspect of cloning that the three of us find troubling, namely, its ability to skew society, create castes, and render blacks even more one-down, is not likely to get conservatives excited in the same way it might our liberal friends," Rodrigo added.

"You two *are* being unkind," Laz said, a slight edge in his voice. "Some of us on the other side of the political spectrum do care about equality. We may not define it in quite the same way as you do, but we do believe in equal opportunity and free competition. The creation of biological supercastes, with a corner on socially created 'merit,' would give at least some of us pause."

Rodrigo's Argument: Two Kinds of Irreversibility and Manipulation of Taste

"I just thought of a second way to rally support among your coreligionists, Laz. Maybe among liberals, too," Rodrigo said. "Had the two of you considered that irreversibility could take one of two forms?"

"Oh?" I said. "What kinds?"

"Well, there's what we might call physical irreversibility. Then, there's a more drastic kind we might call conceptual irreversibility.[50] The first kind refers to technological committing decisions that, once started, are very difficult to turn back. They would cost a large fraction of the gross national product to fix, if we decided we didn't like the result."

"You mean something like Lake Erie?" I asked.

"That's a good example," Rodrigo exclaimed. "For a long time, it was thought that the lake was irreversibly, irretrievably dead—had become so polluted that fish would never again swim there. You would never be able to drink the water or bathe there. It was a dead lake, and we could never bring it back."

"Of course, it hasn't turned out that way after all. The government spent millions of dollars cleaning it up and reseeding it with fish. Today you can swim in it, and the fish are safe to eat," Laz pointed out.

"My point exactly. And this leads to my second kind of irreversibility, namely, the conceptual kind," Rodrigo continued. "With Lake Erie, we all remember how it was before the lake died. We remember that this was much better. So we set about trying to restore things the way they were before. But with conceptual irreversibility, we make changes that are so drastic no one remembers how things were before. Or you change the basis for human preference so that people no longer remember or appreciate that the former state of affairs was better. Now, even if we could bring things back, no one will because no one recalls how things were or considers that they were better."

"I've heard that children in Mexico City paint the sky brown in coloring books," Laz said. "Is that the sort of thing you mean?"

"Exactly," Rodrigo said. "When they grow up, it's highly unlikely that they will join an environmental movement. Unless the city gets lucky, its air will continue polluted forever."

"Can you think of another example?" I asked.

"Consider the flavor of natural vegetables and produce or addictions or physical modification of any human faculty for taste, preference, or desire."

"My parents used to raise vegetables in a little patch in their backyard," Laz said, leaning forward with interest. "They were delicious."

"Have either of you ever tasted the flavor of an organically grown strawberry?" Rodrigo asked. We both nodded, so he went on. "The difference between them and the kind you buy in supermarkets is like night and day. Factory farming produces strawberries that are very large and uniform in color and size. But their flavor is generally disappointing. Once you taste one grown in somebody's pea-patch, you realize there's no comparison."

"But over time, people will lose the incentive to search for the better kind, since they're so expensive and hard to come by," Laz noted. "You lose the basis for comparison. I'm told some people now prefer nondairy creamer to real cream in their coffee. Children prefer soda pop to natural lemonade."

"They also much prefer Disneyland to visiting Switzerland and seeing the real Alps," I interjected. "The whole basis for taste is changing."

"And with TV and theme parks, the change may well become permanent," Rodrigo went on. "Giannina and I were discussing this in case we have children. Some studies say that constant exposure to TV and video games may induce actual changes in the brains and nervous systems of young children, so that books and board games no longer appeal to them. They need constant stimulation and change."

"Almost like an addict," I said. "But you mentioned addiction as a second case of conceptual irreversibility."

"Right," Rodrigo replied. "I don't want to push the comparison too far, but books like *When Society Becomes an Addict* do make the analogy.[51] And as you know, many scientists believe alcoholism and drug addiction are hard to treat because they produce permanent changes in brain chemistry. Even though some addicts do conquer their craving, it's a constant struggle. Many say life was more exciting when they were on heroin or other drugs."

After a moment of silence I asked, "Laz, your argument about reconstitutive decisions and yours, Rodrigo, about the two kinds of irreversibility seem to me to have a great deal of force. I should think both notions would give serious pause even to the most hard-hearted devotee of free-market economics. Not that all conservatives are hard-hearted, of course. I just meant in need of tangible arguments that cloning and other forms of technological reproduction cannot be left to chance and the free market. But, just to play devil's advocate for a minute, why couldn't a decision to proceed with cloning, say, or genetic alteration of the human cell line be reversed? If we decided we didn't like what it ushered in, why couldn't we stop it? I mean, presumably if we are smart enough to produce humans with three eyes or blind, deaf bookbinders, we would be smart enough to change things back if this didn't work out for some reason."

"In some cases we could," Laz conceded. "But the new regime could be seductive—easier, more pleasurable or aggrandizing—so that the lucky few would hesitate to give it up. Even literature teachers sometimes use TV and movies in class, even though deeply ambivalent over them. After a time, the irreversibility becomes conceptual. We lose the ability to conceive of the previous state of affairs as better. Everyone says, 'What's the use?' Or like the frog in a tepid pan of water who doesn't notice that the heat is gradually being turned up, we adapt to our manipulated environment until the very end."

Rodrigo added, "It occurs to me that a third way this could happen is through eliminating possible dissidents. For example, if factory farming drives all the family farmers out of business, no one will be left to raise organic strawberries. If the next generation contains few blacks or jazz musicians—"

"Society will lose its taste for jazz," Laz finished. "And the special qualities of living in a vibrant, multicultural society will be lost. Society will take on a homogeneous, white-bread quality, and no one will miss the way it was before."

"I gave a talk last year at a college town that was nearly all white. It was quite an experience," Rodrigo reflected. "The people were liberal, intelligent, and interested in my ideas. But when I talked about race and civil rights, something was missing. Few of them seemed to have a black or Latino friend. When I walked around the downtown afterward I saw hardly anyone of color and very few poor people. It was very nice, but it had a Stepford quality."

"And your point, I gather, is that the people who lived there had lost the capacity to imagine something better. A rich, textured, multiracial community."

"Well, maybe not entirely. I mean, a major city stood only thirty-five miles down the freeway, completely integrated, with ethnic neighborhoods and restaurants. So the townspeople could have gone there to see a different way of life. But evidently few of them did," Rodrigo said.

"Sounds like a Nordic paradise," Laz said.

"It was. Complete with skiing," Rodrigo replied. We were all silent for a moment as we tried to imagine a world where even conceptualizing a multicultural society would be impossible. Rodrigo broke the silence. "I think Laz is onto something. His argument based on the calculus of choice has something for conservatives, while your and my appeal to equity and fairness in the distribution of vital procreative resources would resonate with the left. How do we effectuate these insights?"

Conclusion: In Which Rodrigo and Laz
Hatch a Plot and I Decide to Sit In

But before we could continue, the waiter arrived to pick up our checks. While the two young friends whispered conspiratorially about something, I quickly paid.

"I got it," I said. "You two may have the lightning-fast minds, but I have the quick hands. Besides, you paid before."

As we left the little restaurant and began searching for taxis to take us home, I learned what Laz and Rodrigo had been discussing. "Professor, do you recall the biblical parable of the ten talents?"[52] Rodrigo asked.

"I do," I said. "In the Book of Matthew, the kingdom of heaven is likened to a wealthy man who leaves his fortune in the care of his servants before taking a trip. Some of the servants invest the money wisely, but one leaves it idle. On his return, the master casts the cautious servant into 'outer darkness,' punishment for not making the best use of his talents. The parable is often cited for the proposition that one should take advantage of the opportunities that capitalism and a marketplace based on investment afford."

"Well, is your friend Rufus religious?"

"I think so," I said. "Baptist, if I'm not mistaken. And despite his humble demeanor, he's president-elect of the AMA for next year."

"Well, well," Rodrigo said, his eyes widening. "We were thinking of making an appointment with him and Ed Maldonado, a friend of mine from law school. Ed is the highest-ranking minority lawyer in Health and Human Services, and he's here today for Laz's ABA section meeting. Maybe we can get something going. Would you like to sit in?"

Notes

1. *See* JAMES BALDWIN, GIOVANNI'S ROOM (1956).

2. *E.g.*, CONTRACT WITH AMERICA: THE BOLD PLAN BY REP. NEWT GIN-GRICH, REP. DICK ARMEY, AND THE HOUSE REPUBLICANS TO CHANGE THE NATION (Times Books, 1994).

3. On artificial insemination, in which semen from a male donor is used to induce conception, see Doe v. Kelley, 1980 Rep. Hum. Repro. 2L II-A-1; People v. Sorenson, 6 Cal. 2d 280, 66 Cal. Rptr. 7, 437 P.2d 495 (1968). For an overview of issues of reproductive control, see MICHAEL H. SHAPIRO & ROY G. SPECE, BIOETHICS AND LAW 326–568 (1981 & 1995 Supp.).

4. *See* JEAN STEFANCIC & RICHARD DELGADO, NO MERCY: HOW RIGHT-WING THINK TANKS AND FOUNDATIONS CHANGED AMERICA'S SOCIAL AGENDA 33–44 (1996) (on the modern eugenics movement).

5. On some of the legal issues of surrogacy, including paternity of the child and enforceability of the contract, see, e.g., In re Baby M, 109 N.J. 396, 537 A.2d 1227 (1988); BIOETHICS AND LAW, *supra* at 158–62 (Supp.).

6. *See generally* BIOETHICS AND LAW, *supra* at 548–64; Gina Kolata, *Infertility Clinics Give Birth to New World of Custom-Made Embryos*, DENVER POST, Nov. 23, 1997, at A-7.

7. On the operation of commercial sperm banks, see BIOETHICS AND LAW, *supra* at 369–71, 501, 531–32.

8. On the so-called Nobel Prize sperm bank, see NO MERCY, *supra* at 39.

9. Derived from a Greek word meaning a "twig" or "slip," *cloning* refers to asexual reproduction of life-forms. Cloning occurs naturally in plants and some lower animals. On cloning in humans and higher animals, including livestock, see I. Wilmut, A. E. Schnieke, J. McWhir, A. J. Kind, & K. H. S. Campbell, *Viable Offspring Derived from Fetal and Adult Mammalian Cells*, NATURE, Feb. 27, 1997, at 810 (describing cloning of Dolly the sheep); Ehsan Maseod, *Cloning Technique 'Reveals Legal Loophole,'* in *id.* at 757; Colin Stewart, *An Udder Way of Making Lambs*, in *id.* at 769 (commenting on Wilmut's method of overcoming problem of differentiation and restoring totipotency of adult cells by means of serum starvation); *Cloning Human Beings: Report and Recommendations of the National Bioethics Advisory Commission* (June 1997) (on file with author); *The Clone Age*, A.B.A.J., July 1997, at 68. *See also* IRA H. CORMEN, CLONING AND THE CONSTITUTION: AN INQUIRY INTO GOVERNMENTAL POLICYMAKING AND GENETIC EXPERIMENTATION (1985); Francis Pizzuli, *Note: Asexual Reproduction and Genetic Engineering: A Constitutional Assessment of the Technology of Cloning*, 47 S. CAL. L. REV. 476 (1974).

10. Edward Berger, *Scientists Must Convene, Now, on the Ethics of Cloning*, CHRON. HIGHER ED., July 18, 1997, at A-44 (sheep, cows, a rhesus monkey). *See also Clone Age, supra*; National Commission, *supra* at iv, 24–25 (approving research on cloning of animals). *But see* Leigh Turner, *The Media and Ethics of Cloning*, CHRON. HIGHER ED., Sept. 26, 1997, at B-4 (pointing out possible immorality of cloning animals).

11. *See* National Commission, *supra* at 1 (as little as one year away); John Robertson, *Liberty, Identity, and Human Cloning*, 76 TEX. L. REV. 1371, 1371 (cloning of first human "might soon follow Dolly"—if certain technical difficulties, such as cellular aging, can be overcome, *id.* at 1375).

12. Conversation with Michael H. Shapiro, Professor of Law, University of Southern California Law Center.

13. Lori Andrews, *Human Cloning: Assessing the Ethical and Legal Quandaries*, CHRON. HIGHER ED., Feb. 13, 1998, at 34.

14. National Commission, *supra* at 1; Pizzuli, *supra* at 481–88. *See also Liberty, supra* at 1391–96 (identifying different uses of cloning—cloning oneself, cloning one's child, cloning a third person, cloning one's parent, etc.).

15. *British Lab Creates Frog Embryo Without Head*, TORONTO STAR, Oct. 19, 1997, at A-22; *Don't Ban Cloning, supra*; Ann Schrader, *Cloned Animal Cells May Aid Lives*, DENVER POST, Apr. 28, 1995, at B-1 (cloning animal tissue to treat Parkinson's Disease); *Cloning Holds Promise*, DENVER POST, May 3, 1998, at G-4; National Commission, *supra* at 29–31.

16. Andrews, QUANDARIES, *supra*; Gina Kolata, *People Cloning Gains Attention, Acceptance in Science Circles*, DENVER POST, Dec. 12, 1997, at A-6.

17. See National Commission, *supra* (recommending ban); Andrews, QUAN-
DARIES, *supra* (describing twenty-two state, three federal bills now under consideration); Robertson, *Liberty, supra* at 1383 (California and Council of Europe enacted bans). On an effort to patent human-animal hybrids, or chimeras, ostensibly
to slow their development, see Mary Hager & Adam Rosen, *A Biotech Roadblock,*
NEWSWEEK, Apr. 13, 1995, at 66; Diamond v. Chakrabarty, 447 U.S. 303 (1980)
(life-forms patentable). *But see* Edward Berger, *Scientists Must Convene Now on the
Ethics of Cloning,* CHRON. HIGHER ED., July 18, 1997, at A-44, (one-third of
bioethics commissioners had no objection to human cloning).

18. Andrews, QUANDARIES, *supra; Gains Acceptance, supra* ("I absolutely think
the tenor of things has changed. People who said cloning would never be done
are now saying, 'well, the risks aren't that great'"). Andrews, QUANDARIES, *supra.*
On Clinton's ban on federal funds, see Rick Weiss, *Clinton Forbids Funding of Human Cloning Studies,* WASH. POST, Mar. 5, 1997, at A-10.

19. Andrews, QUANDARIES, *supra. See also* Gains Acceptance, *supra* (with
cloning "the time frame from horrified negation to 'let's do it' is so much shorter.
This is very, very quick").

20. John A. Robertson, *The Scientist's Right to Research: A Constitutional Analysis,*
51 S. CAL. L. REV. 1203 (1978); CHILDREN OF CHOICE: FREEDOM AND THE NEW
REPRODUCTIVE TECHNOLOGIES (1994); Richard Delgado & David Millen, *God,
Galileo and Government: Toward Constitutional Protection for Scientific Inquiry,* 53
WASH. L. REV. 349 (1975); Cormen, CLONING AND THE CONSTITUTION, *supra* at
34–59; National Commission, *supra* at 93–95.

21. *E.g.,* Pizzuli, *supra* at 493–986; National Commission, *supra* at 29–32; Andrews, QUANDARIES, *supra;* Robertson, CHOICE, *supra.* Cloning is reproduction in
the most literal sense. While not exactly of the coital, conjugal type contemplated
by cases like Griswold v. Connecticut, 381 U.S. 479 (1965), and Eisenstadt v. Baird,
405 U.S. 438 (1992), it would nevertheless seem to fall within a broadly defined
right of reproductive privacy. *See* Roe v. Wade, 410 U.S. 113 (1973) (decision to
bear or not to bear a child momentous and intimate, hence protected by a penum-
bra of constitutional guarantees); Skinner v. Oklahoma, 316 U.S. 535 (1942);
Robertson, *Liberty, supra* at 1372, 1388–1403 (cloning "quintessentially reproductive," *id.* at 1400, so that a complete ban would probably be unconstitutional and
unwise, *e.g., id.* at 1390, 1438, 1440–42). *See also* Laurence Tribe, *Why We Shouldn't
Reject the Idea of Human Cloning,* INTERN'L HERALD TRIB., Dec. 6, 1997, Opinion at
6 (society should not reject the technique merely because it is "unnatural").

22. Pizzuli, *supra* at 508, 510, 516; Joel Feinberg, *The Child's Right to an Open Future,* in WHOSE CHILD? (William Aiken & Hugh LaFollette eds., 1990); Andrews,
QUANDARIES, *supra. But see* National Commission, *supra* at 87 (risks not great).

23. Pizzuli, *supra* at 509.

24. *Id. See also* Vincent Kierman, *Cosmetic Uses of Genetic Engineering May Soon
Be a Reality,* CHRON. HIGHER ED., Oct. 3, 1997, at A-17; Clone Age, *supra* at 70.

25. Pizzuli, *supra* at 510.

26. *Id.* at 510, 516 (cloning for blindness). I am indebted to Michael H. Shapiro for this suggestion.

27. *Id.* at 516.

28. Pizzuli, *supra* at 579–80.

29. Andrews, QUANDARIES, *supra* (quoting the higher figure).

30. Pizzuli, *supra* at 579; Shapiro, MERIT, *supra* at 325, 356 (applying this analysis to the New Biology in general).

31. Shapiro, MERIT, *supra* at 323–325, 344–47.

32. Richard Delgado & Judith D. Keyes, *Parental Preferences and Selective Abortion*, 1974 WASH. U. L. Q. 203; Bioethics and Law, *supra* at 448–51, 512; Rick Weiss, *Anti-Girl Biases in Asia, Studies Show; Abortion Augmenting Infanticide, Neglect*, WASH. POST, May 11, 1996, at A-1.

33. *"A Big Victory for Women," Doctor Defends Rights of Middle-Aged Mothers*, CINCINNATI POST, Jan. 1, 1994, at B-8.

34. Of course, environment, free will, and other intangibles (perhaps even the human soul) guarantee that clones will not be exactly alike—just as so-called identical twins are not.

35. That is, industrialization created Henry Ford and the robber barons; transistors produced Bill Gates; and so on. *See* Lisa Ikemoto, *The Racialization of Genomic Knowledge*, 27 SETON HALL L. REV. 937 (1997); JEREMY RIFKIN, THE BIOTECH CENTURY (1998).

36. *See* NO MERCY, *supra* at 33–44 (some conservatives worried about growth in numbers of minority populations).

37. *See* Andrew Backover, *Jackson Speaks on Minorities' Roles*, WASH. POST, Apr. 11, 1993, at D-3 (on the seduction of athletics for African American and Latino youth).

38. NO MERCY, *supra* at 10–14, 23–25. (Quote at 11).

39. Robert Ourlian, *Addicts Are Offered Cash to Be Sterilized*, L.A. TIMES, Oct. 24, 1997, at B-1. On the sordid history of human sterilization, see PHILIP R. REILLY, THE SURGICAL SOLUTION (1991).

40. THE RODRIGO CHRONICLES, chapter 8 (1995).

41. Text and note 8, *supra*.

42. *See* NO MERCY, *supra* at 39.

43. *See Hypotheses: Get Smart, Will We All Become Geniuses?* LINGUA FRANCA, May/June 1998, at 68; Richard Delgado et al., *Can Science Be Inopportune? Constitutional Validity of Governmental Restrictions on Race-IQ Research*, 31 UCLA L. REV. 128, 130–32, 143–49 (1983).

44. *See* Chapter 2, this volume.

45. Laurence Tribe, *Technology Assessment and the Fourth Discontinuity: The Limits of Instrumental Rationality*, 46 S. CAL. L. REV. 617, 649 (1973); see also CHANNELING TECHNOLOGY THROUGH LAW 17 (1973).

46. Tribe, *Discontinuity, supra* at 655–56.

47. *See* James D. Watson, *Moving Toward the Clonal Man*, 227 THE ATLANTIC 50, 52–53 (May 1971).

48. *See* CORMEN, CLONING AND THE CONSTITUTION, *supra* at 70–74.

49. *See id.* at 63–65, 72–76, 80–84; Berger, *Convene Now*, *supra* (describing 1973 moratorium by recombinant DNA scientists).

50. Michael H. Shapiro first explained this difference to me in a conversation.

51. ANNE WILSON SCHAEF, WHEN SOCIETY BECOMES AN ADDICT (1987).

52. Matthew 25:14–30.

5

Latinos and the Black-White Binary

**Introduction: In Which Rodrigo and I Catch Up
on the News and Each Other's Adventures**

"Rodrigo, here I am," I announced, raising my voice over the din of the airport loudspeaker and voices of fellow passengers waiting at curbside. "How kind of you to pick me up."

"No problem. Giannina's back at the house, reviewing for yet another midterm. Here, let me take that bag."

"Nice car," I said. "Did you have it last time?"

"No, it's new. We tried doing without one, but our schedules are so different now that we needed it in order to have any time at all together. So we got this little beauty."

"It's Italian, right?" I asked.

"Right. Mom and Dad had one when I was growing up, although it was a larger model. Have you ever driven one?"

"I don't think so," I said. "At my age, my tastes run to something a little more sedate."

"You can take it to your hearing tomorrow if you want. I'm staying home. You could drop Giannina off at her law school on the way."

"We'll see," I said as Rodrigo slowed for the short-term parking booth. He showed his ticket to the attendant, who waved him on—"Free, less than 30 minutes"—then I asked, "I gather you've been doing some traveling, too."

"I have," Rodrigo replied. "I just got back from a two-day conference hosted by the Latino law students of a major school. It drew an impressive cast, with speakers like Rodolfo Acuña and Carlos Muñoz, as well as the usual complement of law professors. I've been meaning to ask you about something, if you're not too tired."

"Not at all," I replied. "My flight was nonstop and, despite my best intentions to get some work done, I spent the last half of it sleeping. I'm wide awake—ask away."

"As I mentioned, Professor, the event was richly interdisciplinary. But the panel that sparked the most excitement, among the law types at any rate, centered on the role of racial mixture."

"As a multiracial person yourself, you must have found that one intriguing. Were you one of the speakers?"

"No," Rodrigo replied. "I was on a different panel. But on this one, practically every one was a member of the group called Latino-critical scholars, or Lat-crits, that has sprung up over the last few years."[1]

"I've been reading about them," I said. "They seem to be a spin-off group from critical race theory, which in turn traces its origin to earlier progressive movements, including critical legal studies.[2] What were some of the issues the panel discussed?"

"Mainly interracial marriage and adoption. But afterward some of us were talking about the role of Latinos in American politics. We wondered why this relatively large group, which makes up about 12 percent of the U.S. population, has had so little impact on national civil rights policy. Particularly in areas like immigration reform, bilingual education, poverty, and English-only laws we've been relatively ineffectual, compared to blacks. Some thought it had to do with exomarriage, assimilation, and lack of cohesion in the Latino community, which is made up of so many different national origin groups. But after reading a certain book on the flight home, I've come to think it's something else."

"You mean that one?" I said, pointing to a volume lying in the backseat of the little car, a neat bookmark sticking out.[3] "I saw it when I got in."

Rodrigo craned around. "Yes, that one. I brought it along to show you. Entitled *All Rise: Reynaldo Garza, the First Mexican-American Federal Judge* and written by a Washington, D.C., area biographer, it details the life and career of Reynaldo Garza. It's a good read."

In Which Rodrigo and I Discuss *All Rise* and What It Teaches About the Structure of Civil Rights Thought

"I think I saw a book notice for it the other day," I said. "And of course I'm familiar with some of the judge's opinions, in fact taught some of them in my courses over the years. What does the book say about him? Nothing too harsh, I hope. It's tough being a first of any kind. Sometimes biographers and critics expect more of you than you can possibly deliver."

"It's favorable," Rodrigo replied. "And like all good biography, it helps you understand the person and his or her times—how the circumstances in which he or she lived affected the possibilities for that person's life and thought."

"What's the general thesis?" I asked. As a member of the judge's generation, I was anxious to hear the author's judgment.

"Her thesis is that Judge Garza was able to combine a successful career as lawyer and judge and maintain his Mexican American ties and roots at the same time. The book details his early years as a relatively secure child in a large family of middle-class Mexican immigrants who operated a hardware store in Brownsville, Texas. It shows his early encounters with hardship, racism, and exclusion and the way he fought against those evils by trying harder. It traces his college and law school career at University of Texas, one of only two Mexican American students in his class, then his rise in Democratic politics and the state bar, all concluding in his appointment as the nation's first Mexican American federal judge."

"Wasn't he once offered a cabinet position?" I asked.

"U.S. attorney general during the Carter administration," Rodrigo replied. "He turned it down because he didn't want to uproot his family. Later he was appointed to the Fifth Circuit Court of Appeals. Serving during a time of intense civil rights activity, he handed down many noted decisions, especially in the area of labor law where, according to the author, his familiarity with working-class people and conditions enabled him to write opinions notable for their progressivism."

"He sounds like a commendable human being," I observed. "In some ways he reminds me of some of the early African American federal judges of my own generation who struggled to validate themselves in a skeptical world while trying to hand down rulings that advanced the cause of social justice."

"A difficult balancing act," Rodrigo acknowledged. "But I think that with Judge Garza it was harder, somehow. And this brings me back to what we were talking about at the conference."

"Harder because of who he was, or because of conditions at the time he went on the bench?" I asked.

"Both," Rodrigo replied. "When he was appointed, it was a time of intense ferment, almost all on behalf of blacks. The Chicano movement came only much later. His own community, Brownsville, was more than

80 percent Spanish-speaking. Many people were poor, but according to his biographer this was more because of structural poverty and lack of jobs than because of outright discrimination. Nor did the legal system consider Chicanos a suspect class. Like Indochinese and other Asian groups, they occupied a sort of limbo—minorities but not clearly entitled to the special protection of civil rights law."

"Don't the Lat-crits have a special name for this?" I asked.

"The black-white binary,"[4] Rodrigo replied. "It's an idea that's just now emerging as a means of understanding American civil rights law and the place of nonblack groups in it. The idea is that the structure of antidiscrimination law is dichotomous. It assumes you are either black or white. If you're neither, you have trouble making claims or even having them understood in racial terms at all."[5]

"I think I follow you," I replied. "But, assuming that our system does incorporate such a dichotomy, how does that render nonblack minority groups one-down, as opposed to, say, one-up, compared to blacks?"

"That's the next step," Rodrigo replied. "At the conference, no one had worked that out yet. But it's a vital issue. America's racial future looks increasingly mixed up. Latinos will overtake blacks as the most numerous minority early in the next century. The Asian population is also increasing rapidly, even as multiracial people are demanding their own voice and census category. A simplistic paradigm of racial relations based on an either-or, A or B model, won't work much longer. I've been trying to figure out why this is so. Reading about Judge Garza helped crystallize my thoughts."

"Every time a new movement springs up in the law, it's stimulating," I said. "It almost always leads to changes in the way we think about society and justice. We talked about some of these things before. [Rodrigo nodded.] I remember the ferment when critical race theory was born not too many years ago. And if you can believe it, I was actually around when critical legal studies was born some ten years before that."[6]

"You *have* been teaching a long time," Rodrigo replied, giving me a quick look. "And that's why I want to run past you some things I've been thinking about in the wake of the conference."

"Ask away," I said. "How long does the drive to your place take?"

"About thirty minutes since they built the new airport." Rodrigo eased past a group of slow-moving trucks, accelerated the little sports car smoothly to sixty miles per hour, then said: "You remember, Professor, how critical legal studies early on developed the notion of the fundamental contradiction?"[7]

"Of course," I replied. "At the time a breathtaking breakthrough, it explains many of the strains and tensions running through our system of law and politics. It led to powerful critiques of the public-private distinction, judicial indeterminacy, and rights. Were the Latinos at your conference working on something similar?"

"I think we were," Rodrigo replied, "but without knowing it. And it's that very same black-white binary. People in law are just starting to talk about it. You may have seen an article or two. If one's paradigm includes only one group as deserving of protection, everyone else is likely to suffer. Not only that, even members of one's own group are apt to think of themselves nonpolitically. It's quite a disabling instrument. We may have to blast the dichotomy, embrace the full multifariousness of life, if we're ever going to get anywhere."

"You put it rather dramatically," I said, smiling at my young friend and protégé to let him know I appreciated his enthusiasm for ideas, even if it was sometimes a little superheated. "I suppose any rigid structure inhibits flexibility during times of change. But you started to say this had something to do with Judge Garza."

"I don't want to be too negative," Rodrigo said. "He was a genuine pioneer, for which we should all be grateful. But he never really developed much class consciousness—or, if he did, kept it under his hat. He went around the Mexican American community extolling individualism and telling his countrymen and -women that they could rise and accomplish the American dream through hard work, just as he had.[8] He detested discrimination and slurs aimed at Mexicans, but he attributed them to individual failures on the part of particular Anglos, not on anything systemic. As a young man he worked for the agency that ran the Texas Rangers, despite their history of brutal mistreatment of his people.[9] He sold war bonds, backed America's role in two wars, and encouraged Mexican youths to enlist.[10] He praised all things American, even ruled against the plaintiffs in *Partida v. Castañeda*,[11] an early case attempting to redress segregation and discrimination against Mexican Americans.

"He was reversed by the Supreme Court, as I recall," I said.

"Fortunately," Rodrigo agreed. "Garza began—and even ended—with good social instincts and a love of justice. But the black-white racial binary made it difficult for him to think of himself or his group as a people with a history of conquest and brutal treatment and in need of redress. If you don't have a class analysis—and the binary assures that you don't— all you can do is urge your countrymen to work harder and those who are oppressing them to back off—as individuals, that is. You'll rule against your people, Jehovah's Witnesses, and other minorities and oppose federal welfare programs for the poor and intervention on behalf of prisoners and the institutionalized."[12]

"Didn't I read somewhere that early litigators on behalf of Chicanos and other Latino groups embraced something called the 'other white' strategy?" I asked.

"They did," Rodrigo replied. "It's the logical extension of the kind of thinking the black-white binary predisposes you to. The only way to get relief is to maintain that your client, a Mexican American or Puerto Rican, is white and should thus not be discriminated against."

"Not exactly empowering," I commented wryly. "But I believe you were going to tell me of some other ways the binary does its pernicious work."

"In addition to the way it fetters our own minds," Rodrigo said, "preventing us from articulating, or even imagining, how our victimization is a serious, group-based form of oppression."

"You must do so, and in the most complete fashion possible," I said. "If the binary is to serve as Latinos' fundamental contradiction, you have to spell out exactly how this structure of thought renders your people one-down. Otherwise, it's just simply an observation, a descriptive statement no more useful than 'Many Latinos speak Spanish,' or 'Many have ancestors from Latin America or the Caribbean,' or 'A certain judge with good social instincts stopped just short of a civil rights break-through.'"

"I agree," Rodrigo replied. "Without such an explanation, the insight kind of runs out of gas." He sneaked a peek at his instrument panel, then— "Which reminds me, we'll need a quick stop for fuel before we get home."

"Let me buy," I suggested. "You were kind to come get me in the middle of your evening."

Rodrigo waved my offer aside. "Your listening to my thoughts will be payment enough. We're each other's best sounding boards, I think."

"That we are," I agreed. "So what are your ideas on how the black-white paradigm injures Latinos and other nonwhite groups?"

In Which Rodrigo Sets Out His First Explanation:
The Black-White Paradigm and the Social
Reproduction of Inequality—Doctrine's Role

"As you know, Professor, the mainstay of American civil rights law is the Equal Protection Clause. Rooted in Reconstruction-era activism and aimed at the wholly laudable purpose of redressing slavery, that clause nevertheless produces and reproduces inequality for my people."

"The Equal Protection Clause?" I replied, raising my eyebrows. "That crown jewel in our jurisprudence, centerpiece of justice, and source of civil rights breakthroughs like *Brown v. Board of Education*? It's *this* that you think subordinates and injures Latinos? That's paradoxical, to put it mildly. I think I need to hear more."

"Let me try," Rodrigo replied calmly. "An analogy occurred to me on the plane during the flight home. Consider a different constitutional principle, namely, protection of the right of property. How does that function in a society like ours?"

"I suppose you're going to say that it benefits the haves while disadvantaging or leaving as they are the have-nots, thus increasing the gap between the propertied and those who have less of that commodity."

"Exactly," Rodrigo replied. "And the same is true of other constitutional protections. The Free Speech Clause increases the influence of those who are articulate and can afford microphones, TV airtime, and so on. In the same way, the Equal Protection Clause produces a social good, namely, equality, for those falling under its coverage—blacks and whites. But it leaves everyone else unprotected. The gap between blacks and other groups grows, all other things being equal. Even Judge Garza advocated on behalf of *maquiladoras* and declined to find Mexican Americans a minority group."[13]

"It sounds strange when you first explain it," I said. "The idea of the Equal Protection Clause producing inequality. But you may have a point. As with those other clauses, the black-white paradigm could marginalize Latinos because of the way it and the other civil war amendments were aimed at redressing injustices to blacks, principally slavery."

"I've thought of two other doctrinal sources of inequality," Rodrigo added. "Would you like to hear them?"

"Of course," I said. "I assume they also have to do with the black-white paradigm?"

"They do. The first is the very notion of civil rights. In American law, this means rights bestowed by the civil polity. But Latinos—many of them, at any rate—are not members of that polity. Rather, they want to immigrate here. In this respect they stand on different footing than do blacks. I'm sure you know, Professor, that the plenary power doctrine in immigration law means that someone desiring to immigrate to the United States has no power, enforceable in court, to compel equal treatment.[14] U.S. immigration law can be as racist and discriminatory as Congress wants."

"Immigrants have due process rights, rights to a hearing, that sort of thing," I pointed out.[15]

"But only once they're here," Rodrigo replied. "Not to get here in the first place. Since most Latinos, like Asians, come from somewhere else, this limitation affects them drastically. Yet it is inherent in our liberal notion of civil rights and implicit in the black-white binary. Blacks, even Indians, were here originally or from very early days. Once society decided to count them as citizens, their thoughts and preferences began to figure into the political equation. Even if they were often outvoted and oppressed, their voices at least counted. A Mexican peasant desiring to immigrate in search of a better life, or a Guatemalan village activist fearful that his government wants to kill him, or a Chinese boatperson, does not count. They can come here only at sufferance, only if Congress decides to let them in."

"For example, through a Bracero program, a student visa, or some other category benefiting the United States such as that for investors," I added.

"Judge Garza even cooperated with mass roundups and deportations of undocumented aliens," Rodrigo interjected. "He pioneered mass hearings rather than individualized adjudication of cases, an innovation of which he was quite proud, believing it reduced the misery of the detainees since it shortened the time they had to languish in jail and freed space for other, more serious offenders."[16]

"Since the aliens had not been lawfully admitted, they had few rights, except to bare-bones due process," I said. "Judge Garza's legal training did not equip him with a theory for understanding their predicament in any other terms. It would have taken a judicial genius to pioneer a new approach, especially back then."

"That's true even today," Rodrigo replied, eyeing his gas gauge nervously. "As a society, we seem to have taken a detour on the way to justice. And I'm afraid that you and I will have to take one ourselves, if I don't see a gas station soon."

"I have towing insurance," I said half-facetiously. "But I'm sure we won't need it. What's your other reason?"

"It's related to the one I just mentioned," Rodrigo said, scrutinizing the approaching off-ramp. "No station there. We'll have to wait until the next one. I'm sure you've heard, Professor, of the self-definition theory of nationhood?"

"In immigration law, you mean?" I asked. (Rodrigo nodded.) "I have. Going back to an article and a book by Peter Schuck,[17] the theory holds that nations have the inherent right to decide how to define themselves.[18] Otherwise, according to Schuck, any group could force a nation like ours to undergo radical transformation merely by moving here. This no group has the right to do. Tapping neorepublican principles, the argument has proved influential in the immigration debate by supplying an ostensibly neutral principle for limiting immigration. And I suppose you think there's something wrong with it?"

"I do," Rodrigo replied. "The current contours of the U.S. citizenry are shaped by past immigration policies, which were overtly racist.[19] Recently, those policies have been eased somewhat, but only a little. Thus, to ask a body of citizens like ours what sort of person they would like to let in is to invite the answer: as much like us as possible. If we were a more diverse society, that wouldn't be so bad. But the way things stand, Schuck's self-determination principle merely reproduces more of the same. Oh, good, there's one and it's still open."

While Rodrigo pumped gas and I cleaned the windshield, we continued our conversation:

"So, Rodrigo, you think you have found the DNA, so to speak, that reproduces inequality for Chicanos and Hispanics. A triple dynamic, inherent in Equal Protection doctrine and contractarian politics, that excludes and injures your people."

"Yes, but more than mere doctrine holds us back. If it were just that, we could make gains by working outside the legal arena, by mobilizing and educating, for example. Now, let's see, how do I get a receipt?"

"I think you push that button," I said.

"Oh, there it is," Rodrigo said. "They're all a little different."

"Like Latinos and blacks," I quipped.

Rodrigo smiled, and a few seconds later we were easing back onto the freeway with a full tank of gas. "Something happened at the conference that I think you'll find interesting. It illustrates a second way binary thinking injures Latinos. Would you like to hear?"

Rodrigo's Second Explanation:
The Out-of-Mind Phenomenon

I nodded vigorously. "I love conference dynamics. Something zany happens at almost every one. I can't wait to hear."

"It's not all that earthshaking," Rodrigo replied. "But it seems to me to capture something. The conference, as I mentioned, featured a star-studded cast. Attendance was good, even though the event was held in the law school, near the edge of campus. The curious thing is that only one law professor from the huge faculty of the host school showed up. The dean, who had been scheduled to introduce the keynote speaker, begged off at the last minute, pleading important business, and sent the associate dean instead. He didn't even stay to hear the address itself."

"Maybe they were just busy," I said a little lamely, trying to excuse my colleagues at that other school, several of whom I knew personally.

"I'm sure that's true," Rodrigo conceded. "But suppose the panel had been all black, consisting of Derrick Bell, Cornel West, John Hope Franklin, Leon Higginbotham, and others of that stature. In fact, the Latino speakers were just as stellar in terms of reputation and standing in their fields."

"Are you saying attendance would have been better?" I asked.

"I'm not sure it would have been better," Rodrigo replied. "But I suspect that the law faculty would have put in at least token appearances. They would have gushed over the speakers, shaken their hands, and told them how glad they were that they were here, how much the students needed them, and so on.[20] They would have shown solidarity, mentioned how they had marched with Martin Luther King, engaged in at least a few minutes of chitchat—before, of course, taking off for their offices and their next manuscript."

"I hope you're not saying their failure to show up was a deliberate affront?" I asked.

"More likely just a matter of priorities. On any given day, dozens of major events take place at a large university. The professors probably saw the conference as just one of many possible demands on their time, like that reception for the married students or that lecture on Proust being held across campus. No conspiracy or conscious boycott operated, but the result was the same: They didn't show up. If we'd been blacks, they would have. It's as simple as that."

"I know that faculty pretty well," I said. "What you recount is surprising. They're all liberals and deep-dyed supporters of civil rights."

"I wouldn't doubt it," Rodrigo replied. "The faculty know, on some level, that Latinos have terrible troubles and need help. But the classic, the *essential* racial group is black. If you're a liberal law professor, you donate time to the NAACP Legal Defense Fund. When someone mentions 'civil rights,' you immediately think black."

"And so Latinos are simply out of mind because of the black-white binary," I added.

"We're not part of the mind-set so that people don't think of us immediately in connection with civil rights struggles. Also, many Latinos don't live in cities. They're farmworkers or field hands.[21] But when you think of civil rights, you immediately think of city problems—like gangs, urban blight, segregated, run-down schools, and unemployment—that afflict mainly blacks."

"Puerto Ricans are by and large an urban group," I pointed out.

"True, and some urban programs do include them. But many Latinos, especially in the West and Southwest, fall almost entirely outside traditional civil rights consciousness, even though their struggles with pesticides, insecticides, field sanitation, and education for their kids are just as serious as those of inner-city dwellers."

"I'm beginning to see the force of the black-white paradigm," I interjected. "It looks like it really does render your people one-down."

"And I hope you'll help me figure out more ways that it does. We've touched on two.

"I'm game. What's next?"

Rodrigo's Third Connection: Practical Consequences of the Black-White Paradigm

"I think the paradigm not only has doctrinal and conceptual consequences, limiting the way we think of race and racism. It has highly concrete, real-world ones as well."

"Do you have an example?"

"Let's say you're an employer or administrator of some sort. You're distributing things of value, like benefits, contracts, or jobs. You can give a job, say, to one of two equally qualified candidates. One's a black, the other a Hispanic. You probably give it to the black. The black can sue you. He or she has all those civil rights statutes written with him or her in mind. To be sure, courts have held that Hispanics may also sue for discrimination.[22] But the employer may not know that. And the Equal Protection Clause does not protect brown litigants as unconditionally and amply as it does blacks.[23] The binary makes the black the prototypical civil rights plaintiff. Recall Judge Garza's ruling in the Texas school discrimination case. When people read of Latinos suing for school or job discrimination, they are always a little surprised."

"Latinos ought to publicize this fact," I said.

"That's the problem. We have fewer leaders who could do so. Affirmative action produced a generation of college-trained black leaders and professionals beginning about thirty years ago. Today, these people are mayors of cities and members of Congress. That body boasts a longstanding Black Caucus, but only a much smaller and more recently formed Hispanic one.[24] And despite Judge Garza's breakthrough, the entire federal bench today includes fewer than thirty Latino judges. It contains many more black ones, even though the two groups' numbers are almost the same in the general population. And the reason is simple: Affirmative action started earlier with blacks. Even today, the average employer thinks of affirmative action in black, not Puerto Rican, Laotian, or Chicano terms. A Laotian or Chicano law teaching candidate shows up, and even liberal law faculty members have to remind themselves, 'Oh, yes, they qualify for affirmative action, too.'"

"That's a problem of mind-set and conception," I said. "The way society thinks of a group—or fails to think about it—influences the way it behaves. If you're out of mind because everyone is thinking in dichotomous terms, how will you have your needs noticed and addressed? Listeners may even decide you're at fault for your own predicament, a whiner when you call attention to the way no one attended your conference," I warned my young protégé.

Rodrigo's Fourth Connection: Symbol, Myth, and the Role of the Black-White Binary

"I'll be careful," Rodrigo agreed. "But it's interesting to notice why it's necessary. I think the black-white binary conveys to everyone that there's just one group worth worrying about. People conveniently forget that the early settlers exterminated 95 percent of the Indian population, or that many Puerto Rican, Chicano, and Indochinese families are just as poor and desperate as black ones. Recall how much poverty plagued Brownsville, where Judge Garza grew up. And remember the *colonias* we were discussing the other time. But only the one group, blacks, has moral standing to demand attention and solicitude. Those others don't. And to make absolutely sure they don't, we deploy appropriate myths and images. Asians are the model minority—smart, quiet, sure to rise in a generation or two. Mexicans are happy-go-lucky cartoon characters or shady actors who sneak across the border, earn some money, and then send it to their families back home. No one today could get away with speaking of blacks in comparably disparaging terms. But as recently as the 1960s the Frito-Lay corporation used the logo of a sleeping Mexican bandito, hat pulled over his eyes, dozing under a cactus, and people today laugh at Taco Bell's talking Chihuahua. Even Judge Garza ran across some of that.[25] And the imagery deployed by the political right in the English-only and immigration-reform campaigns is nearly as vicious: Latinos come across as criminals, welfare loafers, and drug dealers. If we were part of the civil rights paradigm, no one would dare do this, at least so openly."

"And you think the black-white paradigm is the reason?" I asked.

"Not alone," Rodrigo replied. "But it supplies the conditions that allow it to happen. If one's prevailing cultural image is not that of a noble warrior, like Martin Luther King, but of someone who takes siestas or steals jobs from deserving Americans, why would anyone want to help you?"

"In some ways, those images of Latinos are even more devastating than the ones society disseminated of blacks. They justify everyone not only in ignoring your misery but also in making war against you."

"I'm sure you've heard of the militarized border that is just beginning," Rodrigo interjected.[26]

"I have, and of the imagery that is being deployed by the political right to justify it—the 'waves of immigrants,' the 'horde of welfare recipients,' the 'tide' of brown-skinned welfare mothers just waiting to have babies here so they can gain citizenship. The unassimilability of Latino people and their dubious loyalty."

"Even though Latino servicemen and -women have given their lives and won medals for heroism far out of proportion to their numbers and exceeding those of every other racial group," Rodrigo interjected.

"Like Reynaldo Garza and his son, war heroes."

"Right. And consider national language. If an immigrant French couple speaks French to each other or English with a French accent, that's considered a sign of high status and culture. A Mexican worker speaks Spanish and he or she is considered stupid or disloyal."

"Here we are," Rodrigo announced, sliding the little car into a driveway. Glancing at a lighted window, he added, "Giannina's still up. You'll have to have a bite with us before retiring."

* * *

A little later I was comfortably ensconced in the hide-a-bed the two young people had graciously opened up for me, reviewing papers for my testimony the next day. As my eyes pored over columns of figures in the plastic-covered binder the lawyer for my side had sent me, my mind kept wandering back to the conversation in the car. I recalled how it had begun with Rodrigo's recounting of Judge Garza's life and career, then continued with his startling announcement that the Equal Protection Clause of the Constitution, with its implicit creation of a black-white binary, functioned as a subordinating instrument and replicator of inequality for Latinos. I recalled how Rodrigo had showed how additional forces operated in concert with that paradigm, magnifying its effect—the out-of-mind phenomenon; geography, asset-hoarding, and political influence; and cultural imagery— some operating on a practical level, others on that of myth and narrative.

As I rather sleepily underlined facts and figures for my testimony tomorrow, I kept coming back to this and other conversations Rodrigo and I had had recently about the role of nonblack groups in America's future. Would a country I had served more than forty years as a professor and civil rights advocate adjust peaceably to a century in which whites began to be outnumbered by blacks and browns? And would those two groups be able to work together toward mutual goals—or would the current factionalism and distrust continue into the future, with the various minority groups competing for crumbs while majoritarian rule continued unabated?

Would the civil rights community prove flexible enough to modify the black-white binary to include other groups? Or would it decide petulantly that broadening vistas to include groups such as Latinos and Asians was too much trouble? For their part, would the young crits be content with a new, richer paradigm, or would they aim at an antiparadigm, in which the very concept of race, and different races, dissolves? *Old habits die hard*, I thought, recalling the nearly all-white law faculty that had failed to show up for Rodrigo's meeting. The more nuanced understanding of race of which Rodrigo spoke would not come easily. I wondered if these issues would be replayed at tomorrow's hearing and recalled, with a start, that a neighborhood group had written my side recently questioning the lack of Spanish-speaking elementary school teachers in two cities within our district.

I checked to see that the alarm clock was set early enough so that Rodrigo, Giannina, and I could continue our conversation over breakfast tomorrow.

Notes

1. On the Lat-crit movement, see Jean Stefancic, *Latino and Latina Critical Theory: An Annotated Bibliography*, 85 CALIF. L. REV 1509 (1997); 10 LA RAZA L.J. 423 (1998). For history and precursors, see *Symposium: Latinos and the Law—20 Years of Advocacy and Lessons for Advancement*, 14 CHICANO-LATINO L. REV. 1 (1994).

2. On critical race theory, see CRITICAL RACE THEORY: THE CUTTING EDGE (Richard Delgado ed., 1995); Richard Delgado & Jean Stefancic, *Critical Race Theory: An Annotated Bibliography*, 79 VA. L. REV. 461 (1993). On critical legal studies, see *Symposium: Critical Legal Studies*, 36 STAN. L. REV. 1 (1984).

3. LOUISE ANN FISCH, ALL RISE: REYNALDO G. GARZA, THE FIRST MEXICAN-AMERICAN FEDERAL JUDGE (1995).

4. *See* Juan Perea, *The Black-White Binary Paradigm of Race: The "Normal Science" of American Racial Thought*, 85 CALIF. L. REV. 1347 (1997); Juan Perea, *Ethnicity and the Constitution: Beyond the Black and White Binary Constitution*, 36 WM. & MARY L. REV. 571 (1995).

5. *E.g.*, Deborah Ramirez, *Multicultural Empowerment: It's Not Just Black and White Any More*, 47 STAN. L. REV. 1995 (1995); Elizabeth Martinez, *Beyond Black/White: The Racisms of Our Time*, 20 SOC. JUSTICE 22 (1993); Trina Grillo, *Anti-Essentialism and Intersectionality: Tools to Dismantle the Master's House*, 10 BERKELEY WOMEN'S L.J. 16 (1995), Ruben García, *Critical Race Theory and Proposition 187: The Racial Politics of Immigration Law*, 17 CHICANO-LATINO L. REV. 118 (1995) (all pointing out inadequacy of current dualistic structure of American social thought on issues of race and ethnicity).

6. On critical legal studies, its themes and history, see *Symposium, supra*; THE POLITICS OF LAW (D. Kairys ed., 1983); see also *id.* (3d ed. 1998) for articles updating the original.

7. On the fundamental contradiction—the notion that we both fear and need others—see Duncan Kennedy, *The Structure of Blackstone's Commentaries*, 28 BUFF. L. REV. 205, 211–13 (1979). *See also* Richard Delgado, *Critical Legal Studies and the Realities of Race—Does the Fundamental Contradiction Have a Corollary?* 23 HARV. C.R.-C.L. L. REV. 407 (1988) (discussing the critical legal studies version and the possibility that a different one explains the predicament of persons of color under American law).

8. ALL RISE, *supra* at 41–42, 68, 125, 170, 175.

9. *Id.* at 34, 37–38.

10. *Id.* at 50.

11. 384 F. Supp. 79 (S.D. Tex. 1974), rev'd, Castañeda v. Partida, 438 U.S. 482 (1977).

12. ALL RISE, *supra* at 58, 119, 130.

13. *Id.* at 112.

14. On this doctrine and its function in immigration law, see Hiroshi Motomura, *Immigration Law After a Century of Plenary Power: Phantom Constitutional Norms and Statutory Interpretation*, 100 YALE L.J. 545 (1990); T. Alexander Aleinikoff, *Federal Regulation of Aliens and the Constitution*, 83 AM. J. INT'L L. 862 (1989).

15. Motomura, *supra* at part I-B; Aleinikoff, *supra* at part II.

16. ALL RISE, *supra* at 33–35.

17. PETER H. SCHUCK & ROGERS M. SMITH, CITIZENSHIP WITHOUT CONSENT: ILLEGAL ALIENS IN THE AMERICAN POLITY (1986).

18. Schuck & Smith, *supra* at 9–41, 116–40; Peter Schuck, *The Transformation of Immigration Law*, 84 COLUM. L. REV. 1, 4–5, 49–65, 85–90 (1984).

19. On racist immigration quotas, see Kevin Johnson, *An Essay on Immigration Politics, Popular Democracy, and California's Proposition 187: The Political Relevance and Irrelevance of Race*, 70 WASH. L. REV. 629 (1995); Michael Olivas, *The Chronicles, My Grandfather's Stories, and Immigration Law: The Slave Chronicles as Racial History*, 34 ST. LOUIS U. L.J. 425 (1990) (racist immigration policies foreshadowed and give support for DERRICK BELL's bleak CHRONICLE OF THE SLAVE TRADERS).

20. *See* TOM WOLFE, RADICAL CHIC AND MAU-MAUING THE FLAK CATCHERS (1967) (on the great attention many liberals shower on black-power and similar celebrities).

21. *See* Regina Austin & Michael Shill, *Black, Brown, Poor, and Poisoned: Minority Grassroots Environmentalism and the Quest for Eco-Justice*, 1 KAN. J.L. & PUB. POL'Y 69 (1991). *See also* Jane Larson, *Free Markets Deep in the Heart of Texas*, 84 GEO. L.J. 179 (1995) (on Texan *colonia* settlements); LUKE COLE & SHEILA FOSTER, TOXIC ASSAULT: THE ENVIRONMENTAL JUSTICE MOVEMENT IN THE UNITED STATES (forthcoming, NYU Press 1999) (on occupational-health issues of farmworkers and others).

22. *Compare* Tijerina v. Henry, 48 F.R.D. 274 (D. N.M. 1969), appeal dismissed, 378 U.S. 916 (1970) (Chicanos may not sue collectively) *with* Castañeda v. Partida, 430 U.S. 482, 494–96 (1977) (same group may sue collectively but only in regions where they are subject to local prejudice), *and* Keyes v. School Dist. No. One, 413 U.S. 159, 197 (1973) (same, in cases brought to challenge de jure school segregation of Latino children). *See also* Hernandez v. Texas, 347 U.S. 475 (1954) (class status upheld for juror-selection purposes).

23. On some of the limitations, see George Martinez, *Legal Indeterminacy, Judicial Discretion, and the Mexican-American Litigation Experience*, 1930–1980, 27 U.C. DAVIS L. REV. 555 (1994); Richard Delgado & Victoria Palacios, *Mexican Americans as a Legally Cognizable Class Under Rule 23 and the Equal Protection Clause*, 50 NOTRE DAME L. REV. 393 (1975) (analyzing procedural difficulties of class-based relief for Chicanos or Mexican Americans under antidiscrimination law). On American courts' peculiar ambivalence over whether Mexican Americans are white, see George A. Martinez, *Mexican Americans and Whiteness*, in THE LATINO/A CONDITION 175 (R. Delgado & Jean Stefancic eds., 1998). On a recent refusal to see anything wrong with excluding Spanish-speaking jurors, see Miguel Mendez, *The Wrong Message at the Wrong Time*, 4 STAN. L. & POL'Y REV. 193 (1993). *See also* Maria Ontiveros, *To Help Those Most in Need: Undocumented Workers' Rights and Remedies under Title VII*, 20 N.Y.U. REV. L. & SOC. CHANGE 607 (1994) (analyzing statutory intersectionality under which undocumented workers fall between the cracks of workplace antiharassment law); Perea, *Ethnicity, supra* (little redress for discrimination based on ethnicity).

24. On the Black Caucus, see ROBERT H. BRISBANE, BLACK ACTIVISM: RACIAL REVOLUTION IN THE UNITED STATES, 1954–1970 (1974).

25. ALL RISE, *supra* at 14–16, 19–20, 24–29, 32–33, 45–49, 89–90.

26. On the new militarized border, see TIMOTHY J. DUNN, THE MILITARIZATION OF THE U.S.-MEXICO BORDER, 1978–1992: LOW-INTENSITY CONFLICT DOCTRINE COMES HOME (1996).

6

Conflict as Pathology

What's Wrong with Alternative Dispute Resolution

I was standing in my pajamas trying to figure how to fold up the little hide-a-bed on which I had spent a surprisingly comfortable night when a familiar voice from behind startled me: "Professor, you're up. Let me give you a hand. How did you sleep?"

My young host deftly snapped the mattress back in place, replaced the couch cushions, and scooped up the bedding, which I had stacked on a nearby chair. "Like a log. I spent a few minutes getting ready for my hearing, then turned in around eleven. How about you two?"

"Fine. We talked for a while about Judge Garza, then called it a night. Did you have any dreams?"

"Not that I can remember. How about you?"

"I actually did," Rodrigo replied. "I don't know if I told you, but Ray and Esmeralda, some good friends of ours, are getting divorced. In my dream, our late friend, Trina Grillo, was warning Esmeralda not to choose mediation. It was one of those mixed-up dreams I sometimes have, with everything out of sequence. I don't think Trina even knew Esmeralda, but she was speaking to her warmly, as though to a friend."

"Oh, what a loss! Trina was a loving, caring person, and, as you know, a leading critic of alternative dispute resolution, particularly for divorcing women. I found her work inspirational."

"Me, too," Rodrigo echoed. "I woke up early, reread her Yale article,[1] and have been thinking about it ever since. Would you like some coffee?"

"Oh, you're up. Here, let me take those bedclothes." The tall, smiling young woman who had just stepped into the room gave me a quick kiss on the cheek, then indicated the espresso machine that was starting to make inviting noises in the next room. "Like some coffee?"

"You know my weakness," I replied, accepting the mug Giannina handed me and pouring myself a steaming cupful. "Rodrigo tells me he's been dreaming of Trina Grillo."

"Another woman?" Giannina replied, smiling at her husband to show she wasn't serious. "He's been worried about our friends Ray and Esmeralda, who seem to be breaking up after nearly seven years together. I gather Trina was giving Esmeralda some sort of lecture on the pitfalls of mediated divorce."

Rodrigo poured himself a mugful of brew, added cream and his trademark four spoonfuls of sugar, and invited me to follow him to their kitchen table. "Have a seat, Professor. This area catches the morning sun, which should come streaming in any minute. Would you like some breakfast?"

"Coffee is fine for now. What were you thinking about ADR?"

"Oh—alternative dispute resolution," broke in Giannina. "We're just about to read up on that in my study group." Closing the door of the refrigerator into which she had been peering, she added: "We have several pieces on our list, including Professor Grillo's. Our civil procedure professor is a great booster. She never misses a chance to plug deformalized justice, which she says saves money and time while reducing the risk and acrimony of a trial. Some of my fellow students and I have our doubts. So I'd love to hear what my dear husband is going to say."

"So, Rodrigo," I said. "Why do you think your friend is about to make a big mistake?"

In Which Rodrigo Argues That Informal Disputing Is Not a Godsend for the Impecunious or Small-Stakes Disputant

After Giannina joined us at the comfortable kitchen table, a cup of steaming tea in hand, Rodrigo began: "Professor Grillo wrote a few years ago, just as alternative dispute resolution—mediation, arbitration, neighborhood justice centers, consumer complaint panels, and so on—was taking off.[2] Her warning was prophetic—as relevant today as it was then."

"She focused mainly on divorce mediation, as I recall," said Giannina.

"Correct," Rodrigo replied. "Although much of what she said applies equally to other methods of deformalized justice, like court-ordered negotiation, arbitration, and consumer complaint boards.[3] Her basic point was that despite its promise of a cheaper, faster, less intimidating means of disputing, deformalization poses special risks for women and other disempowered disputants."

"My professor discussed the supposed advantages in class recently," Giannina interjected. "Informal disputing with the aid of a friendly, trained third party promises a cooperative rather than adversarial means of resolving disputes that otherwise could drag on for months or years and leave the disputants angry and unhappy. It can frame solutions that take context—the particulars of an individual case—into account rather than being limited to fixed categories and rules, as is true in court. Each side gets to tell its story. Displays of emotion are not entirely ruled out. And of course, it's speedier and less expensive than the in-court version."[4]

"All powerful advantages," I acknowledged. "How did Trina deal with that?"

"She showed, with the aid of empirical studies and narratives from practice, that many of the touted advantages were illusory. She also supplied reasons, drawn from social science or psychoanalytical theory, why this is so. Alternative dispute resolution may be speedy and cheap, but if you are a woman or member of a racial minority group, ADR is apt to compound the disadvantages you bring to the bargaining table. Drawing on recent work in communication theory and radical feminist writing on the social construction of sex roles, she argued that mediated divorce poses special problems for women."[5]

"Some people who opt for ADR report that they like it," Giannina added. "My professor mentioned that surveys of consumer satisfaction show that many who go through deformalized dispute resolution feel good afterward."

"Grillo concedes that this may be so in some cases," Rodrigo replied. "Since ADR magnifies power differentials, naturally the more empowered party, who has probably prevailed, is happy. Sometimes weaker parties are happy as well because they feel they got to tell their story. Even though they may have received a worse disposition than the one they would have gotten in court, they may not know this. ADR feels comfortable. The parties get to speak rather than have their position put forward by a lawyer according to prescribed rules of evidence and procedure.

Everything is conducted in ordinary English. The parties meet around a small table, with comfortable chairs, in a conference room somewhere."[6]

"You mentioned that ADR is especially bad for women," Giannina said. "Why is that? And do you think Esmeralda is at risk?"

"She's pretty strong-willed," Rodrigo said. "You can decide whether she needs the warning or not. Grillo's point is that in our society many women are conditioned into an ethic of care and connection and taught that their principal role is that of homemaker and mother. In a face-to-face mediation, they can easily accept too much responsibility for what went wrong. Feeling guilty that the other side is unhappy, they may give in when, had they been represented by a lawyer and gone to court, they might have won."[7]

"Are you two ready for breakfast?" Giannina asked. "We have eggs, muffins, and more coffee."

I looked at Rodrigo. "I am. You know how airplane food is. I had a tiny snack on the flight out, all bread, cold meat, and only a tiny scrap of lettuce. I hope we're not prevailing on you because of your ethic of care."

"Not at all," Giannina said with a laugh. "Usually Rigo is up ahead of me and makes coffee and breakfast. I did the honors this morning because you two were talking and I hate making up that heavy hide-a-bed."

Giannina served up our steaming omelets and offered refills of coffee. As we dove in, Giannina said, "You were going to tell us about your dream."

Conflict as Pathology: What Professor Grillo Might Have Added to the Critique of ADR Had Her Career Not Been Cut Short

"Oh, yes," Rodrigo said. "Trina was warning Esmeralda about mediation, pointing out that divorcing women with children are particularly vulnerable to the power imbalances of ADR. But then, in my dream, she went on to discuss ADR in general."

"What did she say?"

"She said she was planning to explore some of the broader dimensions of deformalization, in particular how changing conditions may be eroding her own fairness-and-formality critique. But she also said she hoped to show that an even more basic premise of ADR—namely, that conflict is pathology, an aberration from a peaceful norm or baseline—is false. Instead, things are the other way around—conflict is normal. She likened this situation to the liberal view of race and racism, which holds that racism is an anomaly in an otherwise fair system, when the crits believe it's just the opposite.[8] Then a noise woke me up."

"Rats," I said. "It must have been me trying to fold up the hide-a-bed."

"Don't worry. I think I caught her meaning. I'd like to run it past you if you have the time."

"Of course," I said. When Giannina nodded, Rodrigo continued.

Fairness and Formality:
Why the Critique May Be Losing Ground

"The first critique—," Rodrigo began.

"The fairness-and-formality one?"[9]

"Right," Rodrigo replied. "It began, as you know, in connection with alternative dispute resolution.[10] The basic idea is that the formal values of American society are aspirational and egalitarian. We have some of the best public values in the world—all men are brothers, every person is an equal moral agent, and so on. The average American knows this and, when reminded, will often act in truly egalitarian fashion, treating a black or a woman, say, with equal dignity and respect."

"But that's not always true in informal interactions," Giannina chimed in.

"No," Rodrigo replied. "In informal settings, with friends, in a bar or a private club, the same person who would behave in a genuinely fair-minded fashion at a Fourth of July picnic, with all the flags flying, feels much freer to tell an ethnic joke or act in a way that will hurt the job chances of a Chicano or African American."[11]

"Women know this by a kind of instinct," Giannina added. "Certain men can be trusted to behave decently in front of others, or on an official occasion. That same man at a party, with others like him, may feel freer to hassle one of us or come on stronger than we want. Is this an aspect of what you mean?"

"It is," Rodrigo replied. "And Professor Grillo's critique of ADR captures just this idea. Formal court adjudication is less apt to be infected with prejudice than the informal variety. In court, you have all those reminders—the flags, the pomp, the judge sitting on high—that this is an occasion when the formal American values of equality, fairness, and so on are to rule. In nonformal settings, fewer such reminders confront the participants. If one is a woman, a gay man, a black, or any other outsider, one should opt for as much formality as one can afford. All this ties in to a leading theory of prejudice,"[12] Rodrigo concluded.

"And you believe this situation may be changing?" Giannina asked.

"Professor Grillo implied so," Rodrigo replied. "I've been puzzling over what she might have meant."

"Perhaps it has something to do with the right-wing surge this country has been experiencing over the last few years," I ventured, "with conservatives attacking affirmative action and multicultural programs on campuses, rolling back voting rights and redistricting for minority candidates, and pressing for immigration reforms, English-only laws and other measures offensive to Hispanics."

"They've also cut out most forms of welfare for the poor," Rodrigo added. "The situation may be flipping."

We were silent for a moment. Then I continued: "I think I see what you mean. The equation of higher values with the public sphere is only contingently, not necessarily, true. In some societies, for example South Africa under the old regime, the official values were racist, namely, apartheid. In that country, if one were a black, one would be better off looking to private sources for relief. Say you were a stranded motorist. An individual South African might stop and help you when the police would drive right by. The government was racist, but an occasional private citizen might be kind."

"And so you are saying that the United States is in the process of becoming more like the former South Africa, with informality being better than formality?" I asked.

"It might be," replied Rodrigo. "Many conservative judges and mean-spirited laws have been put in place. The situation bears watching. Professor Grillo's other observation is even more fundamental. Would you like to hear it?"

I looked at Giannina, who nodded. "I certainly would," I said. "Let me get these plates first."

Conflict as Pathology: Why the Main Normative Premise of ADR Is Wrong

After I helped Giannina carry the plates to the kitchen sink, Rodrigo began: "In my dream, Trina told me that, had she had the opportunity, she would have questioned the most basic presupposition of the ADR movement—that conflict is pathology. All the rhetoric and ideology of the deformalization movement highlight how mediation and its relatives can avoid the tough-as-nails, winner-take-all quality of adjudication.[13] ADR is not adversarial but cooperative. The parties look for a way to solve their problem. Issues of blame, anger, and revenge, if raised at all, are ruled out of bounds. The idea is to go forward together in a search for the best solution to the problem, whether it's custody of the children, a barking dog, or a car that won't run right."

"The whole thing has a sort of therapeutic quality," Giannina observed.

"It does. That's why it appeals so much to social workers and others with similar training," Rodrigo said. "And that's the issue that Professor Grillo told me she would have addressed had she had the chance."

"Conflict as pathology," I mused aloud. "I think you have a point. In a society like ours, conflict is normal, the ordinary state of affairs. Our society is made up of competing classes in endless struggle: consumers and manufacturers; whites and the descendants of former slaves; workers and factory owners. Smoothing conflict over and structuring a dispute resolution system so as to treat its every manifestation as a sign of unhealth is a very big mistake."

"Maybe more than a mistake," added Giannina. "Adjusting divorcing women to their lot, or disappointed consumers to their mistreatment at the hands of General Motors, can take away indignation that might otherwise fuel reform. Richard Abel and others point out that ADR atomizes disputes;[14] Owen Fiss that it deprives courts of the opportunity to articulate public values.[15] Maybe both observations are part of the insight that you, courtesy of Professor Grillo's apparition, are putting forward: namely, that conflict is not pathology but the ordinary and natural state of affairs in a radical, free-market society like ours."[16]

"You mentioned that the two critiques were connected in some way," I said, sensing that our conversation was about to come to a close. "Can you spell that out before we part company?"

Rodrigo looked at his own watch. "I can drop you off on my way, if you like, Professor. It's only a short drive. There's a bookstore on the way you might like to see."

"Thanks. I told the attorneys I'd be there a little early to go over my testimony. But I have time to hear this last point, if you're ready."

In Which the Two Critiques Converge and Rodrigo Predicts the Future of ADR

"I am," Rodrigo replied, draining his cup and pouring himself a refill. "The connecting link is the idea of intersectionality[17] and multiracialism."[18]

"Do you mean the way the U.S. population is rapidly diversifying?" asked Giannina. "With Hispanics expected to take over as the largest ethnic group of color sometime early in the next century, and whites ceasing to be a majority sometime around the middle of it?"

"That and more," Rodrigo replied. "Multiracial people like myself are increasing in number.[19] Some are even demanding their own census category. Black women are asserting their differences from white feminists, as well as from the black, male-dominated civil rights movement. Gays and lesbians of color are asserting themselves.[20] Society is becoming more differentiated."

"And fractious," Giannina replied. "And that is why a dispute resolution system that treats conflict as pathological is less likely to serve us well. But you mentioned something about ADR being on a collision course with itself."

"Oh, yes," Rodrigo replied. "Have the two of you heard the hope that ADR can offer a better form of justice to intersectional people, to black women and single mothers, for example?"

"I have," I replied. "At last year's American Association of Law Schools meeting, a speaker put forward just this view. The idea is that nonformal justice, because it does not have to follow hard-and-fast, bright-line rules designed with stable categories in mind, can do a better job of dispensing justice in nonrecurring, unusual situations or ones featuring nonstandard people, such as black women, gay Latinos, or lesbian single mothers."

"Professor Grillo wrote of this hope," Rodrigo replied, "without endorsing it.[21] But it seems to me that intersectional people who do not fit the cookie-cutter mold should not put their faith in normlessness. Instead, they should insist on new norms. Opting for the normless plasticity of ADR does indeed open the possibility that the mediator will craft a solution that better serves one's needs. But it also exposes one to the prejudices and unstated presumptions apt to come to the fore in exactly that sort of situation. The more one strikes the other participants in the mediation as deviant and outside the norm, the more likely one is to find oneself cut off, foreclosed from expressing certain emotions or exploring the issues dearest to one's heart. This is especially so if the aspect of one's makeup being litigated is controversial, such as the right of gay parents to the custody of their children. To treat a case like that therapeutically, as though the only objective is finding a solution that serves the best interests of the children, is to guarantee a result tinged by bias. If you go to court, you may lose because doctrine is against you. But you may win. The judge may decide to change the doctrine.[22] The jury may decide to nullify the law.[23] At least you will get a hearing. If you opt for ADR you may get no hearing because the mediator and your adversary may unconsciously marshal an entire constellation of attitudes and prejudices to shut you up and trivialize your complaint. At best, you will find yourself treated as an intriguing deviant in need of therapy—or as the one who is breaching the peace and needs to be persuaded to back off."

"And as society becomes more diverse, we will see more and more such cases," Giannina seconded.

"And more and more requests to treat them by alternative dispute mechanisms," Rodrigo added.

"Where the weaker party will be adjusted in the direction of the normal—the straight white male way of seeing or doing things," I added.

"Which is why we must watch out for the notion of conflict as pathology," Rodrigo concluded. "It atomizes and renders invisible those very claims that we should take seriously because they reflect a new, emerging social order. We ought to treat them directly and formally. Doing so confers a benefit on all of society—the opportunity to create new norms that will better serve a diversified people. Invisible, backroom negotiation aimed at a therapeutic result will hurt offbeat disputants in the short term. In the long term, it will deprive society of opportunities to resolve a host of new issues, ranging from gay rights to sex roles in the family, and new norms respecting consumer safety and environmental protection."

"In that sense," I summarized, "conflict may not be pathology but health. And speaking of health, I need to stop taking advantage of your hospitality and think about getting to my hearing. At my age, running through court buildings in search of the right room is a poor prescription for longevity."

"We only need to allow"—Rodrigo looked at his watch—"about ten minutes this time of day. When are you due?"

"Ten o'clock."

"We could have a second cup of coffee unless you need to get there early," Rodrigo offered.

"Okay. I'd much rather spend the time here than in some sterile waiting room. Especially if you have more thoughts on ADR."

The Ideology and Timing of the ADR Movement: In Which Rodrigo Addresses the "Why Now?" Question

"Speaking of timing," Rodrigo began, "have the two of you ever wondered why ADR seems to be taking off right now?"

"I assume you have a theory," I said.

"I do," Rodrigo replied. "Alternative dispute resolution is one of those ideas that appeals to both the left and the right. Republican business leaders love it because it makes lawsuits that might bring bad publicity and high damages go away.[24] Moderate leftists like it because it enables them to think they are cutting down on acrimony and doing something useful for society."[25]

"But in fact they are brushing conflict under the rug," Giannina interjected.

"More than that," Rodrigo replied. "They are atomizing disputes and sidetracking some altogether. In adjusting the dissident to his or her situation, they take groups that are—or should be—spoiling for a fight—the poor, workers, consumers, and civil rights complainants—and offer them, instead, momentary peace. This smoothes things out for the corporate state, which naturally believes we have too many lawsuits because they are the ones getting sued."

"Doesn't the United States in fact have a high rate of litigiousness?"[26] Giannina asked. "My professor pointed out that in Japan the percentage of lawyers is only a small fraction of what it is here. People solve their problems without going to court.[27] She mentioned the notorious hot coffee–in-the-lap case and the jury's extraordinarily high award to the plaintiff."

"Of course our system allows some abuse," Rodrigo conceded, "but look at it from another point of view. Capitalism, ruthlessly pursued, encourages businesses to skirt the line of illegality. Lawsuits are a means of policing that line and assuring that the number of dangerous products is kept down. Much illegal and harmful conduct goes undetected and unpunished. Businesses count on this—normalize it—in setting their profit margin. Naturally, an increase in the number of lawsuits is seen as a sign of social pathology, as something abnormal."

"I know the argument that tort law is efficient; that it encourages businesses to take measures to prevent accidents as the cheapest cost-avoider.[28] So I can see why you oppose ADR for consumers, but what about divorce law? That's a huge area for ADR. In fact it's the main one Professor Grillo was concerned with," Giannina pointed out.

"Divorce law is efficient, too," Rodrigo replied. "It encourages careful calculation of budgets and separate maintenance awards. It encourages separate treatment of separate things, like alimony and child custody. It encourages uniformity of treatment through the development of benchmarks and the possibility of written appellate opinions. By the same token, it encourages parties to settle, because the range of possible outcomes is known in advance. Have the two of you noticed how ADR seems to be taking hold most strongly in those areas of greatest power imbalance between the parties?"

"You mentioned divorce, consumer complaints, and medical malpractice," I replied.

"My professor said that ADR is even beginning to be used in civil rights and environmental disputes," Giannina added.

"In all these areas, powerful parties are able to make lawsuits go away by diverting them. Recent empirical studies, including a large-scale one by Professor Hermann and her colleagues,[29] show that mediation outcomes favor the stronger party even more so than standard, in-court lawsuits," Rodrigo added.

"Well, Rodrigo," I conceded, "you've explained why ADR has caught on so powerfully. Any movement that taps both conservative and liberal impulses is apt to be unstoppable. And you've shown that ADR, for all of its touted advantages, is apt to hurt both disempowered litigants and law reform in general. But why is it catching on now rather than, say, twenty or thirty years ago?"

"Business is ascendant right now," Rodrigo replied. "The gap between the wealthy and the poor stands at one of its widest margins ever. At the same time, a lot of liberals have relatively little to do. The civil rights movement is almost nonexistent, and even environmentalism seems to be at a standstill. Instead of standing around looking at their hands, many liberals are turning into mediators. That way, they can at least tell themselves they are doing something useful—mediating conflict, making it go away."

"A fair number of people on the left are writing books about conciliation and racial healing," Giannina interjected. "Just the other day I saw one by a black writer writing about her first white friend.[30] Until recently, she had been something of a racial activist. Now she advocates loving everybody, including the race that enslaved her forebears."

"And a well known critical race theorist published a book about racial healing.[31] While not quite as unfocused as the other one, this book nevertheless urges the various camps to stop their feuding and learn how to live together," I added.

"A kind of alternative dispute resolution writ large," Giannina commented.

"It's not just the left and liberals who are preaching accommodation," Rodrigo added. "Dick Armey recently accused opponents of his flat-tax proposal, which would reward the rich and punish the poor, of practicing class warfare."[32]

"And of course we've seen how conservatives accuse proponents of ethnic studies curricula at universities, theme houses for minority students, and bilingual education of Balkanization,"[33] I said.

"Curious in a country founded on the idea of popular rule. Thomas Jefferson even thought we should have a revolution every few years," Giannina chimed in. "It's interesting how conservatives cite the Founders and original intent when it suits their purposes and not at other times."

"Speaking of time," Rodrigo said with a start and taking a quick look at his watch, "if we're going to get you to the courthouse on time, we'd better get going."

"I've got my bags right here," I said, standing up and giving Giannina a quick hug. "Thank you for your hospitality. It's ten times better than spending the night in some sterile hotel."

"You were going to tell us how you made it back from exile," Giannina reminded me.

"Maybe I'll tell Rodrigo in the car and let him share it with you later, if you don't mind," I replied. "It's not nearly as dramatic as you might think."

A few minutes later, Rodrigo and I were zooming along the freeway in the direction of the courthouse. I briefly buried myself in my notes, then, when I felt ready, told Rodrigo the story of my return.[34] The ride passed quickly. As we neared the court building, I spied the lawyer for the desegregation group engaged in intense conversation with two others on the steps.

"Uh-oh, Professor. They could be settling your case right now," Rodrigo alertly commented. "Do you want me to wait around and see if you'll be needing a ride to the airport? Settlement, a kind of ADR, might be on the verge of rendering your whole trip here moot."

Rodrigo pulled into the yellow zone while I stepped out and looked inquiringly at the lead attorney. "Come on," she mouthed and waved in my direction.

"Looks like I'm needed," I said to Rodrigo. "They're going ahead after all."

"Great," said Rodrigo. "Give 'em heck." As his little car disappeared from sight, I walked up the courthouse steps with the lead attorney. "I'm glad you're here," she said. "The school district offered to settle, but on completely unsuitable terms. We've got our work cut out for us."

I took a deep breath, squared my shoulders, and got ready for yet another battle on behalf of the poor and oppressed.

Notes

1. Trina Grillo, *The Mediation Alternative: Process Dangers for Women*, 100 YALE L.J. 1545 (1991).

2. *See id.* at *1547–51* (discussing the rise of mediation in family law). On the movement and its development, see Lisa Bernstein, *Understanding the Limits of Court-Connected ADR*, 141 U. PA. L. REV. 2169, 2172–77 (1993) (arguing that ADR programs may work to the detriment of poor litigants); Eric K. Yamamoto, *Efficiency's Threat to the Value of Accessible Courts for Minorities*, 25 HARV. C.R.-C.L. L. REV. 341, 349–54 (1990) (providing historical context for the growth of ADR); Eric K. Yamamoto, *ADR: Where Have All the Critics Gone?* (1996) (unpublished manuscript, on file with author). *See generally* Joshua Rosenberg & H. Jay Folberg, *Alternative Dispute Resolution: An Empirical Analysis*, 46 STAN. L. REV. 1487 (1994) (presenting findings from a commissioned study of ADR in the Northern District of California).

3. On the various settings in which ADR is used, see, e.g., Richard Delgado et al., *Fairness and Formality: Minimizing the Risk of Prejudice in Alternative Dispute Resolution*, 1985 WIS. L. REV. 1359, 1363–66 (providing an overview of the mechanics, claims, and contexts of ADR).

4. *See id.* at 1360 (summarizing claims of ADR proponents).

5. *See* Grillo, *supra* at 1550, 1570–81 (arguing that ADR, despite professedly inclusive aspirations, perpetuates assumptions and stereotypes regarding the superiority of males as ideal workers and proper female emotional comportment).

6. *See id.* at 1548–49, 1551 (discussing studies of divorce showing higher satisfaction rates with mediation than with adversary proceedings); Rosenberg & Folberg, *supra* at 1488–89 (citing a survey finding a two-thirds satisfaction rate among participants in mandatory ADR programs); see Delgado et al., *supra* at 1366 (discussing the informality of process and, by extension, accessibility as one argument proffered in support of ADR).

7. *See* Grillo, *supra* at 1570–71 (positing that women are conditioned to prioritize childcare over wage labor and that mediation may encourage or reinforce this self-conception); 1601–03 (discussing scholarship positing an essential female "ethic of care").

8. *See, e.g.*, Richard Delgado, *Recasting the American Race Problem*, 79 CAL. L. REV. 1389, 1394 (1991) (arguing that racial subordination is an ingrained feature of our cultural and social landscape).

9. *See* Chapter 2, this volume.

10. *See generally* Delgado et al., *supra* at 1367–90 (contrasting procedural safeguards in formal and informal adjudication).

11. *See id.* at 1385–86 (citing psychological research demonstrating that whites tend to exhibit increased prejudice in intimate situations).

12. *See id.* at 1386–87 (discussing the "confrontation" theory, devised by social scientists, of how to curb racism).

13. *See* Grillo, *supra* at 1548–50 (enumerating the reasons advanced for using mediation); Robert B. McKay, *Civil Litigation and the Public Interest*, 31 U. Kan. L. Rev. 355, 372 (1983) ("A case that is fairly settled not only avoids the increasingly expensive burden of a trial, but also avoids the all or nothing result typical of cases litigated to verdict"); Frank E. Sander, *Varieties of Dispute Processing*, 70 F.R.D. 111, 115 (1976) (contrasting the win-lose nature of adjudication with ADR's focus on the relationship between the parties).

14. *See, e.g.*, Richard L. Abel, *The Contradictions of Informal Justice*, in 1 THE POLITICS OF INFORMAL JUSTICE 267, 272–74 (Richard L. Abel ed., 1982) (arguing that ADR magnifies state power at the expense of consumers and other small disputants); Laura Nader, *Disputing Without the Force of Law*, 88 YALE L.J. 998, 998, 1000, 1021 (1979) (noting ADR impedes development of "an active and vital grass-roots . . . consumer movement").

15. *See* Owen M. Fiss, *Against Settlement*, 93 YALE L.J. 1073, 1085 (1984) (arguing that public officials engaged in the adjudication process have an obligation to explicate public values).

16. On the relationship between caregiving and production in a free-market society, see generally Richard Delgado, THE RODRIGO CHRONICLES, chapter 3 (1995).

17. On intersectionality—the problem of things or persons lying at the juncture of two or more legal categories—see *id.* at chapter 6 (1995), and Trina Grillo, *Anti-Essentialism and Intersectionality: Tools to Dismantle the Master's House*, 10 BERKELEY WOMEN'S L.J. 16, 16–19 (1995).

18. On issues the United States will need to face as it moves to an increasingly diverse, multiracial society, see generally Deborah Ramirez, *Multicultural Empowerment: It's Not Just Black and White Anymore*, 47 STAN. L. REV. 957 (1995).

19. *See* Luther Wright Jr., *Who's Black, Who's White, and Who Cares: Reconceptualizing the United States' Definition of Race and Racial Classifications*, 48 VAND. L. REV. 513, 557–58 (1995) (noting that the number of multiracial individuals has increased dramatically in the last two decades).

20. *See id.* at 563–66 (proposing new race classifications, including a category for biracial Americans; Angela P. Harris, *Race and Essentialism in Feminist Legal Theory*, 42 STAN. L. REV. 581, 586–90 (1990); Francisco Valdes, *Queers, Sissies, Dykes, and Tomboys: Deconstructing the Conflation of "Sex," "Gender," and "Sexual Orientation" in Euro-American Law and Society*, 83 CAL. L. REV. 1 (1995).

21. *See* Grillo, *supra* at 1548 (suggesting ADR avoids objectivist errors, enabling "decisions . . . informed by context rather than by abstract principle"); *id.* at 1586–91 (noting the risk for minorities and other disempowered disputants).

22. *See* Romer v. Evans, 116 S. Ct. 1620, 1623 (1996) (upholding protection of gays in the face of a referendum that would have limited rights of political participation).

23. *See* Jeffrey Rosen, *The Bloods and the Crits*, NEW REPUBLIC, Dec. 9, 1996, at 27 (describing an increase in jury nullification in criminal trials in which the defen-

dant is black and the jury is dominated by persons of the same color). For an argument that this is as it should be, see generally Paul Butler, *Racially Based Jury Nullification: Black Power in the Criminal Justice System*, 105 YALE L.J. 677 (1995).

24. *See, e.g.*, PETER HUBER, LIABILITY: THE LEGAL REVOLUTION AND ITS CONSEQUENCES (1988) (discussing high costs of the U.S. tort system). On capital's eager embrace of nonformalism, see Richard L. Abel, *Conservative Conflict and the Reproduction of Capitalism: The Role of Informal Justice*, 9 INT'L J. SOC. L. 245 (1981).

25. *See, e.g.*, Rosenberg & Folberg, *supra* at 1510 (reporting that the ADR process used in the Northern District of California saved participants time and money, improved the efficiency of trial preparation, and increased prospects for early settlement).

26. *See* Marc Galanter, *Reading the Landscape of Disputes: What We Know and Don't Know (and Think We Know) About Our Allegedly Contentious and Litigious Society*, 31 UCLA L. REV. 4, 36–61 (1983) (analyzing and disputing this contention by comparing levels of litigation in the United States over time and with other countries).

27. *See id.* at 57–61 (examining cultural and institutional explanations for the low rate of litigation in Japan).

28. *See* RICHARD A. POSNER, THE ECONOMIC ANALYSIS OF LAW 230–31 (3d ed. 1986) (arguing that the tort system "prices behavior in such a way as to mimic the market").

29. *See* MICHELE HERMANN, THE METROCOURT PROJECT FINAL REPORT (1993). *See generally Symposium, Gender, Empiricism, and the Federal Courts*, 83 GEO. L.J. 461 (1994) (containing articles by various authors, including Vicki C. Jackson, on the impact of various forms of disputing on women); Lisa G. Lerman, *Mediation of Wife Abuse Cases: The Adverse Impact of Informal Dispute Resolution on Women*, 7 HARV. WOMEN'S L.J. 57 (1984) (arguing that mediation in abuse cases fails to protect women); Proceeding, *What Happens When Mediation Is Institutionalized?* 9 OHIO ST. J. ON DISP. RESOL. 307 (1994) (including comments by Leonard Riskin and Michele Hermann).

30. *See* PATRICIA RAYBON, MY FIRST WHITE FRIEND: CONFESSIONS ON RACE, LOVE, AND FORGIVENESS 84–101 (1996).

31. *See* HARLAN L. DALTON, RACIAL HEALING: CONFRONTING THE FEAR BETWEEN BLACKS & WHITES (1995).

32. Dick Armey, *Ground Rules for Flat Tax Debate*, WASH. TIMES, Feb. 14, 1996, at A-14; see also G.A. Pollin, *Class Warfare Stuff and Nonsense*, WASH. TIMES, Apr. 14, 1996, at B-5.

33. *See* DINESH D'SOUZA, ILLIBERAL EDUCATION 236–42 (1991) (decrying fragmentation on campuses); JEAN STEFANCIC & RICHARD DELGADO, NO MERCY: HOW CONSERVATIVE THINK TANKS AND FOUNDATIONS CHANGED AMERICA'S SOCIAL AGENDA 12 (1996) (citing comments by leaders of the official-language movement).

34. In the concluding chapter of RICHARD DELGADO, THE COMING RACE WAR? AND OTHER APOCALYPTIC TALES OF AMERICA AFTER AFFIRMATIVE AC-

TION AND WELFARE 148–65 (1996), the Professor takes early retirement and departs for Mexico rather than face a "citizenship audit" sparked by the government's belated discovery that his father had been an illegal alien. After passage of a bill withdrawing citizenship from children born in the United States of undocumented aliens, the Professor receives a form query, prompting Rodrigo to offer to defend his mentor and friend for free. *See id.* at 151–52. Instead, the Professor, whose family is grown, packs his office, grades his last set of bluebooks, purchases a Winnebago, and returns to his ancestral country. *Id.* at 148–52. The birth of a grandchild, however, causes him to make a series of trips to the States, and he decides to explore the possibility of a return. While carrying out genealogical research in the national archives, he discovers that his ancestors were Chichimec Indians, who ranged as far north as what is now Texas and Arizona. He writes a letter to the Immigration and Naturalization Service, calling its attention to this fact and the possibility that his own father may not have been an illegal alien, after all. The agency, after a long silence, writes him that he is no longer on their "active list" and is free to return at any time.

7

Rodrigo's Book of Manners

How to Conduct a
Conversation on Race

"Rodrigo?" I said, looking up at the tall, smiling young man who had materialized, as though by magic, as I sat in a self-absorbed stupor in the airport boarding area, a half-read newspaper in my lap.

"Professor!" my young friend and protégé beamed, shaking my hand warmly. "I hoped you'd be on this flight. And here you are! You're going to the Crit conference, I gather?"

"I am, indeed," I replied. "The dean paid to bring me back, but I would have gone even if she hadn't. Are you going, too?"

My friend gestured toward a conference program under one arm, then said: "My connecting flight got in a half-hour ago. I've been wandering the concourse looking for a bookstore to pick up something for the flight. But I'd much rather talk with you. Want to sit together? The plane was nearly empty coming in."

"I'd love to," I said. "Uncharacteristically, I've got my speech all ready, so I was going to do nothing but finish this newspaper and maybe catch a nap. But I'd much rather get caught up on what's been happening with you. Is Giannina along?" I cast an eye around the waiting lounge, but the familiar face of Rodrigo's companion was not in view.

"She's home, recovering from the moot court competition. She wanted to come but decided to pass up the conference on condition that I take good notes and share everything with her later. If she had known we'd run into you, nothing would have kept her away. I think you're her honorary uncle and role model."

"If so, she's in some trouble, I'm afraid. I've been attacked in print more times than I can even remember, just this last month." Then, craning my neck and pointing at a slim gray-and-red volume under Rodrigo's other arm, I asked: "What's that you're reading?"

"Oh, that" Rodrigo replied. "Farber and Sherry's, *Beyond All Reason.*[1] Subtitled [Rodrigo looked down] *The Radical Assault on Truth in American Law,* it criticizes critical race theory and radical feminism, which the eminent authors refer to as 'radical multiculturalism.' They attack Derrick Bell, Mari Matsuda, Catharine MacKinnon, and Richard Delgado. Even you and I come in for some criticism."

"I know," I said, a little wryly. "It's one of the attacks on me I was referring to before."

Just then, our conversation was interrupted by the loudspeaker announcing that our flight was boarding. "Let's see if we can switch seats," Rodrigo said. "What's your assignment?"

I gave him my boarding pass. Seconds later, my young friend was back from the counter, new passes in hand. "The flight's only half full. We've got a window and an aisle," he said. "That way, we'll have an empty seat to hold our stuff. Can I help you with those bags?"

After a short delay, during which two courteous plainclothes airport security agents pulled us aside, went through our scanty luggage, and asked us about our destination and purpose for travelling, we boarded our plane.

"That's never happened to me before," Rodrigo said. "We must have triggered a profile of some sort. Oh, here are our seats."

We placed our bags in the overhead compartments and sat down, trying to ignore the anxious looks of nearby passengers. "I'm sure we did," I replied. "Two men of color, one from overseas, meeting at a transfer point and carrying relatively little luggage. I read that this sort of thing happens all the time."[2]

"At least they were polite and didn't cause us to miss our flight," Rodrigo said. They probably let us off easy because of all the law review articles they found in our bags—that and your speech. Scarcely a drug dealer's or terrorist's paraphernalia."

"A good story for Giannina," I said.

"I'm going to call her as soon as I get to the hotel," Rodrigo replied.

"Give her my best," I said.

Radical Multiculturalism and the Assault on Truth

We buckled up. After the flight attendant finished the safety demonstration, I asked Rodrigo what he thought of the Farber and Sherry book.

"Thought-provoking," Rodrigo replied, "even if it didn't treat our side particularly gently. Building on their previous work, the authors take issue with race-crit scholarship, particularly narrative analysis or legal storytelling. They also part company with radical feminism. But critical race theory seems to be their main target."

"That was my impression also," I said. "They accuse us and feminists like MacKinnon of cultural relativism and playing fast and loose with such cherished concepts as merit, the rule of law, and Western rationalism. Lacking in common sense and respect for knowledge, we are part of what they call 'the sleep of Reason.'[3] All this they illustrate through a string of provocative-sounding quotations, divorced from context, from major critical writers, ignoring what came before, and calculated to make us sound ridiculous."[4]

"A cheap trick," Rodrigo replied. "Although, unlike some of our detractors, they at least get the quotes right and try to substantiate most of the charges they level. They point out, for example, that we emphasize the role of history and context in evaluating whether legal rules are fair or not, which we do, although I don't see how it follows that we are cultural relativists who reject all truth whatsoever. They also note how we weave stories and narratives into our scholarship."[5]

"Which, of course, mainstream figures like Lon Fuller and Norval Morris have been doing for years," I interjected.[6]

"Indeed," Rodrigo acknowledged. "Farber and Sherry even accuse two crits of attempting to overturn the foundations of American legal thought[7] merely because they point out that conventional bibliographic categories and legal indexing systems are slow to change and incorporate new terms like indeterminacy, postmodernism, interest convergences, and consumer protection."[8]

"I should have thought anyone would acknowledge that," I quipped. "You should see how the *Index to Legal Periodicals* classified my latest article."

"That piece at least developed a rational argument, with examples and reasons. But Farber, Sherry, and others say that much of our work is therapeutic, focusing excessively on feelings and unconscious forces lying beneath the surface of social discourse, like standpoint, perspective, and the invisible sort of self-interest that can tip an argument.[9] All this supposedly goes against the Enlightenment tradition of rational argument, in which the speaker or writer lays all his or her cards on the table and doesn't spend much time analyzing why the other side plays its hand the way it does."[10]

"Good gamblers have always done just that," I mused. "Slaves, too. Hegel pointed out that dominated people tend to be better observers of their masters than the latter are of them. They have to be, since the master's moods and habits could spell the difference between survival and death. But the slave owner does not need to know much about what is going on in the slave's mind since the owner can rely on force."

"Exactly," Rodrigo replied. "No conservative seems to waste much time analyzing minority culture or ways of knowing. Except, of course, when a few law professors start to write in a different voice and to win readers."

"Or advocate controls on hate speech and pornography," I interjected. "Then they are ready to attribute base motives to us."[11]

"Or ignorance," Rodrigo agreed. "Farber and Sherry, for example, write that our willingness to entertain limitations on face-to-face racial slurs and name-calling on campus shows disdain for Enlightenment values and rational discourse. We are said to ignore that free speech has been a huge benefit for minorities. If we knew our own self-interest, we would not be attempting to bridle speech."[12]

"That accusation I found more than slightly odd," I said. "Oh, here we go." We were silent for a moment as the plane began gathering speed for the takeoff. We watched the ground rush past, then the plane lifted, banked slightly, and soon we were climbing smoothly, clouds rushing past. The pilot's voice came on announcing our destination and estimated time of arrival. We loosened our safety belts slightly, then I continued: "But Farber and Sherry also find fault with us for incorporating stories and narratives into our scholarship. Do you think this is connected to their relativism complaint?"

"I think so," Rodrigo replied. "They don't reject narrative scholarship entirely, just the kind that they believe plays on emotions and deforms an ambiguous reality so that it has only one interpretation. These and other defects they lay at the doorstep of some of our most noted narrativists, such as Derrick Bell and Patricia Williams, for her famous Benetton story. These first-person narratives, they say, are troublesome because the reader cannot apply to them the ordinary criteria of legal scholarship. One can't be sure a story such as Williams's is authentic, typical, and true. Indeed, they charge that minority tales, such as the ubiquity of racism, are not typical or true. For example, they say minorities have better chances than Euro-American white males of getting jobs as law professors."[13]

"That would surprise me," I said.

"But my point is that it's hardly typical," Rodrigo replied. "No reasonable person could think that applicants of color have a better chance of winning a job, or a promotion, than similarly credentialed whites, everywhere and at all times."

"I agree," I said. "But the relativism charge is only one of many they level at us. Another is that our critique of merit is potentially anti-Semitic and anti-Asian."[14]

"Supposedly by calling into question conventional criteria such as IQ tests and the LSAT, we are disparaging those other two minority groups because that is the ladder up which they have climbed. The critique of merit is anti-Semitic and anti-Asian since the critics—that's us—have no explanation, other than unsavory theories, such as Asian mimicry or Jewish pushiness, for the success those groups have enjoyed," Rodrigo said.

"A curious charge, since I don't know anyone in the Crit camp who would say those things," I said. "They put words in our mouths, then take us to task for what they think we must be saying."

"Even Richard Posner, in an otherwise gushing review in *New Republic*, thinks they went too far. The essence of anti-Semitism, he writes, is preoccupation with Jews, something the crits are not guilty of. Of course, he pretty much agrees with everything else they said."[15]

"And goes on to deliver a few zingers of his own," I added. "Our side has certainly been coming in for criticism these days. After a honeymoon period, in which the press was notably generous toward the fledging movement, critical race theory has been taking some knocks. Some of this criticism seems principled. But some strikes me as mean-spirited or unfair. Some critics rely on selective quotation, as you mentioned. Others choose one example of what they consider bad scholarship, such as the Benetton story—which I don't think is bad scholarship, by the way—and attribute it to the entire movement. Posner, for example, criticizes the author of *The Imperial Scholar* for trying to ride white liberals out of the civil rights movement, then goes on to declare that the author of that article, a Chicano, is white and has no business writing about the poor community and people of color.[16] Talk about a double-bind!"

In Which Rodrigo and I Discuss How to Conduct a Racial Conversation: The Imperial Scholar and Beyond

After a pause for the flight attendant to take our orders for beverages ("Coffee for me, cream and sugar," replied my young seatmate; "Orange juice for me," I said), Rodrigo put his tray down and began: "It seems to me, Professor, that just as Farber, Sherry, and others[17] feel free to lay down rules for our side, we should be able to propose our own versions, especially when some of our critics, like Farber, Sherry, and Posner, take liberties themselves."

Rodrigo paused, took a sip of coffee, then grimaced slightly.

"Bad?" I asked sympathetically.

Rodrigo nodded. "I'm not used to the mass-produced variety. I'm afraid I got addicted to espresso overseas, where it's practically the national drink."

"I miss good coffee," I said. "But I've had to cut way back—doctor's orders. But back to what you were saying. I agree. It's tit-for-tat. The rules should be subject to negotiation. If it's fair for one side to call the other to task for being overly rhetorical or playing fast and loose with statistics, why shouldn't the other have a say when it believes the first is being unfair? If it's open season on crits, we should at least insist that those taking shots at us obtain a license and obey the hunting rules."

When Rodrigo nodded, I looked at him encouragingly and asked, "And what might those be? I imagine you have given this some thought."

Rodrigo Propounds an Overall Theory for Racial Discourse

"I have. Giannina and I were talking about this the other day after a meeting of her study group. One of them asked if we had read a certain article by Stephen Gey on hate-speech regulation,[18] which she had read for a legal writing assignment. Later, Giannina and I discussed the article, which is long, detailed, and fairly contentious. The author trots out some of the standard objections to hate-speech regulation but goes on to attribute paranoia, fear, cowardice, and other rude character traits to writers like Mari Matsuda and Charles Lawrence, who are merely trying to make campuses safer for undergraduates of color."

"And you say this suggested a theory of racial discourse?" I prompted.

"It did," Rodrigo replied. "It occurred to me that the law reviews are sort of adjuncts to the courts and so are ideally suited to serve as a testing ground for new theories and criticism."

"We've certainly seen evidence of the criticism part," I replied. "But go on."

"Well, as with structural analysis of statutes and the Constitution, this view suggests certain features for law review discourse. Giannina and I were talking of this after her group left."

"Yes, yes," I said, impatiently. But before Rodrigo could continue, another flight attendant materialized at our row, pushing a heavy rolling cart. "Would you gentlemen like some lunch?"

"What are we having?" I asked, while Rodrigo eagerly cleared space on his tray. I regretted not having asked for my usual vegetarian meal when placing my flight reservation.

"You have your choice of pasta primavera or a cheeseburger," the attendant said. I delightedly ordered the noodles, while my omnivorous friend opted for the cheeseburger. ("And more coffee, please.") The attendant put down our trays, after which we ate in tacit silence for a few minutes.

"How's your burger?"

"Great," replied my ebullient companion. "After the coffee, I feared the worst. But this is actually quite good. Would you like a bite?"

"No. I'm trying to cut down on meat. But you were going to tell me your theory of racial discourse. You mentioned that the law reviews are testing grounds for new theories, which I assume would imply relatively wide latitude in what is said and, presumably, how one goes about saying it. Right?"

Taking one last bite of his burger and wiping his lips, Rodrigo said, "Yes, although despite the wide latitude—or maybe because of it—certain maneuvers ought to be avoided. Just as when men and women engage in conversation, men have to be careful not to dominate, similar rules should apply when people talk about race."

"A sort of racial etiquette," I observed. "You know, that article you mentioned earlier, *The Imperial Scholar*,[19] addressed one aspect of racial conversation. Controversial at the time, its advice now seems almost commonplace. And in a way, the author's suggestion—that the white giants who were then dominating racial discourse back off a bit and allow new scholars of color who were springing up to show their stuff—is a kind of rule of conversational etiquette. It says, in effect, that when you are having a conversation, look around you and see who has been speaking. If too many people of one sort are not talking, shut up for a while or try to draw them out."

"The author of that early article drew an analogy to the doctrine of standing, according to which persons who are most immediately affected by a controversy ought to be the ones who bring suit."

"And so one rule would be that scholars who write about race should check up from time to time to make sure that they have standing—or at least that minorities, who have the most immediate stake in the controversy, are not shut out entirely. At least their views should be treated respectfully and not dismissed outright. The idea would be that minorities are apt to know, and care about, the right things. Not in every case, of course, but in most."

"Some of our critics seem unaware of this rule," Rodrigo replied. "For example, Richard Posner both invoked and transgressed it in the space of a short review essay.[20] Farber and Sherry come perilously close, in practically making a career out of scolding a group of scholars that is merely trying to work for racial justice.[21] Toward the end of their book, they engage in a little imperial scholarship of their own, when they attempt to draw a hierarchy between responsible and lunatic-fringe race-crits.[22] Some of your and my best friends fall in the loony group, although others receive their grace."

"A sensible rule," I said. "But do you think that law review discourse should adhere to every rule of evidence, procedure, discovery, and so on? That seems like a heavy burden."

"Not in every detail," Rodrigo replied. "But a lawsuit is in some respects a kind of conversation. Two parties put forward their own stories of what happened. The legal system has devised rules about how that conversation should take place, including not speaking at the same time, answering contentions directly and in numbered paragraphs, not suing unless you have a stake in the litigation, and so on."

"I'd love to hear how you think they apply," I said.

Prudential Rules Based on Public Adjudication

"Consider this: Just as public adjudication limits standing to those who can show an injury in fact, courts have developed a host of nonconstitutional doctrines that, though not strictly compelled by the Constitution, apply as counsels of prudence."[23]

"And you think that these should apply in ordinary discourse about race and civil rights?" I asked.

"Maybe not in every detail, but certainly by analogy. Consider the rule that litigants must present a live case and controversy, rather than some abstract question.[24] This would counsel against work like that of another critic of hate-speech rules.[25] This author lays out, in highly abbreviated form, his conviction that the rules violate the First Amendment, then goes on to analyze at great length why substantive equality is bad and offends our libertarian sensibilities."

"But the debate over hate speech has little to do with various forms of equality," I offered.

"Of course," Rodrigo replied. "And a system of hate-speech controls might equally be seen as promoting process as outcome equality. That other debate simply is not in the minds of most hate-speech theorists like Matsuda or Lawrence."

"So the critic you mentioned violates the rule dealing with cases and controversies. Maybe the one against ripeness, as well."[26]

"Precisely," Rodrigo replied. "He speculates what our side *might* or *must* be saying rather than asking us—or better yet, waiting until we say something on the subject. It's like the straw man argument in ordinary discourse. The author posits that the other speaker must be saying something indefensible, and demolishes it, even though the other speaker may not be saying that at all."

"Do you think Farber and Sherry are guilty of that?" I asked.

"Yes, although some of the other critics are worse. But Farber and Sherry do commit this sin when they accuse us of latent anti-Semitism because we critique conventional standards of merit that have served Jews well."

"That's a big leap," I replied. "Jews might do well under any revised system of merit as well, including one that is fair to minorities."[27]

"None of us implied in the least that they would not," Rodrigo agreed. "What's more, Farber and Sherry transgress the rule regarding cases and controversies when they say we have no account of Jewish success. That's true, but why do we need one? Most people of color very much want to be allies with Jews in the struggle for civil rights.[28] But to require that Latinos and blacks have at the ready a complete explanation for the wholly commendable success some Jews have enjoyed in education and the professions, as a price for coalition, is plain weird. Minorities want Jews' help precisely because we need their brains and energy. If a minority leader like Farrakhan expresses anti-Semitic thoughts, criticism can be leveled at him. But to impute such ideas to all of us simply because we want fairer promotions standards at work is to place words in the mouths of people who show no inclination whatsoever to speak them."

The copilot's voice came on, telling us to expect choppy air. After tightening our seat belts, I said, "I hope that's not a metaphor for what lies ahead. But you mentioned other rules. What are they?"

"A third that I think applies, also by analogy, is the rule against mootness,[29] which counsels against dredging up disputes that have already ended and are unlikely to recur. In ordinary discourse, this would dictate that someone who critiques another's work look for the latest, and most complete, expression of it, not an earlier version that that author might have abandoned."

"Or refined," I added. "Most writers I know elaborate a thesis in an early essay, then develop it in later ones. That's true of leading work on hate speech, interest convergence, narrative theory, and a host of critical race themes."

"Some of our critics do appear to overlook that policy," Rodrigo added. "The author we mentioned earlier, who approached hate speech by means of his favorite philosophical category, picked on one or two ten- or fifteen-year-old articles by prominent hate-speech writers, ignoring the more recent and sophisticated versions those same authors have put forth."

"Farber and Sherry do something like that when, toward the end of their book, they set out what they consider to be dominant 'stock stories' of the crits. They either haven't been reading very carefully or else stopped with our very early stuff, for many of these stories have not been heard in critical circles for years. Some are more typical of liberalism."[30]

"They also charge that critical race theorists essentialize, drawing conclusions from the black experience when the population of color in the United States today is almost equally split between blacks and non-blacks," Rodrigo added. "But if we ever did that, we emphatically are not guilty of it today. Lat-crits, Asian-American scholars, and gay and lesbian activists within critical race theory have been developing their own theories under the CRT umbrella while maintaining friendly relations with blacks. Antiessentialism emerged as a key theme within critical discourse as early as Angela Harris's 1990 article.[31] The first CRT bibliography, published in the *Virginia Law Review* nearly a decade ago,[32] listed it as one of the movement's principal themes. Farber and Sherry stray as well when they identify a simplistic, additive model of intersectionality according to which a black women, for example, must be doubly disadvantaged because of her status as an African American and a woman. None of us says this today. Even early analyses of intersectionality expressly disavowed this model."[33]

"So you're saying that some of our critics make the mistake of relying on old sources, of dealing with issues that are, as you put it, moot. But what about the doctrine forbidding collusive suits.[34] Do you think that has any application? It seems to me it is related to the other prudential rules you have been discussing."

Rodrigo paused as the flight attendant came by to ask if we would like refills of coffee. Rodrigo nodded vigorously, reminding him that he liked extra sugar. I wondered if Rodrigo ever sleeps. I asked the attendant for a cup of tea, after which Rodrigo continued as follows: "I was thinking about that rule just now. The idea behind it is similar to the one that underlies the rule against advisory opinions. Courts don't want to hear cases that lack adversariness because the parties are basically on the same side—that is, trying to accomplish the same thing. In political writing, this would correspond to an author's writing an article that lavishly praised someone from the same camp."

"For example, to gain tenure or curry favor with a more senior scholar," I said.

"Or to solidify a friend's reputation."

"Which the average reader might not be aware of as a conflict of interest," Rodrigo added. "Posner's gushing book review of the Farber and Sherry book comes to mind."[35]

"Although I don't know that there's anything wrong with writing a favorable review per se, even for someone who is on your side, so long as you disclose that somewhere," I said. "Posner doesn't and goes on to sneak in several barbs of his own, even more vituperative and mean-spirited than the ones Farber and Sherry aim at us."[36]

"That does sound a little collusive," Rodrigo agreed. "Although he might reply that he was going to use them anyway and just chose this opportunity to do so. But I agree his essay is collusive in the sense that he professes to be reviewing the Farber-Sherry book, but really he is reviewing us."

"And doesn't disclose that, so his readers can't take it into account," Rodrigo concluded. "But speaking of smuggling in one's point of view, did you notice how another reviewer, Jeffrey Rosen, accused one of us of something similar?"[37]

"Do you mean in his *New Republic* review essay?"

"The very same," Rodrigo replied. "One of his charges was that critical race theorists like Bell, Williams, and Delgado, who sometimes write in the narrative vein, laid down theories of law as storytelling that the O.J. Simpson Dream Team used to acquit their famous client. In his view, Johnnie Cochran 'unwittingly' embraced 'the critical race theorists' theorem' and was thus a virtual puppet of those academics who pulled the strings in the trial."[38]

"I thought it one of his strangest observations. Cochran was a highly successful defense attorney long before critical race theory arrived on the scene. To say we colluded with him, or he with us, to do what defense attorneys have long done, namely, frame theories of a case that weave facts and law to the benefit of their client, is preposterous. Moreover, to say that Cochran did all this unwittingly gives him too little credit. Finally, it overlooks that he had different motives and methods for telling his client's story from those of the critical race theory storytellers. He did it for instrumental reasons—to persuade the jury and win acquittal; the scholars, to probe and test social theories and accounts of racial reality."

Rodrigo and the Professor Discuss Procedural and Evidentiary Rules That Can Serve, by Analogy, as Guidelines for Discussions of Controversial Subjects Like Race

We stopped to help the flight attendant gather our empty plates and cups. Then I asked Rodrigo: "I think you said some nonconstitutional doctrines also offer insights for racial discussions?"

"I think they do, also by way of analogy. Courts and legislatures have devised a panoply of rules having to do with how arguments and evidence are presented. One group discourages the dismissal of claims, especially novel ones, without adequate consideration."

"Hmmm," I said. "I haven't taught civil procedure since my early days as a law professor. But I do remember the rule against granting summary judgment unless it appears to a legal certainty that the party against whom the motion is made cannot possibly prevail. Then there are the rules discouraging motions for a more definite statement or granting a demurrer or motion to dismiss for failure to state a claim except when it appears that the plaintiff cannot state any ground on which relief can be granted. What's more, the right to amend should be liberally granted when the plaintiff has such a motion granted against him or her."

Rodrigo brightened. "Those were many of the same ones Giannina and I were discussing. You must have read our minds."

"You mustn't assume we old-timers don't know anything," I said, a little archly. "Just because we can't talk high crit-talk or cite the latest Europeans, it doesn't follow that we don't know a little doctrine here and there."

"I wasn't implying that," Rodrigo said, blushing slightly. "You really know your stuff. I just meant that those are the rules anyone would come up with who was looking for analogous authority for not showing the door too quickly to someone, like a crit, who is putting forward a new theory."

"And do you think our detractors do that?" I asked.

"Stephen Gey and others certainly do, in my opinion, when they invoke classic First Amendment doctrine to reject arguments for bridling

hate speech, ignoring that the controversy presents a host of issues dealing with equality and thus requires a balancing of interests. Their argument is similar to a demurrer. Look how poorly hate-speech rules fare
when judged by the one standard, they say, as though that were the only
possible one. Of course, when you add human-dignity interests, you get a
different equation. As with a demurrer, dismissal should not be granted
because a claim can be made based on these other interests and values."

"What about Farber and Sherry?" I asked.

"They generally are more careful not to dismiss us merely because we
deviate in some respects from the old paradigm. But they do fall into the
trap of applying the old way of judging to the newcomers, whose ideas
are aimed at changing, not functioning within, the old paradigms."

"Do you mean the way they dismiss these approaches as departures
from the rule of law and on what they call 'Reason'?" I asked.

"That and more," Rodrigo replied. "Crits and radical feminists are asserting that conventional legal discourse encodes white male supremacy,
so that reform cannot occur without altering the basic structures and
premises of legal argument, such as the reasonable man standard or the
concept of color blindness.[39] This strikes Farber and Sherry as going to
the very heart of the way law does things—as though this way could not,
and will not, ever change.[40] They come close to saying, 'This is law; work
within this system or you will be saying things that cannot be heard, that
don't register.' But, of course, some very basic principles of law *have*
changed. Not so long ago, women and unpropertied men were not entitled to vote, and courts were saying that separate can be equal in pupil assignment rules or railroad-car seating. At one time blacks were persons
whom the law need not respect. Today, they are. The same might happen
to seemingly bedrock principles of antidiscrimination law, such as the
color-blind maxim, the rule requiring intent as proof of discrimination,
and other premises of the liberal state."

"Deployment of demurrerlike arguments to rule new movements out
of bounds begs the question," I summarized. "It's like saying, 'What you
are urging is new, so we needn't listen to it just because of that.'"

"Exactly," said Rodrigo. "It's like overzealous use of Rule 11,[41] which
provides for sanctions for frivolous claims or ones not based on a good-
faith investigation by the attorney into the relevant facts and theories."

"Many have pointed out how the rule can easily discourage law-re-
form cases and ones judges may disfavor, such as civil rights.[42] Most
now agree that Rule 11 should be used carefully, so as not to discourage
innovation."

"That would counsel that writers like Posner be careful about calling an entire school of scholarship loony[43] merely because he has not heard about it before. It would also argue against that style of refutation that merely offers a string of snippets, taken out of context, without the supporting argument and evidence the other scholar marshaled for his or her conclusion."[44]

"As Posner, Gey, and even Farber and Sherry do," I added.[45]

"Rosen, as well," Rodrigo added.[46] "For example, several scholars hold up for ridicule statements by some of us doubting whether Enlightenment political philosophy is good for persons of color. To them, its goodness is so self-evident that they overlook the reasons why scholars of color put it in question."[47]

"These reasons include its color-imagery, embrace of universalism—which can easily work to the disadvantage of those, like women or working-class people, who were not part of that ideal picture the architects had in mind—and the ease by which some of its leading figures endorsed slavery and conquest."[48]

"As with Rule 11, these writers seem to think those charges are flyspecking and that any attack on Enlightenment ideals is outrageous and frivolous," Rodrigo said.

"They really should examine the basis for those claims before rejecting them out of hand," I added. "Crafted during a period of European supremacy and black slavery, it would not be at all surprising if Enlightenment theories harbored at least a tinge of race-coding. Yet some of our critics treat the merest suggestion that political theories laid down during that grand period might be a source of racism and classism as tantamount to heresy—practically self-refuting, as Judge Posner put it. We should not reject that as an area of inquiry, any more than scholars looking for an explanation for the Holocaust should close their eyes to Western complicity—to the tacit toleration of Swiss bankers or British accommodationists, for example."

"I seem to recall Posner guilty of something similar when discussing the idea of white privilege.[49] According to prominent feminist scholar Peggy McIntosh, white folks carry with them a nearly invisible backpack of privileges, customs, and courtesies that they can rely on every day, for example, when out shopping, that folks of color cannot assume will be extended to them. She lists forty-six examples," said Rodrigo.[50]

"I remember her discussion," I said. "Farber and Sherry are equally dismissive of it."

"Posner rejects the idea of white privilege without evaluating any of her examples or telling us why. I wanted to hear more, but the famous judge seemed to think the whole idea so outlandish as not to be worth discussing."

The pilot announced the beginning of our descent. As we checked that our safety belts were tightened and raised our seat backs to the upright position, I added: "Speaking of dialog, it occurs to me you might want to send your suggestions to the national commission. As you know, under eminent African American historian John Hope Franklin, a multiracial group conducted a national discussion on matters of race, including a series of town hall meetings across the country. Now that its successor group is gearing up, naysayers and conservative columnists are weighing in against it, committing many of the mistakes you have pointed out."[51]

"Do you think it would do any good?" said Rodrigo, brightening up.

"I do," I replied. "Discussions about race often founder on just the shoals you have pointed out. Anything that can enhance the quality of discussion, moving it beyond the predictable exchange of solemn maxims and thought-ending cliches, should be welcome. But we digress. Let's hear any more wisdom you've culled from the rules of civil procedure."

"This shouldn't take long," Rodrigo said. "One source is the set of rules that govern the pleading of damages, including mitigation. Some commentators, including Richard Posner in his review of Farber, and Jeff Rosen in his review of five crit books, point out that things are getting better for blacks and Chicanos, as though this proves that discrimination is over."

"Of course, it doesn't," I chimed in. "Things are getting better for whites, too, so that the gap between them and us in health, income, family assets, longevity, educational attainment, and many other indices of well-being is staying the same or growing. It's like saying that a burglar who breaks into a house and steals the jewels should be entitled to a reduced sentence because he straightened out the furniture or showed the family that they needed a security system. But the rules pertaining to damages have a lesson for our side, as well. Sometimes we fail to detail our specific grievances and damages stemming from, for example, slavery or conquest, remaining content with simply asserting generalized loss. The rule requiring enumeration of special damages, ones that do not stem ineluctably from the type of harm alleged, would counsel our being a little more careful in this regard."

"Good point, Professor. It would certainly allay some of the impatience conservatives and uncommitted people sometimes display over our sometimes nebulous assertions of cultural damage resulting from events that happened a long time ago."

"Second- and third-generation pathology traceable to the Holocaust is just beginning to be studied.[52] Perhaps we could tap this line of research," I pointed out.

"Maybe so," said Rodrigo with interest. "My colleague, Laura Goldstein, is doing some work in this area. Perhaps I'll have a talk with her. She's sympathetic to critical race theory, even taught a seminar in critical race feminism until last year, when we hired Mary Bergeron."

We both heard a bump. "Must be the landing gear," I said. "Do you have any final analogies?"

"Just quickly," Rodrigo replied. "There's the rule about observing precedent. In our setting that would counsel applying the same standard to your targets as you do to your friends. For example, one shouldn't attack storytelling by scholars of color without noticing that some famous majority-race scholars have done the same thing to great acclaim. Moreover, who has not run into the conservative or anti-PC detractor who begins by recounting: 'I know a story'. . . and then tells of a mythical professor who was so hounded by PC fanatics that he hung up his coffee cup and retired.[53] No one seems able to identify this professor. How well do these stories hold up under Farber and Sherry's criteria that stories be authentic, typical, and true? Presumptions and burdens of proof should be the same for both sides, unless justified by a good reason. Farber and Sherry, for example, warn that standpoint epistemology leads to relativism and, potentially, Holocaust denial.[54] But they overlook that some of the most ardent embracers of objectivism and the Western canon feel free to minimize the results of slavery, Mexican conquest, Indian massacres, and even Japanese American prison camp internment, merely because these happened some time ago. The movement in the federal system and many states toward notice, and away from nitpicky code pleading implies that the scholarly community should be less concerned about scholarship that fails to state a claim in the most familiar manner— that is, in the form of a case-crunching, six hundred–footnote article, with a predictable linear structure that begins with a review of every single relevant case and authority—and receptive to the newer modes of scholarship, such as the essay and chronicle, which may be full of analysis and new ideas and, in that sense, even more useful than the usual fare."

Seconds later, with a slight bump we were on the ground. "Perfect timing," I said. After waiting for the noise of the braking engines to die down, I told Rodrigo, "This has been most stimulating. Although I am sure some readers will quarrel over this or that one of your analogies, you have managed to extend the reasoning of *The Imperial Scholar* to new realms. Many have called for rules of engagement in law review and similar writing. Looking to rules already laid down strikes me as a fruitful approach."

"As usual, you're too kind, Professor."

The plane rolled to a stop. The pilot announced our arrival; the passengers stood up and began unloading their carry-on baggage.

Standing up and stretching his lanky frame, Rodrigo grinned and said, "And as for sending these ideas around, I think I will. These discussions of race between the left and the right already carry too much baggage. Maybe we need a fresh start."

I smiled, glad to see that for all his brilliance, Rodrigo still had a playful streak and, at the end of an intense two-hour conversation that ranged over large areas of constitutional and private adjudication and sketched the outlines of a new, inclusive theory of racial dialog, he was still capable of drawing on his abundant youthful levity.

Notes

1. DANIEL A. FARBER & SUZANNA SHERRY, BEYOND ALL REASON: THE RADICAL ASSAULT ON TRUTH IN AMERICAN LAW (1997).

2. Larry Bleiberg, *Profiling Latest Weapon in Airline Security Arsenal*, PITTSBURGH POST-GAZETTE, Mar. 2, 1977, at F-5.

3. BEYOND ALL REASON, *supra* at 3–4, 6–7, 21, 23–29, 36–39, 48, 142.

4. *E.g., id.* at 32.

5. *Id.* at 23–27, 31–34, 36–40, 47–51, 55–66, 75–77.

6. *See* Lon Fuller, *The Case of the Speluncean Explorers*, 62 HARV. L. REV. 616 (1949); Norval Morris, *The Tropical Bedroom*, 57 U. CHI. L. REV. 773 (1990).

7. BEYOND ALL REASON, *supra* at 26–29.

8. Richard Delgado & Jean Stefancic. *Why Do We Tell the Same Stories? Law Reform, Critical Librarianship, and the Triple Helix Dilemma*, 42 STAN. L. REV. 207 (1989).

9. *E.g.*, Henry Louis Gates, *Let Them Talk*, NEW REPUBLIC, Sept. 20 & 27, 1993, at 37.

10. BEYOND ALL REASON, *supra* at 6, 12, 14, 29, 34–48, 95–116.

11. *E.g.*, Steven G. Gey, *The Case Against Postmodern Censorship Theory*, 145 U. PA. L. REV. 193 (1996) (charging proponent of hate-speech regulation with censorship, paranoia, and reluctance to engage in robust give-and-take).

12. BEYOND ALL REASON, *supra* at 40–45, 122, 126, 141–420.

13. *Id.* at 38–40, 55–60, 72–90, 95, 96–117.

14. *Id.* at 52–71.

15. Richard Posner, *Beyond All Reason* (book review), NEW REPUBLIC, Oct. 13, 1997, at 40–42.

16. Posner, *supra* at 42–43.

17. Edward Rubin, *On Beyond Truth: A Theory for Evaluating Legal Scholarship*, 80 CALIF. L. REV. 889 (1992); Mary Coombs, *Outsider Scholarship: The Law Review Stories*, 63 COLO. L. REV. 683 (1992).

18. Gey, *supra*.

19. *See* Richard Delgado, *The Imperial Scholar: Reflections on a Review of Civil Rights Literature*, 132 U. PA. L. REV. 561 (1984).

20. Posner, *supra* (rejecting argument by Delgado that white scholars who were dominating civil rights discourse begin moving on to other fields, but later questioning the standing of this same scholar to engage in civil rights writing because he is supposedly white!).

21. *See* Daniel Farber, *The 200,000 Cards of Dimitri Yurasov: Further Reflections on Scholarship and Truth*, 46 STAN. L. REV. 647 (1994); Daniel A. Farber, *The Outmoded Debate over Affirmative Action*, 82, CALIF. L. REV. 893 (1994). *See also* Suzanna Sherry, *The Sleep of Reason*, 84 GEO. L. J. 453 (1996).

22. BEYOND ALL REASON, *supra* at 140–42.

23. On these prudential doctrines and their role in constitutional and public adjudication, see LAURENCE TRIBE, AMERICAN CONSTITUTIONAL LAW 108 et. seq. (2d ed. 1988).

24. *Id.* at §§ 3–7, 3–14.

25. *See* Gary Goodpaster, *Equality and Free Speech: The Case Against Substantive Equality*, 82 IOWA L. REV. 645, 660 (1997).

26. On ripeness, see Tribe, *supra* at § 3–10. Ripeness is the rule against adjudicating a case where a prospective examination suggests future events may alter its makeup so fundamentally that a later decision may be more apt.

27. For example, a revised system might decrease reliance on the SAT and other standardized testing, emphasizing instead evidence of leadership ability, originality of mind, and entrepreneurial skills. In all these measures, Jews might prove to be as much above average as they are now on conventional criteria.

28. On this historic alliance, see JACK GREENBERG, CRUSADERS IN THE COURT: HOW A DEDICATED BAND OF LAWYERS FOUGHT FOR THE CIVIL RIGHTS REVOLUTION, (1994); *A Crusader in the Court: Comments on the Civil Rights Movement*, 63 UMKC L. REV. 207 (1994).

29. *See* Tribe, *supra* at § 3–11. The rule against mootness provides that a case is moot, and hence nonjusticiable, unless the one mounting a challenge confronts harm or a significant prospect of it in the future, *id.* at § 3–11.

30. *E.g.*, their critique of these scholars as proponents of multiculturalism or wrapped up in feelings, when many if not most crits are nationalists and concerned more with material determinism than feel-good philosophy. BEYOND ALL REASON, *supra* at 12, 129–31.

31. Angela Harris, *Race and Essentialism in Feminist Legal Theory*, 42 STAN. L. REV. 581 (1990).

32. Delgado & Stefancic, *supra*.

33. BEYOND ALL REASON, *supra* at 129–30. *But see* Harris, *supra* at 588; Paulette Caldwell, *A Hair Piece: Perspectives on the Intersection of Race and Gender*, 1991 N.Y.U. L. REV. 365.

34. Tribe, *supra* at § 3–12.

35. Posner, *supra*. Conservative scholars, Farber, Sherry, and Posner decry civil rights activism and innovation.

36. *Id*. at 42 (critical race theorists are poor role models); 43 (grasp of social reality is weak); 43 (their lodgment in the law school is a disgrace to legal education).

37. Jeffrey Rosen, *The Crits and the Bloods* (book review), NEW REPUBLIC, Dec. 9, 1996, at 27.

38. *Id*. at 34–36.

39. *E.g.*, Neil Gotanda, *A Critique of "Our Constitution Is Color-Blind,"* 44 STAN. L. REV. 1 (1991).

40. BEYOND ALL REASON, *supra* at 23–32, 95–116.

41. Fed. R. Civ. P. 11.

42. *E.g.*, Georgene Vairo, *Rule 11: A Critical Analysis*, 118 F.R.D. 189, 234–41 (1988); Carl Tobias, *Rule 11 Recalibrated in Civil Rights Cases*, 36 VILL. L. REV. 105 (1991).

43. Posner, *supra* at 40 (" Radical legal egalitarianism is distinguished by having a rational fringe and a lunatic core").

44. *E.g., id*. at 41 ("In the case of critical race theory, however, criticism is almost secondary. One has only to illuminate the target").

45. *See id*. at 41; Gey, *supra* at 243; Farber & Sherry, *supra* at 97.

46. Rosen, *supra* at 33 (quoting Rodrigo as saying, "Minorities should invoke and follow the law when it benefits them and break or ignore it otherwise." Rosen concludes that this language was directly linked to the defense team strategy in the Simpson case).

47. *E.g.*, Farber & Sherry, *supra* at 29, Posner, *supra* at 41.

48. *See* RICHARD DELGADO, THE RODRIGO CHRONICLES, chapter 7 (1995).

49. Posner, *supra* at 43.

50. Peggy McIntosh, *White Privilege and Male Privilege: A Personal Account of Coming to See Correspondences through Work in Women's Studies*; reprinted in CRITICAL WHITE STUDIES 291 (Richard Delgado & Jean Stefancic eds., 1997).

51. Stephen A. Holmes, *Critics Say Clinton Panel About Race Lacks Focus*, N.Y. TIMES, Oct. 12, 1997, at 1; William Powers, *Oh My! (Angela Oh's Activities on the Presidential Commission on Race Relations)*, NEW REPUBLIC, Aug. 11, 1997, at 9.

52. Betty Booker, *So Many Secrets: How Holocaust Survivors' Children Confront History*, RICHMOND TIMES, Apr. 28, 1997, at C-1.

53. *See* JOHN K. WILSON, THE MYTH OF POLITICAL CORRECTNESS (1995).

54. BEYOND ALL REASON, *supra* at 12, 109–10, 119.

8

Rodrigo's Committee Assignment

A Skeptical Look at Judicial Independence

**Introduction: In Which Rodrigo Encounters
Me in an Embarrassing Situation and I Learn
About His Unusual Committee Assignment**

I had been sitting glumly on the cold, hard bench in the long marble hall of the city courthouse when a familiar voice shook me from my reverie:

"Professor! What are you doing here?"

"Rodrigo," I stammered, rising, then awkwardly shaking the hand of my young friend and protégé. "I might say the same. You're the last person I expected to see here. I'm waiting for my lawyer. What about you? Are you here to represent someone?"

Rodrigo laughed, then said, "No, I'm here for a meeting in the chambers of the chief judge. It's for a regional bar committee that the dean volunteered me for." Looking up at the sign overhead labeled CRIMINAL DIVISION, Rodrigo added incredulously, "You aren't being charged with something, are you?"

"I'm sorry to say I am," I said, hanging my head. "For the first time in my life. I haven't even had a parking ticket in twenty years, and now this."

"What did you do—I mean, allegedly?" Rodrigo asked.

I sighed. "It's a long story." Rodrigo gestured that he wanted to hear, so I went on. "I was crossing the street in front of the law school in the com-

pany of a brilliant student named Raul, who was having a crisis of conscience. A Puerto Rican, he had come to my office to talk about dropping
out of school in order to fight, shoulder to shoulder, as he put it, with his
brothers and sisters in the *barrio*. He said he couldn't see spending two
more years studying cases about giant corporations and insurance companies when his people needed him now."

Rodrigo nodded sympathetically. "I had a student with a similar
lament just last week. And then what happened?"

"Everything happened so fast I'm not really sure. We stepped into the
street, I heard a screech, and a bicycle messenger went flying. He suffered
nothing worse than a cut knee and a torn pant leg, but a police officer,
who must have been practically on the spot, cited us for reckless endan-
germent."

"That's a class-three felony," Rodrigo said, suddenly serious. "Was the
light in your favor?"

"I honestly can't recall, although I've crossed that street hundreds of
times, and I always look. I assume the walk sign was on. But the messenger swears it wasn't and that we cut him off."

"They're really throwing the book at you," Rodrigo said. "I would have
thought that for a first offense they'd let someone like you off with a jaywalking ticket and a warning. Maybe make you pay for the messenger's
pants and Band-Aid."

"I would have thought so, too," I said. "I forgot to tell you Raul has
long hair and was wearing a red bandanna around his forehead and carrying a boom box."

"I can't believe it," Rodrigo said, clapping his hand to his forehead.
"Professor, they're charging you with TNB."

"That's what my lawyer thinks, too," I said. "Typical nigger behavior,
in the cynical police phrase.[1] The mayor's been on a campaign to crack
down, not just against jaywalking and loud radios but any manifestation
of black disorderliness or cultural self-assertion. It's a misguided application of James Q. Wilson's broken-windows theory."[2]

"What were you wearing?"

"A business suit. But I'd taken off my tie and left it in my office, probably out of a misguided subconscious desire to show solidarity with Raul."

"And now they're charging you, who have led an exemplary life and
are a model of civic responsibility," Rodrigo said. "I still can't believe it.
What are you facing?"

"Oh, maybe a week or two in city jail, followed by community service
of some sort—probably a traffic guard in front of a school. The commu-

nity service part I don't mind. The jail time I could do without. The law school would have to get someone to teach my classes."

"Has the dean done anything?"

"She wrote a strong letter to the prosecutor and the chief judge, all to no avail. And—can you believe it—the district attorney assigned to prosecute me turns out to be one of my former students. She seemed a little sheepish at the plea-bargain conference, but refused to drop or lower the charge. My lawyer thinks her office is on a tough-on-crime binge and wants to make an example of me."[3]

"What do you know about the judge?" Rodrigo asked.

"We drew Judge Ingersol."

"Oh, no! Isn't he the one who—"

"The very one," I said. "Last year he let a burglar with an otherwise clean record off on bail, and he went on a crime spree that included two vicious rapes. The law-and-order folks got up a petition to have the judge impeached, and when that failed, launched a campaign to recall him."[4]

"And ever since then, I bet, he's been tough on crime and criminals," Rodrigo said, completing my thought.

"Maximum sentences on everything, and no bail, ever. Oh, here's my lawyer."

Rodrigo stood while I introduced him to Jerome Steinglass, another former student and ex-prosecutor who knew the court system well. After a few pleasantries, my lawyer said, "We've been continued, I'm afraid. Until the afternoon session. The court clerk just told me." When I must have grimaced, he added, "But she promised to get us on first thing. Why don't we meet right here at quarter of one?"

I looked at my watch. "I guess it can't be helped. Would you two like to join me for lunch in the cafeteria downstairs?"

My lawyer demurred, but Rodrigo said, "Sure. My meeting's not for an hour. I was just going to take in a session or two—of your judge's court, actually. But I'd much rather talk with you."

Steinglass disappeared with a wave, and minutes later Rodrigo and I were walking through the line of the cavernous cafeteria in the basement of the building, examining the food. "What are you having?" I asked.

"These scallops look good," Rodrigo said, helping himself to a big ladle full. "How about you?"

"A club sandwich, I think. I don't usually eat meat, but I feel a need to gear myself up for my ordeal."

"I'm sure it won't be as bad as you think," Rodrigo said, as the cashier punched in the numbers for his food. "The mayor's office would look pretty silly if his get-tough policy locked up a famous, elderly law professor for jaywalking." He handed the cashier his credit card, then said, "I'll be glad to serve as a character witness, if you like. It'd be my privilege, and I'll be just down the hall if you need me."

"Thanks," I said. "I'll tell my lawyer. Although it's sort of a role reversal."

"Right," Rodrigo said with a quick smile. "It wasn't too long ago that you were writing letters of recommendation for me.[5] Life is funny."

"That it is," I admitted, following him out the line. "Now tell me about that committee of yours."

In Which Rodrigo Tries to Convince Me
That the Issue of Judicial Independence
Contains More Than Meets the Eye

"Is this table okay?" Rodrigo asked. When I nodded, he set down his tray, then pulled out the chair for me to sit. I remarked once again about his courtesy toward my aging frailties—I hadn't had someone pull out my chair for some time. *His European background comes out at the oddest times,* I thought. After setting down my own plates and handing my tray to a passing waiter, I settled back while Rodrigo began as follows: "The association just set up this committee consisting of several lawyers, me, one other law professor, and the chief judge of this court.[6] It had been considering doing something on the subject for some time, because of the hue and cry over judicial activism and soft-on-crime judges, mainly by conservative pressure groups,[7] and concern on the part of progressives about the judiciary's independence. Hmmm," said Rodrigo, taking a bite full of his steaming food. "Not bad for a cafeteria. I guess I'm hungry. I walked all the way over from the hotel. How's your club?"

"Great," I said, swallowing and putting the sandwich down on my plate. "I must confess I miss meat, even after more than a year. Oh, what we do on doctors' orders. But go on."

"As you might have guessed, the culminating event was the write-in campaign to get rid of Judge Ingersol."

"Whom I'll be meeting in"—I looked at my watch—"fifty-five minutes. But I gather things were building even before that."

"Long before," Rodrigo replied. "Everyone remembers what happened when Roosevelt threatened to pack the Supreme Court, which was bent on invalidating New Deal legislation, and those early efforts to impeach judges, often initiated by politicians eager to discredit a judicial appointee of the opposing party. The first impeachment of a federal judge took place in 1804 when the Federalists brought charges against John Pickering. The very next year, the Jeffersonians responded by unsuccessfully attempting to impeach Supreme Court Justice Samuel Chase in highly publicized hearings."[8]

"But that kind of politics went on years ago. Surely, judges today cannot be impeached for purely political reasons."

"That's debatable," Rodrigo replied. "Seven federal judges have been impeached and convicted in U.S. history, three as recently as the 1980s. A number of those featured flimsy evidence and dubious circumstances."[9]

"I remember hearing something about a judge in Nevada who was impeached even though the state bar association found he was a victim of a federal vendetta,"[10] I said, checking my watch.

"Judges face immense pressure to appear tough on crime—or low on activism.[11] When they stray, they feel the heat," Rodrigo said. "Even lawyers with immaculate records, who have dedicated their professional lives to fighting racism and discrimination, face an uphill battle for positions in government. Look at the example of Bill Lann Lee—just last year, Republicans blocked his appointment as assistant U.S. attorney general.[12] Don't worry. I can see the clock," Rodrigo indicated. "I won't let you be late."

"I'm sure Steinglass would come get me in the unlikely event we lost track of time," I said. "Go on."

"Well, much of the concern today stems from pressure groups, as I mentioned. But others worry about lawyers who criticize judges for the way they rule. They think it's undignified and demeans the judiciary in the public's eyes. A few deplore mandatory sentencing or urge that we get away from requiring judges to stand for reelection, as some states do. They think the process is too politicized and causes judges to decide cases with an eye on how they will look to the electorate. Recently, the national bar association got up in arms when President Clinton threatened to call for the dismissal of a federal judge who freed a defendant charged with drug-running because of an illegal search and seizure."[13]

"I've seen editorials in *ABA Journal* deploring that sort of thing,"[14] I said, then added, squaring my shoulders, "as well they should."

"And you probably know that the national association commissioned a study group to look into the issue. It released its report, just last year."[15]

When Rodrigo paused, I asked, "And what's your role in all this? I hope you're not against judicial independence."

"Well, as I mentioned, the dean nominated me. And I'm afraid I *am* supposed to present the critical or skeptical view, whatever that is."

"A daunting assignment!" I exclaimed. "On two counts. First, I can't remember a single piece of writing by a leading crit on the subject. It's like writing against motherhood or apple pie. But more fundamentally, I don't see how anyone can be against judicial independence. Even a race-crit like you. Need I remind you I'm facing jail, merely because of one those right-wing campaigns the judicial independence movement is aimed at countering? I'm afraid I'm going to be a very hard sell. But go on—what's your flaky, out-of-touch, radical critique of this liberal legalism?"

Rodrigo Presents Eight Doubts About Judicial Independence

"I decided there's not just one perspective," Rodrigo began, pushing his plate away to give himself more room. "Ranging from the neoliberal view, which would highlight a few reservations, to the deeply distrustful—"

"All the way to the legitimizing myth, I imagine," I added.

"Exactly," Rodrigo seconded. "I've actually made a list." Looking down at a piece of paper he pulled from his pocket, he said, "I've identified eight separate critiques."

When Rodrigo looked up, I said, "This better be good. Especially as I'm likely to end up an unwitting victim of the hysterical right-wing surge. My own protégé, trying to put me in jail," I groused, then smiled to let Rodrigo know I was joking.

"Oh, Professor, nothing's going to happen to you," Rodrigo replied. "I'd bet a fine, at worst, and a few weekends of community service. You'd look dashing in a crossing guard's uniform."

"My law students will be highly amused."

"You can use the experience in class," Rodrigo smiled. "Maybe in a hypothetical about the reasonably prudent crossing guard."

"Cold comfort," I said. "Maybe I'll let you take my place. But let's hear your arguments."

Judicial Independence as a Deflection

Rodrigo glanced down again at his list. "I didn't mean to make light of your predicament. The first way to look at judicial independence is as a deflection."

"Do you mean from other issues that really matter—or from other, more valid ways of looking at the judicial function?" I asked.

"Both. Consider the way the debate obscures how a host of invisible forces constrain legal decisionmaking. Most judges are white, male, middle-class, able-bodied, and moderate in their social and political views.[16] No one considers this an affront to judicial independence, although it has a tremendous influence on how cases are decided. Judicial independence enthusiasts take the judiciary, as currently constituted, and then spend a great deal of time and indignation clearing the way for them to act as freely as possible. It's a little like planting your garden with only one kind of seed and then suing the supplier when the flowers come up slightly different heights because of variations in the soil or sunlight. Giannina thought of the metaphor."

"I hope you're not saying that judicial independence is unimportant," I said. "I'm on trial before a basically good, honest judge. I know him slightly—he was on our board of visitors. To use Giannina's metaphor, he represents a good seed. If left alone, I'm confident he'd do justice. But I'm worried precisely because in trying me he might be looking over his shoulder at special interest groups that want to see me behind bars."

"I see your point," Rodrigo conceded. "Maybe we can say that judicial independence, like all liberal legalisms, both advances and retards the cause of justice. A mixed blessing, it can operate for good or for ill. The good part is easily stated: When things work the way they're supposed to, a fearless, wise judge exercises an independent mind in rendering justice. And this, of course, actually happens on occasion. *Brown v. Board of Education* comes to mind. But, that being said, one immediately thinks of the many cases when judges, completely without pressure, handed down cruel, racist rulings simply because they didn't see them that way at the time.[17] Their class situation and range of experiences allowed them to do business as usual. And 'as usual' meant radically unjust."

"Robert Cover wrote about that," I mused.[18] "But you mustn't overstate. Sometimes judicial independence can take your eye off the ball. But other times, it keeps you focused on it exactly. What's your next criticism?"

Judges as Peculiar Objects of Mercy

"I'll try not to. Overstate, I mean," Rodrigo said. "My next one isn't so much a criticism as an observation. It's just that judges are, by and large, anything but an oppressed class. Highly paid and educated, they enjoy some of the highest occupational prestige of any profession. Most of them live in nice homes, send their children to good schools, and retire millionaires. They have good fringe benefits, medical coverage, and solvent pension systems. Some of them have lifetime security."

"Like tenure in our line of work," I replied dryly.

"Better," said Rodrigo. "They can't be removed, except for blatant misconduct. And their salaries cannot be reduced while in office, as ours can under some systems of posttenure review. No one is threatening to burn down their churches or set crosses afire on their lawns. The police do not routinely harass them if they are caught walking or jogging in the wrong neighborhood."

"And your point, Rodrigo, is . . . ?"

"Oh, it's that dashing around, making a fetish of defending judges against unkind words or the occasional removal from office is an odd allocation of resources. No one speaks of the need to protect the independence of dentists or accountants even though they do valuable work, too, or waxes indignant over devices to control the jury—such as voir dire, judgment n.o.v., sequestration, gag orders, or jury instructions that run on dozens of pages and spell out in minute detail what they are to do—or ones that control lawyers. I'm thinking of judicial chastisement, sarcasm, injunctions to 'move things along, counsel,' and even contempt citations when a lawyer has done something a judge doesn't like, even if the lawyer did it on principle. Nor does anyone see an affront to judicial independence when a higher court exercises *its* independence to slap down a lower one."

"So, you think we're guilty of selective sympathy," I said.

"Something like that," Rodrigo replied. "I'm sure this argument alone won't persuade you, especially because you want Judge Ingersol to be independent when he hears your case. I just point out how easy it is to get caught up in a crusade on behalf of judges, when other actors may be equally deserving. Do you want to hear my next point?"

Judicial Independence, Like Many Liberal Rallying Cries, Is a Paired Platitude

"I do," I replied. "I hope it's more impressive than your last one."

Rodrigo winced, then said, "I'll let you decide. Do you recall the critical legal studies position on indeterminacy?"

"Of course," I replied. "It holds that legal reasoning, especially of the case-law variety, never, or almost never, dictates a single conclusion.[19] By picking one argument or line of authority, the lawgiver can make one outcome appear inevitable and just; by another, he or she can rationalize the opposite result. This open-textured quality, first pointed out by the legal realists in the early part of the century, allows a wide scope for politics and disguised personal predilection on the part of the decisionmaker. Critical legal studies refined this critique and applied it to a host of areas, including torts, contracts, constitutional, and labor law."

"And have you considered how the same thing may apply to policy arguments?" Rodrigo asked.

"I suppose it could," I said. "There's the old joke about how you can almost always find an opposite proverb for any situation. Look before you leap. He who hesitates is lost. Birds of a feather flock together. Opposites attract. And so on."

"Well, consider how judicial independence is set off against other maxims that we also subscribe to and trot out from time to time: Judicial accountability and restraint. Strict construction. Law as the least dangerous branch. Checks and balances. The will of the people should not be lightly set aside."

"So you're saying that judicial independence is part of a matrix of values that surround the judiciary and its functioning. When we want to limit a judge's prerogative, we pick one of the narrowing kind. But when we like what they're doing—such as when they intervene on behalf of discrete and insular minorities—we forget these other maxims and genuflect toward judicial independence. We praise judges for their courage in interceding on behalf of weak, impotent, voiceless groups."

"You put it better than I could have myself," Rodrigo said. "And in that respect, judicial independence is like other vague but noble sounding liberal legalisms, such as free speech. They conceal what is going on, diverting discussion of the content of what the speaker is saying—whether progressive or regressive—into a *procedural*, free-speech controversy: 'I've got my rights.' By the same token, we sometimes need to look at what judges are *doing* with their independence, or what those advocating restraint are promoting. Chanting over and over that judges should be free—or accountable, for that matter—obscures what they are actually doing."

"Which can often be good," I pointed out.

"Or bad," Rodrigo countered. "As when the Supreme Court backtracked from *Brown v. Board of Education*[20] or cut back on affirmative action,[21] search and seizure law,[22] liability of police who engage in highspeed chases,[23] and the right to abortion.[24] Not to mention your own case."

"Which would have come out fine, without those pressure groups looking over the shoulders of good judges. No, Rodrigo, you haven't converted me yet. Let's hear your other arguments."

Judicial Independence as a Check and Balance

"My next one," Rodrigo said, looking down at his list, "is not so much an argument against judicial independence as a comment about its place in our political system. Do you remember how we were saying that platitudes come in pairs? [I nodded yes—after all, it had been only ten minutes ago—*these youngsters must think we old-timers have no faculty of memory left at all!* I thought.] Well, at least one of those platitudes has a broad, political dimension. I'm sure you've heard how our system is one of checks and balances?"

"Of course," I said. "Early Federalist writing sets out the theory. To reduce the risk of tyranny, the three branches are created coequal, each limiting the power of the other. And to me, at least, this is not only a very good thing but an excellent reason for an independent judiciary. Who else could rein in an out-of-control Congress or curb a president bent on skullduggery, like Nixon during the Watergate crisis?"

"But notice two things," Rodrigo said. "First, both sides invoke checks and balances with equal conviction. Conservatives say we need to be able to vote judges out of office, precisely because they consider this a vital check on an out-of-control judiciary that is unresponsive to the will of the people."[25]

"While liberals say the opposite, namely, that these pressure groups are diminishing the ability of judges to serve as an independent check on the behavior of other branches, such as the police."

"A perfect standoff," Rodrigo said, "both sides invoking the same value, certain the other is wrong in hijacking it to support its position."

I paused, then said, "On this one, Rodrigo, I agree with you. The checks-and-balances notion is too abstract to yield much in the way of concrete results. I don't think judicial independence is a mere rhetorical flourish. After all, I'm facing some uncomfortable results of its failure. But I do agree one can't decide individual cases by reciting a broad political maxim laid down two hundred years ago."

"As we said earlier, you have to get down to specific cases. Are you ready for my next argument?"

"I'm waiting."

The Role of Structure

"Consider some ways structure plays a role in judging, aspirationally and as a limitation."

"I'm intrigued," I said. "I love structural arguments. Unlike ones based on rhetoric or high-flown abstractions, they sometimes actually get somewhere."

"I think you'll agree this one does," Rodrigo said. "Notice how judges can't be truly independent. If so, they'll get reversed. Even before that, if too independent, they won't get confirmed. In this age, that doesn't take much independence at all."

"I can certainly think of examples," I said. "One Supreme Court nominee got thrown out because he smoked marijuana decades earlier.[26] And you know what happened to Lani Guiner[27] and Bill Lann Lee.[28] Too leftist for the Republicans in Congress, they saw Clinton abandon them or, in Lee's case, beat a strategic retreat and name him only to an interim position."

"Real renegades don't even make it that far," Rodrigo went on. "It turns out the independence we tout means only a narrow thing: in no particular ideology's thrall while leading an average life and doing ordinary, bureaucratic 'normal science.' "[29]

"The demography of the federal bench, at least, bears you out," I conceded. "I certainly wish it was more diverse. I wouldn't mind having a minority judge this afternoon," I added wistfully.

"As we mentioned, the bench contains very few disabled people, Marxists, labor organizers, minorities, or gay and lesbian people. Real independence would mean judges with a wide range of life experience. It would mean upholding draft resisters, at least on occasion; affording a sympathetic hearing to against-the-grain groups; giving careful consideration to Ruth Colker's antisubordination interpretation of Equal Protection jurisprudence."[30]

"Is this your other kind of structural independence?" I asked.

"It is," Rodrigo answered. "Do you remember when we were discussing the idea of structural due process?"[31]

"In connection with cloning and human procreative technologies?"

"Exactly," Rodrigo replied. "Popularized by Laurence Tribe, but foreshadowed in Continental philosophy, structural due process means that in contentious cases falling in a zone of moral flux courts should afford the most complete, open hearing. Later, when society has decided where it stands on an issue, say women's or gay rights, they may afford more streamlined treatment under codified rules. Until that time, we ought to give those cases the broadest scope, allowing every point of view to be heard. Liberal rules of evidence, intervention, and burdens of proof ought to be applied. At this early stage, we don't know where we stand on the issue. We thus do ourselves a favor by forcing the most open treatment. Later, when we know the geography of the area, we can give litigants more cursory, standardized treatment."

"Not a bad idea," I said, "at least in theory."

"But my point is that this is exactly what we do not do," Rodrigo said. "It would require a kind of meta-knowledge on the part of judges, something most lack as narrow specialists. Consider, for example, their disappointingly wooden, mechanistic dismissal of hate-speech cases brought under campus speech codes."[32]

"Or the cross-burning case," I interjected.[33] "Scalia's opinion sounds like a commercial outline or a cribsheet of 1950s free-speech law. It gives scant attention to the interests of the black family on whose lawn the cross was burned. The same is true of the two district court decisions striking down campus speech codes."[34]

"Although those were cases presenting novel, emerging issues of great social importance, the judges treated them as though someone proposed a rule limiting bookshops to a hundred square feet. Touting the independence of judges—even as they demonstrate so little of it—is a little like praising the independence of notaries, car mechanics, or accountants."

"Professor, you're more of a crit than you may realize. Independence is a cry judges raise only when they are doing something that others question. Most of their work is routinized, bureaucratized butchery. Robert Cover was right—they do operate on a field of pain and death."[35]

"Yet act blithely ignorant of that," I said. "Otherwise, they would slow down when operating in the zone of moral flux, when doing something novel and socially important."

"Instead they seem to hurry up," Rodrigo said. "Or throw up their hands and say, 'We can do no other. Our hands are tied. The mighty First Amendment decrees. . .'"

"Sometimes, people and pressure groups participate legitimately in constitutional value-making," I commented. "That same author had a name for this."

"Jurisgenesis," Rodrigo said. "The idea that norms come from many sources, not just the judiciary. They come from the work of small groups, even individuals. We all participate in norm-making, in our daily lives, in what we do."

"And your point, I suppose, is that none of this is illegitimate or an affront to political principle."

"Not at all," Rodrigo said. "You have to look at what the pressure group is doing. The Freemen, for example, go too far when they declare that the government is totally illegitimate and then try to set up their own court system. But patriot groups are perfectly within their rights to insist that we have too much taxation, or that this or that judge exceeds his or her mandate in requiring them to pledge allegiance in school or at the commencement of a civic proceeding."

"You crits do make common cause with the strangest people," I said, shaking my head. "What's your next argument?"

The Cash Value of Judicial Independence

"Historically, judicial independence simply has not been worth that much," Rodrigo began. "In the hundred years between *Dred Scott*[36] and *Brown v. Board of Education*,[37] very few judges exercised their independence to rule against Jim Crow or segregated schools, beaches, and public facilities.[38] They blandly did 'ordinary science,' which meant ruling against integration."

"The same happened during other times of stress," I added. "Few judges stood up against McCarthyism or the Salem witch trials, even fewer against slavery. And everyone knows that the German judiciary and bar meekly went along with the excesses of Nazism and the Holocaust.[39] Cases like *Buck v. Bell*[40] and *Dred Scott*[41] mar the careers of some of our most eminent judges, who seem to have gone right along with the spirit of the times. If they had independence, they chose not to exercise it."

"A black or gay judge would not have handed down *Plessy v. Ferguson* or *Bowers v. Hardwick*,"[42] Rodrigo said. "Or been less likely to," he added.

"I can certainly think of a prominent one today who might," I added mildly, not wanting to make too much of it.[43]

"Still, people make a big thing of the occasional case in which a judge stands up for principle—"

"Like Harlan's dissent in *Plessy v. Ferguson*,"[44] I interjected.

"Right!" Rodrigo exclaimed. "Neglecting the hundred cases where they uphold the unjust law. Or, in Harlan's case, upholding anti-Asian laws.[45] His liberality toward blacks evidently did not generalize, his Asian jurisprudence being as jingoistic and racist as that of the rest of the justices. I was just reading an article on this."

"I think I saw it. It was by a young Asian scholar, if I recall, and won some sort of prize."

"That's the one," Rodrigo said. "The Thurgood Marshall Prize, if I remember correctly."[46]

"Right. But I hope you're not saying Harlan's remarkably humane opinion was dimmed in some way by his failure to reach the highest degree of sainthood in other cases?"

"No, not dimmed," Rodrigo said. "It does show, however, that we need to beware the celebratory tendency. Some judges' countermajoritarian rulings may not be as brave as we like to think. I'm sure you know of Derrick Bell's analysis of *Brown v. Board of Education* as a majoritarian exercise."[47] I nodded yes, and Rodrigo continued: "And another scholar speculated that Justice Harlan may have written as he did in *Plessy* because he had a black brother.[48] Not having an Asian brother, he lapsed back into business as usual when the Chinese Exclusion cases came before him."

"So you're saying that true judicial independence is rare, often explained on simple material terms."

"Rather than ideal ones," Rodrigo added. "Or may serve to promote stasis, to assure that the gap between our ideals and current reality doesn't get too great."

"'Contradiction-closing cases,' Bell calls them."[49]

"Which allow business as usual to go on, because now we can point to the exceptional case and say, 'See, our system is really fair and just. See what we just did for minorities or the poor.'"

"Overlooking that the rest of the time, we tolerate a system that excludes them from jobs, schools, friendship networks, homes in the suburbs, and many of the good things of life. But I still believe in judicial independence. Judges aren't perfect, and Harlan or Holmes may have suffered a black eye now and then. But I'd rather have a judiciary that can act fearlessly, at least every now and then, than one constantly looking over its shoulder at what the demagogues, letter writers, newspaper editors, and right-wing fanatics are saying. In fact, in about [I looked at my watch] fifteen minutes, I hope my judge is willing to exercise a little independence. Otherwise this absurd charge could stick, and I might actually do time for jaywalking, if you can believe it."

"I have nothing against judicial *courage*," Rodrigo replied. "That's always a good thing. It's characterizing the virtue as *independence* that I think is misleading."

Just then, the waiter arrived to tell us that the dessert line now contained their specialty, carrot cake with pistachio frosting. We looked at each other. Rodrigo seemed interested, so I said, "What the heck. If I'm going to jail, I might as well have a good last meal." Rodrigo picked up his tray, and I followed him to the line. After we returned to our tables, Rodrigo continued:

The Ordinary and the Extraordinary: The Example of Race

"On the subject of courage, consider courts' race jurisprudence. I know you may feel differently in light of your own experience, but history shows that judicial independence has not been of great help to minorities. Courts sometimes hand down helpful opinions, to be sure. But some of the worst—*Plessy, Dred Scott, McClesky v. Kemp*,[50] *Bowers v. Hardwick*—came down when the Court was not under great pressure. And some of the best—*Brown, Hernandez*,[51] and in Australia, *Mabo*[52]—were handed down when it was. Pressure can, of course, make courts rule even more regressively than they would otherwise; consider how right-wing pressure or Southern resistance brought about the *Adarand*[53] decision, the reversal of *Metro Broadcasting*,[54] or *Brown II*.[55] Liberals who worry about judicial independence seem to assume that without pressure courts will do the right thing. But unpressured, business-as-usual judging is the real problem, not the pressured kind."

"You and I once discussed how systemic evils like racism, which are deeply imbedded in the fabric of society, are very hard to see and correct.[56] We called it the empathic fallacy, if I recall."

"Right," Rodrigo said. "It consists of believing that we can easily and quickly rid ourselves of error and injustice by merely naming and calling attention to it. Experience shows that this does not happen. The voice of the reformer goes unheard or dismissed as incoherent or absurd.[57] It's only when ten thousand voices are shouting in the streets that we begin to pay attention."

"And that's what people call 'pressure,'" I said ironically.

"When a black judge gets a black case, this looks abnormal, so that white attorneys almost invariably call for the judge to recuse himself. In one case, Leon Higginbotham decided to stick it out and remain on the bench.[58] A huge furor ensued, with few riding to his rescue. With business as usual—white judges hearing white cases—hardly anyone raises such a stink. But the mere possibility that a black judge might give sympathetic treatment to one of his race raises hackles. And the reaction in Higginbotham's case—no one called *that* an affront to judicial independence, which it was. The famous African American judge's critics thought it stood to reason that he should step down, and they were upset when he refused."

"And as we mentioned before, when black jurors decline to convict a black defendant, law-and-order types are outraged and demand reforms so that this cannot happen again.[59] No one speaks of *jury* independence, even though the jury's role in our scheme of justice is as ancient and vital as that of the judge."

"Judicial independence is really a misnomer. Our paradigm does not allow for it. A high majority of cases brought by prosecutors result in conviction. Few cases are overturned on appeal—"

"Unless they're from a maverick judge or liberal circuit, like the ninth," I cracked.[60]

"Right. Robert Bork and his friends, who seek a constitutional amendment allowing for congressional overturning of court judgments[61] really want to constrain judges who display any sort of legal thought other than the normative or traditional. They want to make judges toe the line, act in predictable ways."

"But wait a minute," I said. "Doesn't that cut the other way? If you are a social reformer, would you not welcome judicial independence? That way, judges would be free to act in nonnormative ways, as you call them."

"In theory, yes," Rodrigo conceded. "Although liberals and the ABA rightly stand up for the concept of judicial independence, they are not defending it in any real sense, because judges have almost never acted independently. The entire structure of the legal system, from stare decisis to judicial demography, judicial ethics, and socialization, assures this."

"So, the whole thing is a legitimating myth?"

"Yes and no," Rodrigo answered. "It's better to have it than not. But having these little side skirmishes from time to time, even if the right side wins, sets us back. They enable us to pat ourselves on the back and relax, overlooking the other ninety-nine out of every hundred cases when the judge does the predictable thing."

"Given his or her background, ethnicity, social status, and role."

"Exactly," Rodrigo said. "If the ABA report had considered how the culture of law, for lack of a better word, determines the outcome of particular cases, it would have reached a more disheartening conclusion."

"But what's wrong with that?" I asked, beginning to be aware of a looming shape that had approached our table.

"Hello again," said Rodrigo, looking up at the figure who had materialized at our tableside. It was my lawyer.

"Hi," said Steinglass. Then to me: "We're on, but not till two o'clock. And you'll be glad to know the prosecutor wants to meet with us fifteen minutes before. She may be ready to deal. Sanity may have returned."

"That would be a relief," I said. Then after a pause: "Won't you join us? You remember Rodrigo from this morning. He teaches at the public school the next state over and is in town for a committee meeting. In the chambers of the chief judge, in fact."

"Welcome back," Rodrigo said shaking hands. "Congratulations on that plea bargain."

"I won't celebrate until it's signed and delivered," said my lawyer. "Maybe I'll get a cup of coffee and join you in a minute."

Judicial Independence as Civility: A One-Way Street

While waiting for my lawyer to return, I turned to Rodrigo. "We may not have very long. By my count, you've got one more argument left."

"Actually, your friend might have something to say on it. It's that in one of its aspects, the call for judicial independence is hypocritical. Maybe that's too harsh—I should say one-sided."

"One-sided?"

"I mean that one of the complaints the judicial independence crowd makes is that harsh criticism, especially from lawyers, tarnishes the image of the legal system, detracting from the majesty and dignity of the courts."

"Well, that of judges, anyway. They're not the courts. I mean, there are other players as well, including the lawyers, the parties, the juries, the reviewing court. . . "

"I know. The complaints are a little selective. But they are also one-sided. Had you noticed how many judges feel free to belittle or admonish a lawyer who is presenting a novel claim or taking too long to present an established one?"

"Rule 11 cases present some notorious examples," I said.[62] "In fact, I was reading an article just the other day entitled *Scorn*, in which the authors point out how freely some judges belittle, dismiss, or ridicule lawyers who do something out of the ordinary, such as bring a novel case, say, for comparable worth."[63]

"I think I saw it, too," Rodrigo said. "If I'm not mistaken, the authors argued that scorn and satire are never warranted out of the mouths of powerful figures like judges."

"Sounds like you two have been having a good time." It was Steinglass, a smile on his face and a huge plastic cup of coffee in his hand.

"Have a seat," I said. "How much time have we got?"

When Steinglass said, "About thirty minutes, don't worry—I've set my wrist alarm," I summarized our discussion, explaining Rodrigo's task on the committee and his thesis that judicial independence serves as a legitimating myth. I repeated, in summary form, Rodrigo's eight observations, including that judicial independence can serve as a deflection and that judges are a peculiar object of mercy. I reiterated his point that the judicial-independence norm, like many, is a paired platitude and, as such, perfectly indeterminate; and, as a further example of it, that one can just as easily argue judicial independence as an aspect of or danger to a system of checks and balances. I mentioned his argument that real judicial independence would lead to judges' applying some variant of structural due process but that they rarely do so, instead affording most cutting-edge cases irritable, cursory treatment. Finally, I outlined Rodrigo's example of race jurisprudence and what it showed about the low cash value of judicial review and independence, and concluded with his observation that civility—one component of the judicial independence rallying cry—seldom cuts both ways, as judges feel free to be as uncivil as they like toward lawyers and parties who do something that offends them. "He ties it to a whole theory of humor," I said. "I know this from a previous discussion."

When Steinglass looked interested, Rodrigo said, "Yes, satire and scorn are never justified, except against the high and mighty, those who abuse power and authority.[64] The powerful, such as judges, may never rightly wield those tools against those of lesser power and station. One root of humor is *humus*, 'bringing low, down to earth.' The classic satirists, like Swift, Voltaire, and Mark Twain, realized this, reserving their barbs and slings for the pompous and self-important. They never made fun at the expense of the lowly, such as beggars or the blind."[65]

"So you're saying that judges can dish it out but can't take it," Steinglass said. Rodrigo nodded.

"Something like that."

The lawyer went on: "I've certainly seen cases like that, including a DUI I argued just last week. The judge was as sarcastic as a human being can be, merely because my client, a physician who was on medication, refused to take a Breathalyzer test."

"Judges like to affect false modesty," Rodrigo interjected. "'We're the least powerful branch. We defer to political questions. In diversity cases, we are oh-so-careful not to overstep on state sovereignty. We are bound by precedent. All we do is read and apply the statute.' But try attacking or criticizing one, and the iron fist comes out of the velvet glove. The false modesty disappears. You can get thrown in jail for contempt, condemned by your bar association for unseemly expression."

"Thanks for the summary," Steinglass said. Then looking over at me: "I gather that you, Professor, have your doubts about what this young fellow is saying. I do, too. If you'd like to hear what a practicing lawyer thinks. . . "

When Rodrigo and I both nodded eagerly, he continued as follows: "I actually taught trial practice at the Professor's school for several years. So although I'm not as well versed in critical thought as you are, Rodrigo, I've read a little in political theory and the new clinical jurisprudence. And if you'll allow me, I'd like to make a case for judicial independence that goes beyond the liberal pieties you usually hear."

"Please do," we said in unison. Taking a deep draft of his coffee and a quick glance at his watch, Steinglass began as follows:

Steinglass Makes the Case for an Independent Judiciary *and* an Independent Bar, and We Conclude on a Note of Reconciliation

"Do you two know about the host of books that have come out recently on the role of the professions in Nazi Germany under the Third Reich?" We both nodded a little uncertainly, so Steinglass continued: "Books by Robert Jay Lifton,[66] George Annas,[67] and Michael Stelloeis[68] highlight how little the German bench and bar and Nazi doctors did to stop the atrocities that were occurring there during the years leading up to World War II."

"I've read some of them," Rodrigo said. "I've even heard it theorized that concern over the excesses of statism in Germany underlay our Supreme Court's decision in *Hickman v. Taylor*,[69] the work-product privilege case."

When Steinglass looked a little uncertain, I chimed in, "The idea is that Justice Jackson and at least one of the court clerks who participated in that landmark 1946 decision upholding a lawyer's zone of privacy had recently returned from taking part in the trials at Nuremberg of Nazi war criminals. One of the impressions they brought back with them was the craven behavior of the German bar and judiciary, which, unlike ours, follow a nonadversarial or inquiry-based model in which the lawyers and judge cooperate in trying to reach the truth. Unlike here, where the lawyers are the zealous advocates of their clients' cause and try to vanquish the other side, German lawyers, at least during that period, considered themselves arms of government and allies of each other and of the judges."[70]

"Oh, now I see the connection," Steinglass said, his face lighting up. "And it illustrates my point perfectly. Without a work-product privilege in our recently adopted rules of civil discovery, lawyers would be able to pry secrets out of each other. Mental impressions, legal strategy, and office memoranda would be required to be shared with the other side.[71] That degree of cooperation would be suffocating, would start us on the road to groupthink, and would be incompatible with the sort of feisty, combative system we now have. With all its bumps, warts, and inefficiencies, it's still the best system in the world. Certainly it's the best guarantor against statism and Big Brother yet invented. And that's why judges must be independent."

We both started as Steinglass's alarm went off suddenly. "I have it set loud," he explained. "I have to be able to hear it even in a noisy corridor. We've got a few more minutes."

All three of us were silent for a moment. Then Rodrigo said: "A powerful example. And I agree that judicial independence can serve as a vital bulwark against excesses of statism and atrocities like those we saw in Germany. Even though once or twice in our history, it didn't work as intended. For I think I see a way of reconciling my own critique and Mr. Steinglass's insight. Do we have a minute to sort of pull things together?"

I looked over at my lawyer, who nodded.

"It just struck me that judicial independence has a double aspect," Rodrigo began.

"Both advancing and retarding the search for justice?" I said, hearkening back to something we had said earlier.[72]

"Yes. It's one of those mechanisms whose value is hard to pin down because it's capable of doing great good in individual cases while doing the opposite in the large run of them."

"Hmmmm," I said. "That helps make sense of cases like mine, where one wants the judge to be able to work free from outside pressure. But insisting that the judiciary be always and forever insulated from criticism can paralyze political instincts and allow atrocities. Criticism—at least of the kind directed upward, toward authority—is the best guarantor of liberty."

"I'll buy that," Steinglass said. "Even though I'm up for a judicial appointment myself, the idea of rules against criticizing judges strikes me as a dangerous precedent."

"As for myself," I said, sensing that we were about to conclude our discussion, "I like your idea of judicial *courage*, Rodrigo. Maybe the best guarantor of liberty is to pick judges who believe in something and then train them to stand their ground when unfair criticism comes their way."

Just then, a slender, uniformed young man approached our table. "Mister Steinglass, Professor. Excuse me. The court is now in session. But the district attorney decided to accept your plea bargain. Ten hours of community service plus restitution for the biker's medicals. You can all go home. Just mail these papers in. Just among the three of us, the judge thought the whole thing pretty silly. In fact, his precise words were, 'I'll be glad to take the heat on this one.'"

Notes

1. On this and similar code words and epithets used in police communications, see interview with Anonymous Police Officer in a major U.S. city ("TNB"); Report of the Independent Commissioners on the Los Angeles Police Department (1994) ("Warren Christopher Commission"), 71 ("Gorillas in the Mist"), 72 ("the natives," "monkeys slapping time," "huntin' wabbits"), 73 ("Don't cry Buckwheat," "cholo," "don't transfer me any orientals"); Marvin Zalman & Larry J. Siegel, CRIMINAL PROCEDURE: CONSTITUTION AND SOCIETY 332 (group of officers in an Ohio department had designated themselves a "special nigger arrest team"—SNAT). *See also* John P. Crank, UNDERSTANDING PUBLIC CULTURE 123 (animal), 206 (beater), 207 (racial epithets in general), 211 (nigger), 213–215 (we-they attitude) (1997); Paul Chevigny, EDGE OF THE KNIFE: POLICE VIOLENCE IN THE AMERICAS (1995) (on police violence in general); Jerome Skolnick, *A Sketch of the Policeman's Working Personality*, in JUSTICE WITHOUT TRIAL 41 (3d ed. 1994) (on racism and prejudice in police work). On race profiling, in which police use an individual's race to decide whether to stop and question him, see Harvey A. Silverglate, *'Race Profiling' Inflicts Injustice on Individuals*, NAT. L.J., June 22, 1998, at A-20. On stereotyping, rude treatment, and police harassment of black males, see D. Marvin Jones, *"We're All Stuck Here for a While": Law and the Social Construction of the Black Male*, 24 J. CONTEMP. L. 35 (1998). *See also* Richard Delgado, THE RODRIGO CHRONICLES, chapter 8 (1995) (on social construction of black crime as threat).

2. *See* James Q. Wilson & George L. Keiling, *Broken Windows: The Police and Neighborhood Safety*, THE ATLANTIC, Mar. 1982, at 29.

3. *See* John Kifner, *Thousands Call on City Hall to Confront Police Brutality*, NY TIMES, August 30, 1997, at A-1 (detailing Rudolph Giuliani's crackdown on crime and some of its unintended consequences, including an increase in police harassment and brutality).

4. *See* John C. Yoo, *Criticizing Judges*, 1 Green Bag 2d, 277–81 (Spring 1998), on various recent efforts to impeach and chastise judges.

5. *See* CHRONICLES, *supra* at chapter 1. (Professor recommends Rodrigo to various LL.M. programs on the young man's return to the States).

6. Compare Rodrigo's committee with the national version, which issued a major report only last year. AMER. BAR ASS'N, COMMISSION ON SEPARATION OF POWERS AND JUDICIAL INDEPENDENCE, AN INDEPENDENT JUDICIARY (1997).

7. *See id.* at 46; Stephen B. Bright, *Political Attacks on the Judiciary: Can Justice Be Done Amid Efforts to Intimidate and Remove Judges from Office for Unpopular Decisions?* 172 N.Y.U. L. REV. 308, 313 (1997). On judicial independence generally, see Federal Judicial Independence Symposium, 46 Mercer L. Rev. 637 (1995); *A Symposium on Judicial Independence: Safeguarding a Crown Jewel: Judicial Independence and Lawyer Criticism of Courts,* 25 HOFSTRA L. REV. 703 (1997). *See also House Passes "Judicial Activism" Bill,* THE THIRD BRANCH, May 1998, at 1 (describing measure backed by "the right wing" to curb judicial initiative and discourage prisoner suits).

8. Mary L. Volcansek, JUDICIAL IMPEACHMENT 5 (1993). Although Chase was indicted by the House on charges that he treated defendants who violated the Alien and Sedition Acts leniently, the Senate acquitted him, and Chase continued to serve on the highest court until his death in 1811. The Constitution mentions impeachment six times. Article 1, section 2, provides that the House bring impeachment charges, and the next section gives the Senate the power actually to try the case.

9. The three federal judges impeached and convicted by the Senate during the 1980s were Judge Harry Eugene Claiborne (U.S. District Judge, Nevada), African American Judge Alcee Lamar Hastings (U.S. District Judge, Florida), and Judge Walter L. Nixon (U.S. District Judge, Southern District of Mississippi). *Id. See* ABA, *supra* note 9, at 47–48. On state impeachment, see Jerome B. Meites & Steven F. Pflaum, *Justice James D. Heiple: Impeachment and the Assault on Judicial Independence,* LOYOLA U. CHI. L. J. 741 (1998).

10. Claiborne, a maverick judge who mistrusted government, had jousted with the federal government and various agencies several times in the past. Claiborne claimed he was targeted by government officials and that the ensuing bribery charges were entirely founded upon the word of a convicted felon protecting his own interests. Even after Claiborne's impeachment by the Senate, the Nevada Bar Association found that he was a victim of a "federal vendetta." IMPEACHMENT, *supra* at 24, 63.

11. Mario Cuomo, *Some Thoughts on Judicial Independence,* 72 N.Y.U. L. Rev. 295, 299–302 (1997); ABA, *supra* at 22–23, 49; YOO, *supra* at 279–82. On the recent campaign to punish federal judge Harold Baer for suppressing illegally seized evidence in a drug case, see BRIGHT, *supra* at 324, 326–27; ABA, *supra* at 5–6, 15–18 (describing this and similar cases of judges hounded because of unpopular decisions); ACTIVISM, *supra.*

12. John M. Broder, *Clinton, Softening Slap at Senate, Names 'Acting' Civil Rights Chief.* NY TIMES, December 16, 1997, at A-1.

13. ABA, *supra* at 15.

14. Jerome J. Shestack, *The Risks to Judicial Independence* (editorial), ABAJ, June 1998, at 8; *What Is Judicial Independence,* 80 Judicature 73 (Sept.-Oct. 1996). *See also*

Archibald Cox, *The Independence of the Judiciary: History and Purpose*, 21 U. DAYTON L. REV. 566 (1996).

15. ABA, *supra* (decrying politicization and harsh criticism of judges and the judging functions and suggesting measures to cope with them).

16. On the racial composition of the U.S. judiciary, see Sherrilyn A. Ifill, *Judging the Judges: Diversity, Impartiality, and Representation on State Trial Courts*, 39 B.C. L. REV. 95 (1997).

17. *See* Richard Delgado & Jean Stefancic, *Norms and Narratives: Can Judges Avoid Serious Moral Error?* 69 TEX. L. REV. 1929 (1991). *See also* Robert Cover, JUSTICE ACCUSED: ANTISLAVERY AND THE JUDICIAL PROCESS (1975).

18. ACCUSED, *supra. See also Norms, supra*.

19. *See* David Kairys, *Legal Reasoning*, in THE POLITICS OF LAW 11 (D. Kairys ed., 1982).

20. *See* 349 U.S. 294 (1955) (*"Brown II,"* ordering desegregation of southern schools at "all deliberate speed"); Milliken v. Bradley, 433 U.S. 267 (1977) (rejecting metropolitan-wide remedy for segregated schools).

21. Adarand Constructors, Inc. v. Peña, 515 U.S. 200 (1995).

22. Illinois v. Krull, 480 U.S. 340 (1987); United States v. Leon, 468 U.S. 897 (1984) (good faith a defense to an otherwise illegal, warrantless search).

23. County of Sacramento v. Lewis, 118 S.Ct. 1708 (1998).

24. Planned Parenthood v. Casey, 504 U.S. 833 (1992).

25. Dan Carney, *Striking Controversial Provisions, House Waters Down B.11 Limiting Federal Judges' Powers*, CQ WEEKLY, Apr. 25, 1998 at 10–14. *See* also Robert Bork, SLOUCHING TOWARD GOMORRAH: MODERN LIBERALISM AND AMERICAN DECLINE 117 (1996) (criticizing activist judges and urging amendment to allow congressional override of federal court decisions with which that body disagrees); ABA, *supra* at 44 (opposing this proposal).

26. On the rejection of Supreme Court nominee Douglas Ginsburg for this very reason, see Editorial, *Behind the Ginsburg Smoke*, N.Y. TIMES, Nov. 10, 1987, at A-34.

27. For a step-by-step account of her confirmation struggles, written by the candidate herself, see Lani Guinier, LIFT EVERY VOICE (1998).

28. On Mr. Lee's difficulties, see BRODER, *supra* at A-1.

29. Coined by THOMAS KUHN, THE STRUCTURE OF SCIENTIFIC REVOLUTIONS (1962), the term refers to inquiry conducted within the reigning paradigm—safe, incrementalist, and familiar.

30. *See* Ruth Colker, *Antisubordination Above All: Sex, Race, and Equal Protection*, 61 N.Y.U. L. REV. 1003 (1986).

31. *See* Chapter 4, this volume.

32. *E.g.*, U.M.W. Post v. Regents of University of Wisconsin, 774 F. Supp. 1163 (E.D. Wis. 1991); Doe v. University of Michigan, 721 F.Supp. 852 (E.D. Mich., 1989). *See* Richard Delgado, *Campus Antiracism Rules: Constitutional Narratives in Collision*, 85 NW. U. L. REV. 343 (1991).

33. R.A.V. v. St. Paul, 505 U.S. 377 (1992).

34. U.M.W. Post and Doe v. University of Michigan, *supra*.

35. Robert Cover, *Violence and the Word*, 95 YALE L.J. 1601 (1986).

36. Dred Scott v. Sandford, 60 U.S. (19 How.) 393 (1857) (holding that blacks were not intended by the Framers to be citizens with rights that white people are bound to respect).

37. 347 U.S. 483 (1954).

38. Leon Higginbotham, SHADES OF FREEDOM: RACIAL POLITICS AND PRE-SUMPTIONS OF THE AMERICAN LEGAL PROCESS (1996); *Norms, supra* (obliviousness of many judges).

39. *See* Michael Stelloeis, THE LAW UNDER THE SWASTIKA: STUDIES ON LEGAL HISTORY IN NAZI GERMANY (1998).

40. 274 U.S. 200 (1927) (upholding state-ordered sterilization of mental defectives).

41. 60 U.S. (19 How.) 393 (1857).

42. 478 U.S. 186 (1986) (upholding punishment of sodomy).

43. I was thinking of Justice Clarence Thomas, author of numerous opinions that have set back the fortunes of minorities and the poor. For an analysis of Thomas's jurisprudence, see Stuart Taylor Jr., *The Problem with Clarence Thomas*, 19 LEG. TIMES, June 1996, at 21.

44. 163 U.S. 537, 552 (1896) (Harlan, J., dissenting against separate but equal ruling on grounds that the Constitution should be color-blind).

45. Gabriel J. Chin, *The Plessy Myth: Justice Harlan and the Chinese Cases*, 82 IOWA L. REV. 151 (1996). *See* Pat Chew, *Asian Americans: The 'Reticent' Minority and Their Paradoxes*, 36 WM & MARY L. REV. 1 (1984) (on law's neglect of the Asian minority).

46. Chin, *supra*.

47. Brown v. Board of Education *and the Interest Convergence Dilemma*, 93 HARV. L. REV. 518 (1980) (hypothesizing that the government ruled as it did in the famous case to advance Cold War imperatives).

48. James Gordon, *Did the First Justice Harlan Have a Black Brother?* 15 U. NEW ENG. L. REV. 159 (1993).

49. Derrick Bell, *The Supreme Court, 1984 Term: Foreword—The Civil Rights Chronicles*, 99 HARV. L.REV. 4, 32 (1985).

50. 481 U.S. 279 (1987).

51. Hernandez v. Texas, 347 U.S. 475 (1954).

52. Mabo v. Queensland (No. 2) (1992) 175 CLR1 (upholding aborigines' land claims against doctrine of *terra nullus*—that at the time of settlers' arrival, Australian land was essentially unowned and ripe for taking).

53. Adarand Contractors Inc. v. Peña, 515 U.S. 200 (1995).

54. Metro Broadcasting v. F.C.C., 497 U.S. 547 (1990) (upholding minority preference in issuance of broadcast licenses).

55. Brown v. Board of Education, 349 U.S. 294, 301 (1955) ("*Brown II*"—implementation decision, permitting desegregation to proceed at "all deliberate speed").

56. RICHARD DELGADO, THE COMING RACE WAR? AND OTHER APOCALYP-TIC TALES OF AMERICA AFTER AFFIRMATIVE ACTION AND WELFARE, chapter 1 (1996).

57. *Id.* at 12–81. *But see* Frank B. Cross & Emerson L. Tiller, *Judicial Partisanship and Obedience to Legal Doctrine: Whistleblowing on the Federal Courts of Appeal*, 107 YALE L. J. 2155 (1998) (a maverick judge can sometimes shame the others into obeying precedent).

58. On Higgenbotham's ordeal, see JUDGING, *supra* at 114.

59. *E.g.*, Jeffrey Rosen, *The Bloods and the Crits*, NEW REPUB., Dec. 9, 1996, at 27 (decrying O.J. Simpson's acquittal and laying blame on critical race theorists who devised notions of law as storytelling).

60. *See* Jerome Farris, *Judges on Judging: The Ninth Circuit—Most Maligned Circuit in the Country—Fact or Fiction?* 58 OHIO ST. L.J. 1465 (1977) (describing recent pattern of reversals of Ninth Circuit decisions); Editorial, *Decency and the Arts*, DENVER POST, June 27, 1998, at B-9; David G. Savage, *9th Circuit Rebuked Again*, A.B.A.J., July 1998, at 40. *See also* Bob Egelko, *Judge Accused of Misconduct for Writing Dissenting Opinion*, BOULDER DAILY CAMERA, July 8, 1995, at B-3 (liberal judge J. Anthony Kline accused of judicial misconduct by state commission for dissenting, on grounds of conscience, from a 2–1 ruling concerning the erasure of past rulings in a case).

61. See SLOUCHING, *supra* at 117 (setting forth this proposal); CUOMO, *supra* at 300 (criticizing it).

62. Fed. R. Civ. P. 11, permitting courts to punish parties and attorneys who file frivolous lawsuits or motions.

63. *See* Richard Delgado & Jean Stefancic, *Scorn*, 35 WM. & MARY L. REV. 1061 (1994). Comparable worth is a novel legal theory that holds that jobs of similar complexity—such as nursing and telephone repair—should be paid comparably, even though one is a traditionally female occupation and commands lower pay by market rates.

64. *Id.* at 1062–63.

65. *Id.* at 1063–65.

66. Robert J. Lifton, THE NAZI DOCTORS: MEDICAL KILLING AND THE PSY-CHOLOGY OF GENOCIDE (1988).

67. *See* George J. Annas, THE NAZI DOCTORS AND THE NUREMBERG CODE: HUMAN RIGHTS IN HUMAN EXPERIMENTATION (1992).

68. Cited in full, *supra*.

69. 329 U.S. 497 (1947).

70. Arthur Miller first pointed out this connection to me.

71. Hickman v. Taylor, 329 U.S. at 509.

72. Text *supra* (liberal legalisms simultaneously advance and retard the search for social justice).

9

The Problem with Lawyers

I looked up from signing the flyleaf of my book for a gray-haired gent ("Just make it out to Ezra, please"), when a familiar, smiling youth reached out to shake my hand.

"Rodrigo! What on earth are you doing here?" I exclaimed.

"Giannina and I are in town for a Women's Law Caucus meeting. She's representing her school, while I'm tagging along. We saw a notice about your book tour and decided to try to track you down."

"I'm glad you did. What a wonderful surprise!"

"New book, I see," Rodrigo said, craning his head sideways.

"I asked the publisher to send you a copy. I hope you like it. You're in it, actually."

"Oh?" Rodrigo said quizzically. "I think you're in Giannina's new play, too, although she hasn't let me see it yet. Any chance you could join us for a bite later?"

"I'd love to. Business is slowing down here. I signed a couple dozen books this morning, but only one or two the last hour. When is Giannina free?"

"In about twenty minutes. We agreed to meet here. But there's a little restaurant practically next door that someone told us about. We could go there later, if you like."

"Sounds good to me," I said, looking around to catch the store owner's eye. "What if we wait for her in the meeting room over there. It's not busy right now."

Seconds later, we were seated at the long table, littered with current newspapers and magazines, where I had read from my book earlier that day. "She can see us in here," I said, indicating that the store's entrance was in full view. "So, what's new with the two of you?"

"I'll let her tell you what's new on her end. I just got another assignment." Rodrigo pulled a small pile of papers and reports, with yellow slips of paper sticking out, out of his briefcase and laid them on the table in front of us. "If I hadn't met you, I was going to work on these while waiting for Giannina."

"What's all that about?" I asked, glancing at some of the titles on the table.

"The dean put me on the curriculum committee. Laz is the chair. She asked us to decide what, if anything, the law school should do in response to these reports." Rodrigo held up one of the volumes. "Are you familiar with this one, Professor? I think it came out just as you were leaving the country."

I half-stood, peered at the thick paperback volume in Rodrigo's hand, and said, "The McCrate Report.[1] They issued it in draft form just as I was packing up. It caused quite a stir. As I recall, it argued that legal education should be more practical. A number of my colleagues applauded it. Others damned it, because they thought it threatened innovative scholarship and teaching."

"And had you seen this other one?" Rodrigo asked.

I leaned forward again. "Oh, Judge Harry Edwards's article.[2] He sent me a reprint, which got forwarded. Boy, has he changed. Did you know that we knew each other?"

"No. But it stands to reason," Rodrigo replied. "You're of the same generation. So you know he leveled quite a blast at law review scholarship, charging that a high proportion of it has little to do with law and judging."

"I don't know what got into him. He was quite a scholar before he went on the bench. Maybe I'll write him sometime. What's that other one?"

"It's the Paul Carrington article.[3] We discussed it one time before. It accuses critical legal studies scholars—and, by implication, critical race theorists and radical feminists—of nihilism."

"I remember. He said their message was cynical, counteraspirational, and went against the central ethos of the law. People who write that way should either move over to other departments or leave the academy entirely. And so your dean asked you to look at all three?"

"She did. We're supposed to report on the implications they harbor for the way we teach and write. Her memo came accompanied by a number of news clippings about public discontent with law and lawyers."

"Some of that was building when I left. The major newsmagazines have been covering it, even in their international editions, which are the ones we get down there. But it's not just the public who are discontent. Lawyers are disenchanted with law practice, as well. Some are leaving for other lines of work."

"She asked us to look into all that. Giannina is really interested and has opinions of her own."

"Speaking of Giannina, how's her first year of law school going? I hope she hasn't given up her writing."

"By no means. She did well in her midterms. But she says the first year is so weird she writes for relief. She's finished most of a play that she refuses to let me see. I think it's about law school, and I'm sure we're both characters in it."

"Uh-oh," I said. "Reminds me of the time my younger daughter wrote a crime mystery for a high school English class. It was so realistic the teacher called home. My late wife and I had to do a lot of talking to persuade the teacher we weren't running some sort of crime ring out of our home!"

Rodrigo laughed.

"But tell me your thoughts on these three critiques. I assume you have a theory?"

"I do. But would you like a cup of coffee? I saw an espresso maker over there."

I caught the store owner's eye to ask whether it was okay. He nodded yes, so we busied ourselves with the ingredients and chrome custom maker.

"Just like the old days," I said.

In Which Rodrigo and the Professor Review Law's Laments

As we mixed the condiments into our coffee, Rodrigo began: "You asked if I had a theory, Professor. As you know, the two dominant currents in legal education today are, first, the McCrate–Harry Edwards critique of legal education and scholarship as not practical enough, and, second, deep discontent with law and lawyers, both on the part of the public and of lawyers themselves. My thesis is that these two are related, although not at all in the way most people might think. And the connecting link is legal formalism."[4]

"Legal formalism?" I said. "You mean teaching and scholarship that emphasize cases and rules over policy, interdisciplinary approaches, and critique? The Langdellian idea that law is a science with only one right answer? Rigorous, hard-nosed Socratic teaching?"

Rodrigo nodded animatedly, whether in response to my answer or his own double-size mugful of coffee, I could not tell. In any event, I went on: "So are you saying that we need more formalistic classroom teaching and boring, doctrinal scholarship? I certainly hope not."

"Quite the contrary, Professor. Formalism and extreme preoccupation with doctrine are what's causing all the trouble."

"That's a relief," I replied. "But I hope you can spell out the link in convincing fashion, for you are definitely swimming against the tide. In fact, you are saying the opposite of what the ABA report and my old friend Harry Edwards are."

"I'll be happy to," Rodrigo replied. "But first consider what the public is saying about us lawyers, and also the complaints lawyers themselves are raising over the way law is practiced."

"I'm all ears," I said. "I haven't practiced in quite a while, as you know. But I have always done a little consulting, mostly in school desegregation cases. So I'm vitally interested in the profession's fortunes and image."

In Which Rodrigo and the Professor Analyze the Public's Disenchantment with Law and Lawyers

"Let's take the public's attitudes toward lawyers first," Rodrigo began. "If you'll just give me a minute—" Rodrigo rustled through some papers. "Oh, here we are. These news clippings turned out to be only the tip of the iceberg. I bet you've seen this one."

I peered at what he was holding up for my benefit. "*Time*'s international edition featured something like it just last month. Yes, come to think of it, the picture is the same. It's the ABA president, saying that the profession isn't as bad as it's made out to be."

"The public doesn't trust us. It sees us as ambulance chasers feasting off the misfortunes of others, more interested in money than justice, prolonging suits in order to drive up our fees. A poll—if I can just find it . . . oh, here it is. A Gallup poll rated lawyers below druggists, clergy, doctors, dentists, and college teachers for honesty and ethical standards. We ended up toward the bottom, not much above professional admen and used-car salespersons. In another survey of confidence in institutions, law firms rated dead last, behind every branch of government, the military, major companies, Wall Street, the press, colleges and universities, the medical profession, and TV news. Only 3 percent of the public said they trusted lawyers the most. Fifty-six percent said lawyers tend to recommend more legal work than is necessary because it increases their fees, 73 percent that there are too many of them, and that the excess number causes disputes to be taken to court when they shouldn't be."[5]

"Sounds dismal," I said. "But you can prove almost anything with statistics. Studies have shown that the way a pollster frames a question shapes the answer. Maybe the public associates lawyers with trouble—with divorces, drunk-driving tickets, and other hassles. Maybe it's a case of shooting the messenger."

"I wish that were all," Rodrigo replied. "But other surveys showed that the public views lawyers as of uneven character and quality, mercenary, deficient in compassion, caring, ethics, and honesty, and engaged in undignified advertising.[6] Lawyer-bashing jokes are legion."

I winced. "I know. I'm a law professor, but when I'm in the United States a certain type of person makes it their business to let me know at parties what they think of lawyers, as though I were some sort of media-hungry, ambulance-chasing personal-injury shark."

"The same happens to me. I tell them I'm an Italian lawyer, which I am. That usually shuts them up, because they have no idea whether their stock criticisms hold true elsewhere. Oh, look here. Here's one on parents. Professor, would you want your new grandchild to be a lawyer someday?"

"I'd be honored," I said.

"Most parents wouldn't. This poll [Rodrigo held up another printout] shows that when parents were asked which of eight professions they would encourage their son or daughter to go into, only 5 percent said law. Ten years ago, the figure was twelve. Among the top five lawyers people today said they admire most, one is fictional and two are dead."[7]

"I love fictional lawyers," I quipped. "Some of my best friends—"

Rodrigo rolled his eyes. "The dead lawyer is Thurgood Marshall. The fictional ones are Perry Mason and Matlock.[8] Miller Brewing Company aired a commercial featuring a 'Big Lawyer Roundup,' in which cowboys are shown lassoing a hotshot divorce and an overweight tax lawyer.[9] Oh, here are some other polls. On these we rank only slightly ahead of prostitutes, politicians,[10] and used-car salesmen in honesty and integrity.[11] Three-fourths said that the large number of attorneys is hindering the country's economy."[12]

"A stunning indictment," I replied. "Especially when you hear it all at once. We obviously have some work to do." I pointed toward the other folder, which lay on the table in front of Rodrigo. "But I think you mentioned another side to the story."

In Which Rodrigo and the Professor Discuss Lawyers' Own Discontents

"Not so much that as another count to the indictment, I'm afraid," Rodrigo continued. "Not only is the public fed up with law and lawyers, our colleagues are as well."

"Everyone pines for the good old days," I interjected. "Except for women and minorities of color. My law school class boasted only four women and three students of color in addition to myself. Even outstanding graduates like Sandra Day O'Connor and my friend Santos Keller had trouble getting jobs. Surely, you are not going to maintain that conditions for today's lawyers are worse?"

"I'll let you decide," Rodrigo said, opening a second folder. "Here's a study of lawyer satisfaction. Nearly 40,000 lawyers a year are leaving the profession, almost as many as are entering it. A Maryland State Bar Association survey showed that more than one-third were unsure they would continue practicing law. *Time* cited a major increase in working hours and greater stress as eroding quality of life for attorneys.[13] Firms today often require that lawyers perform two thousand to twenty-five hundred hours of billable work—"[14]

"Which, as we both know, means many more hours than that on the job," I interjected.

"Of course. One can't bill for time spent eating, talking with colleagues, or going to the washroom. That figure, by the way, is almost one-third greater than it was a decade ago. Many attorneys routinely put in twelve-hour days."[15]

"The strain has gotten to the point that books are now warning students away from law school," I added. "While browsing at a bookstore in the airport I noticed one entitled, *Full Disclosure: Do You Really Want to Be a Lawyer?*[16] It stood next to another entitled *Running from the Law: Why Good Lawyers Are Getting Out of the Legal Profession.*[17] Both warned that law practice is becoming all-consuming, lawyers have no family life, and that law is repetitive and dull. Older lawyers say the profession is not as enjoyable as it once was. It leaves little time for leisure or contemplation. They said it is a business today, not a learned profession.[18] I went back for my law school class's forty-year reunion the other day. All my friends were saying the same thing. Some were retiring or even going into other lines of work."

"A whole new industry counsels lawyers who are unhappy with their situation," Rodrigo interjected. "They see lawyers who are unhappy at work and complain that they feel like hamsters in a cage. Some are depressed or even suicidal.[19] Some good students don't even try for law jobs."

"I bet you have something on that right there," I said, indicating a pile of neatly clipped computer printouts nestled in Rodrigo's folder.

"Indeed," Rodrigo said. "One ABA study showed"—Rodrigo looked down—"quote: 'a deterioration in the lawyer workplace that will likely continue until law firms and other employers begin to address the management practices that are causing the problem.'[20] Lawyer dissatisfaction is increasing; more attorneys describe themselves as seriously discontent than did in 1984."

"I have the impression this is even more true of women," I added.

"It is," Rodrigo said. "And it's on the rise for partners and senior associates as well as for sole practitioners and very young attorneys. Lawyers say the work atmosphere is not warm or personal; that they have difficulty advancing; that the work is monotonous and pressured. Many describe themselves as burned out or overstressed. An ABA survey found that more than half of second-year associates in big firms were dissatisfied.[21] Even the big paycheck can't compensate for the long hours and tedious detail. According to one analyst, 'Many of the smartest college students don't know exactly what they want to do, so they turn to one of modern society's last refuges for the generalist—law school.'[22] Those who do well win summer clerkships, then first-year associateships making one hundred thousand dollars a year or more. But then they learn how solitary law practice is, with so many hours passed in the library. Little time is spent with clients, or in learning to be a wise counselor. One adviser says: 'There's an incredible amount of dissatisfaction out there. They'd come in and shut the door and literally start crying. So many wanted to leave, too, but felt they couldn't. There's a conspiracy of silence among people who doubt that the law is for them.'"[23]

"Graduates of mine have told me they love the law and their jobs," I added—"right up until the day they quit. One writes me regularly about life on her strawberry farm. One of my top students, she had been in line to become partner at one of the most prestigious law firms in Washington, D.C."

"Here's another one," Rodrigo said. "A recent survey of lawyers in New Jersey showed that 23 percent are certain they will leave law practice before they retire. The same percentage of North Carolina lawyers said that if they had to do it all over again they would not become lawyers. A report by the Young Lawyers Division, entitled 'At the Breaking Point,' found that lawyers in their early years perceive law practice as almost unbearably intense. Associates juggle several projects at the same time, working nine to twelve hours a day in the office and still taking work home."[24]

"Many lawyers prop themselves up with drugs or alcohol," I added.[25]

"Many divorce. Some marriage counselors and psychiatrists have practices devoted exclusively to unhappy attorneys.[26] One laid the blame on changes in the structure of law and law practice. Forty or fifty years ago, some who entered law were motivated by money. But more were attracted by the intellectual challenge and opportunity to help people and society. Back then, law practice allowed you actually to fulfill those aspirations. Today, it does not. Law and legal education take broad-based humanists and generalists. They turn them into narrow, driven specialists."[27]

"Did you find anything on specialization? Law today is much more specialized than it was when I was starting out."

"I did. A number of the reports mentioned how unsatisfying it is for many young associates to work only on one piece of a project, over and over again—say, document retrieval or analysis of damages. They complain that they never see clients or even the attorneys who are working on the other parts of the case."[28]

"I've read of a felt decline in civility," I said. "Some articles complain of hate speech directed by lawyers or judges against other lawyers.[29] Others report dirty tricks and cutthroat tactics, things that old-time practitioners never would have tolerated."[30]

Rodrigo was silent for a moment. Then: "It just occurred to me that the two critiques may be connected. If lawyers believe the public hates and distrusts them, their job satisfaction will obviously suffer. Almost nine of every ten attorneys do believe the image of the profession has been deteriorating. The O.J. Simpson so-called disgrace didn't help, according to one study.[31] A legal magazine asked attorneys, 'Is the public becoming more antilawyer?' Eighty-six percent answered yes. Only 12.1 percent said no.[32] And just the other day, a justice of the U.S. Supreme Court lamented 'legal capitalism'—the excessive influence of the profit motive in the practice of law."[33]

"Ironic!" I exclaimed. "The Court has been a bastion and protector of corporations and capitalism."

"Scholars such as Mary Ann Glendon report the same thing—that law is overcommercialized.[34] Oh, here's another poll. Seventy percent of California lawyers would choose another line of work; three-quarters would not want their children to be lawyers.[35] Sol Linowitz says that today's lawyers and law firms no longer think of law as a helping profession. They are hired guns for whom winning is everything. Work leaves little quiet time or opportunity for creativity. No one reads for pleasure any more."[36]

Just then a knock at the door caused us to start. "Giannina!" Rodrigo exclaimed. "We didn't see you. Come in."

I leapt to my feet. "I'm so glad to see you." The slim, dark-haired young woman set down her backpack and gave me, then Rodrigo, quick hugs. "I'm starved. My panel went almost a half-hour long. Have you two been entertaining each other?" Giannina looked down at the mess of papers on Rodrigo's desk. "Law's troubles again? How was your flight?"

"Fine. I got in just yesterday. Saw my other daughter and her fiancé, and this is my third bookstore. Now I want to get caught up on the two of you."

"No babies yet on our side," Giannina said with a laugh. "How's your grandchild?"

"Fine. My daughter, too. I'll have to introduce all of you sometime. But for now, can I take you two out to dinner? Talking makes me hungry. And your friend here seems able to eat any time." I looked over at Rodrigo, who nodded vigorously. "Maybe we can find a quiet place," I said. "Rodrigo has been regaling me with tales of despair. But he promised to tell me his theory of why the profession has been in such a tailspin. Earlier, he mentioned a paradoxical equation. Have you heard it?"

Giannina said, "I don't think so. But Rodrigo is never at a loss for theories. He and Laz have been slaving away on this committee. Although I must say, the first year is a peculiar enough experience that it practically begs for reform. I can't believe the Socratic method. Professors seem to believe that not telling you something is more educational than telling you. And the way lawyers write—it's deplorable."

A published poet and playwright, Giannina wrinkled her nose in disgust. "I just got through Moot Court," she said. "The idea seems to be that when writing a brief, the flatter and more boring, the better. My writing instructor is actually not too bad. She knows how to put words on paper pretty decently and sometimes lets me get away with a metaphor or simile. But the structure of a brief—I can't believe it. It goes against all the rules of good writing. I thought of using a flashback technique in my reply brief. My instructor told me to get rid of it, for no good reason other than it just isn't done."

I gave her a sympathetic look and added, "I know. Hang in there. Will a bit of dinner help?"

**In Which the Professor and Giannina Hear
Rodrigo's Thesis About Law's Discontents
and Attempt to Find an Explanation for
Women's and Minorities' Disenchantment
with Law and Law School**

A few minutes later we were seated in the quiet Japanese restaurant that Giannina's friends had recommended. The waiter took our orders, vegetarian tempura for Giannina, some sort of fish stew for my omnivorous friend Rodrigo, and udon noodles ("It doesn't have MSG, I hope?") for me. The waiter filled our teacups and departed.

"Now, Rodrigo," I said. "Why do you think that doctrinalism is responsible for law's woes? It's really quite counterintuitive. I love policy analysis and critical thought, as you know. But it seems to me that turning out technically well-trained lawyers is a law school's central mission. If lawyers knew their craft and made fewer mistakes, maybe the public and judges would like us more."

"We all have to know our craft," Rodrigo agreed. "The question is what that craft is. Carrington, McCrate, and Harry Edwards speak as though critical theory and interdisciplinary scholarship are not part of it. In that respect, they are completely wrong—one hundred percent off. It's the ignoring of all these Realist-based approaches and the obsession with doctrine and law-as-science that is responsible for our predicament."[37]

"I don't mind doctrine," Giannina said quietly. "But I've noticed that most of the professors, including even some of the young ones, cut off discussion when it wanders too far afield, begins to get into politics or feelings. Even though the classes are plenty challenging, a sameness is beginning to set in. How does this case square with that? Can this doctrine and that be reconciled? What difference in the court's result would it have made if the plaintiff were blind, left-handed, or a child? All my fellow students are beginning to comment on this. So, I'm curious why you think a steady diet of this is bad for you."

"Me, too," I chimed in.

Rodrigo took a deep draft of his tea. "Laz and I were talking about this the other day.[38] In fact, it's his idea that something is wrong with doctrinalism. But it's because he loves law and economics and thinks the curriculum slights his favorite approach. All the public-law courses, he said, teach about the majesty of *Brown v. Board of Education, Marbury v. Madison*,[39] and all the other big liberal cases, over and over, with very little about judicial restraint and other notions dear to conservatives. We're buddies, even though he's the sponsor of the local Federalist Society, as I may have mentioned."

"And yet you're best friends," I marvelled. "For a conservative, he seems genuinely to like minorities."

"His family grew up poor. Anyway, we had a good long talk, after which I did some more thinking. I think formalism—the sort of thing Judge Edwards and Paul Carrington admire and the McCrate Report champions—is responsible for law's laments in a number of ways."

"We'd love to hear them," Giannina and I broke in simultaneously.

Rodrigo's First Connection: The Mechanical Quality of Doctrinalism and Scientific Jurisprudence as Responsible for Law's Discontents

"I realize this is paradoxical," Rodrigo began. "But I believe that legal formalism—the kind of law teaching and scholarship that all three of our authorities hold up as the ideal—makes matters worse, not better."

"That certainly *is* paradoxical," I agreed. "Everyone thinks the opposite. This had better be good."

"You can decide for yourselves," Rodrigo replied levelly. "It's like prescribing that someone go stand in the rain to get rid of a cold. The exaggerated focus on doctrine and case law contributes to law's low estate in at least five separate ways."

"Your discussions always seem to break down into four or five parts," Giannina interjected with a wry smile. "You're like one of my professors. Everything is either a three- or a four-part test."

"Sounds like a doctrinalist," Rodrigo replied with a smile. We all paused as the waiter set our plates down before us. "This looks good," Rodrigo said, dipping a fried shrimp in a sort of yellowish sauce. "A five-course meal to go with a five-part analysis. My favorite evening."

"Mine, too," I said, patting my stomach a little ruefully. "And how do McCrate, Harry Edwards, and Carrington prescribe exactly the wrong cure?"

"The first way those three giants—who, incidentally, are quite correct about the problem—err is by overlooking the mechanical quality of law-as-doctrinalism."

"It can make for a dull classroom," Giannina chimed in. "Several of mine are that way. The professor never gets to the big issues, the ones the students are dying to discuss. But how does that cause the laments we were discussing earlier?"

"It's not responsible for all of them," Rodrigo replied. "For that, we need the other critiques I'll share with you in a minute. But mechanical jurisprudence goes hand in hand with emotional insensitivity and under-development. It's the famous hired-gun mentality that the public accuses us of, in which a lawyer seems to most people equally prepared to take either side of a case, with no personal attachment or conviction."

"I don't agree," I said. "In criminal law, for example, our system holds that every defendant is entitled to a lawyer. If lawyers decided on which side justice lay and refused to take the other, half the cases would have no lawyer."

"It's not a case of black and white," Rodrigo conceded. "Rather, a subtle quality of mind sets in. Lawyers come to resemble mere craftsmen, going through the paces, citing cases and precedent, highlighting the worst-case scenario, and so on, when the client's life or property may be on the line. Good lawyering is more an art than a science. Under the apprenticeship system that prevailed until not so long ago, lawyers learned to use intuition and creativity to solve problems, more than they do in today's Socratic classroom. Even Paul Carrington acknowledges that technocratic learning can 'dehumanize' and that law professors need to teach the 'effective use of intuition going beyond technical knowledge'[40] and precedent if their students are to do justice. The apprenticeship system, which included hands-on learning in a practical setting, was a much better way to teach imaginative lawyering."

"Clinical classes might offer that," Giannina interjected. "I'm really looking forward to taking some of those next year. Unfortunately, our school is thinking of closing one of its three clinics. The immigration clinic just lost its funding due to federal cutbacks."

"Bad news," Rodrigo commiserated. "Because clinical classes *do* help. But they must offer theory, too. Otherwise they can easily become mere cookie-cutter exercises in which an experienced practitioner drills a student in the practitioner's favorite way of doing things—as bad as formalism, if not worse. Both teach instrumental reasoning: If you want to get from A to B, use C or D. Cite the right holding. Bring your case under a certain rule. The means by which an attorney can achieve an end for his or her client should be independently morally justifiable. Yet the ends should be, as well. As Sol Linowitz says, we are a profession that can no longer say no to the desires of a client.[41] The action may be technically legal, but it may be an abominable thing to do to the other side. The mechanical approach says, go ahead and do it."

"I'm not sure I'd go that far," I said. "It seems to me a lawyer needs to know technique just as much as he or she needs to have a firm grasp of values. If you have the right values but don't know the precedents or statutes, your advocacy is going to suffer. I think your critique needs more than that, Rodrigo, to convince me, at least."

"There *is* more," Rodrigo replied. "Mechanical jurisprudence goes hand in hand with some unlovely traits, including hyperaggressiveness and extreme obsession with production—billable hours and rainmaking over all. Law schools' focus on borderline cases—which, of course, are the only ones in the casebooks—fosters a litigator's mentality. Lawyers learn to love to fight, in part because the cases on which they cut their teeth are ones in which someone staged a full-scale battle with someone else. The curriculum neglects planning, negotiation, prevention of the mess in the first place. We don't train law students to be wise counselors and conciliators but rather killers. The focus on appellate cases is one reason why."

Rodrigo was quiet for a moment. I took a bite of my noodles, swallowed, then said: "You said something about obsession with production."

"Oh, that's right," Rodrigo said, offering Giannina, then me, a morsel of his own steaming dish. After depositing small portions neatly on our plates with his chopsticks, he continued. "If citing cases and filing papers is all there is in life, then the only thing that separates you from the next lawyer is doing more of it. With case law, you go round and round in little circles like a hamster on a treadmill."

"Witness the rise of the Rambo-lawyer," I added with a shudder. "The lawyer who places winning above all. Older lawyers say that there weren't that many of them just fifteen years ago. Maybe the return to case law and doctrine has something to do with it."

"I suspect it does," Rodrigo agreed. "But the means of production, the conditions of making a livelihood, also have taken a turn for the worse, so that even more humane teaching couldn't solve all of our problems. Doctrinalism is a discourse of power, of mastery. Like positivist thought in early social science, it serves the rise of specialization and profit in our capitalist society. The rise of the megafirm, the introduction of departments within firms, and the decline of the generalist all are aspects of the same thing. If doctrinalism is a cause of all this, it is also a symptom of something broader."

"With *that* I think I agree," I said. Giannina, too, nodded vigorously, then added, "Formalism is a discourse of mastery. The case method and Socratic teaching foster arrogance, rather than humility, rewarding the confident, snap answer rather than the thoughtful, modest response. I see it in my classroom every day.[42] The competitive individualism that these traditional methods foster carries over into daily life. All my classmates notice they have become more argumentative. Three couples are divorcing in my first-year class alone, and the year isn't yet half-finished. It stands to reason that the habits of mind the traditional classroom inculcates could carry over into practice and replicate overzealous, uncollegial advocacy and relations inside the bar."

"Older practitioners complain that civility is declining and that lawyers treat each other with less respect, both in and out of the courtroom," I went on. "The educational goal may be to develop effective advocates, but doctrinalism offers no stopping points, no built-in checks. Confrontationalism and rabid advocacy increase at the expense of interpersonal decency, communicative skills, empathy, and justice. Negotiation, counseling, problem solving, compromise are fast becoming lost arts. In my day, many professors emphasized these things. Today, I get the impression few do."

"Maybe that's part of the reason why women are unhappy with the law and the legal classroom," Giannina said. "I was just reading professor Guinier's study.[43] It mirrors some of the complaints I've read about from young women in the bar. If so, things won't change until we learn to teach differently.

"Agreed," Rodrigo said. "And on the scholarly side it would counsel that we shy away from the Carrington–Harry Edwards critique of impractical scholarship. And this concludes my first point. Should we order dessert? I think I can go through my other points a little more quickly."

I looked at my watch. "I'm due at my daughter's at ten. So I've got some time, if you two do."

Giannina nodded and summoned the waiter, who materialized quickly, dessert menus in hand. We ordered—candied yams for my rail-thin friend, mango sherbet for Giannina and me. After the waiter departed, Rodrigo resumed as follows:

Rodrigo's Second Connection: Extreme Doctrinalism Dehumanizes Clients and Legal Problems (the Anarchy-and-Elegance Critique)

"The second connection is related to the first. Legal formalism fosters dissatisfaction with the legal profession, among both the public and lawyers, because it mistakenly tries to make law a science. This it can never be. For law deals with people and the myriad fact situations in which they find themselves, not the orderly and relatively predictable phenomena of, say, chemistry or physics. The attempt to map scientific epistemology onto a humanistic subject matter naturally produces frustration. People are not like molecules, solar systems, or microbes; their behavior is not like that of liquid in a tube or objects on an inclined plane. Chris Goodrich, who spent a year at Yale Law School in a program for journalists and writers, wrote about how law, with its elegant structures of rules and principles, struggles to come to terms with an unruly world.[44] He marveled at how well it did so. But I think if he had stuck around for another year or two, or better yet visited a busy city court, he would have been more cautious in his praise. Formalism tries to make law a science, reducing human factors and fact patterns into preexisting forms, called precedent, minimizing the role of judgment, experience, politics, love, compassion, discretion, and what our friend Duncan Kennedy calls 'intersubjective zap.'[45] Critical legal studies tells us that these other things are all there is—something that I don't agree with—but even the more modified scientism of legal process and Paul Carrington manifestly give less scope than CLS and Derrick Bell do to politics, history, compassion, instinct, and all the rest."

"That's certainly true," Giannina replied. "I've been reading Duncan Kennedy in my reading group."

"Didn't you meet him last year?" Rodrigo asked.

"No, I was out of town when he spoke. You told me he was amazing."

"He was. Judges, however, being busy bureaucrats with large caseloads, do not much like that role or those other forms of scholarship, much preferring to think of themselves as technicians whose hands are tied when they send prisoners to jail, deny welfare rights to the poor, reduce recovery for consumers injured by dangerous products, and so on. The public also feels that something is wrong when a person finds his or her own lawyer taking the other side and spelling out the worst-case scenario. They want a friend, but they get a laboratory technician. 'Mr. Jones, I'm sorry, but your test shows you have cancer. Please make an appointment next week with the doctor.'"

"Hmmm," said Giannina. "Now that I think of it, dissatisfaction with law as currently practiced and taught may be part of a more general movement, visible in many disciplines, away from rigid, pseudoscientific approaches and toward 'softer,' more modest, interdisciplinary ones. This new emphasis came on the heels of widespread criticism, mainly from philosophers and critical social scientists, some in Europe, of positivist epistemologies and their false embrace of objectivism. In the old, discredited paths, social scientists would try to see human behavior as subject to unvarying rules, independent of social context. These *dominant discourses*, as they came to be called, ultimately failed because they ignored subjectivity, perspective, and positionality. They simply could not deal adequately with the heterogeneity of social life and the situated, contingent nature of knowledge."[46]

"Well put. But I assume you mean human knowledge, not physics and mathematics," I said, resolving to push Rodrigo and her as long as possible.

"But even knowledge in the hard sciences is constructed and has an element of convention," Rodrigo said. "There is a real world, of course. But the way we choose to describe it is contingent and subject to differing constructions at different times."

"Granted," Giannina broke in. "But I'm still not sure whether all this has anything to do with the public's dissatisfaction with law and lawyers. Science clings tenaciously to past paradigms, embraces objectivism, and yet the public has a generally high regard for scientists. Why is this a special problem for lawyers?"

"Aside from the habits of mind it creates, it predisposes you not to put the human dimensions of the client's problem first. You end up talking about funny things like the 'material elements' of a cause of action. You slice the client's problem up into little pieces, so that they end up hardly recognizing it. Good lawyering requires engagement, judgment, and knowledge of human beings and their motives. It requires the ability to see the world as it really is, in shades of gray, acting fearlessly in situations of factual uncertainty and even moral ambiguity."

"I know what you're going to say," Giannina said, excitement in her voice. "Good lawyering requires great literature; psychology; social science; even religion. All these may be better models for what lawyers do—good ones, anyway—than science." I recalled that during her pre–law school life Giannina had been a successful poet and playwright, publishing a number of volumes and even winning a prize or two.

"So," Giannina went on, "you think that the illness in lawyers' souls comes from *denial*—the failure to deal straightforwardly with a complex reality."

"Yes," Rodrigo said. "Formalism leaves you with no moral anchor. You go out into the world, confront its anarchy, and quickly become cynical. Doctors deal with sick people; lawyers, sometimes anyway, with bad ones. But formalism looks the other way, concealing all this. It's as though doctors were trained only in science, not in how to take care of sick people."

"I had a doctor like that once," Giannina shuddered. "He was a terrific technician but had a horrible bedside manner. I quickly changed to another."

"Would you folks like some coffee?" asked the waiter, who had materialized at the side of our table. "We have cappuccino, decaf, and herbal teas."

"Decaf for me," I said.

"Make mine the real thing," said my high-energy young friend.

"I'll pass," said Giannina. Then after the waiter left: "Although you can't do that in a Socratic classroom."

"It's a different discourse," said Rodrigo with a wink. "In restaurants, no one pretends that every diner is the same. One that did would quickly go out of business. But Socratic professors make that very mistake. If you teach law exclusively by the appellate case method and do not make the human aspects of lawyering explicit, your students end up with a highly parochial view of their profession. Law becomes a narrow exercise, reduced to a mechanistic set of principles. But law is a social institution. The crits who are calling attention to law's contingency and political underpinnings may be speaking for widespread discontent in the legal community. Far from teaching cynicism or neglect of craft, the new critical scholars may be in tune with the public and its needs. In that sense, Carrington, McCrate, and Harry Edwards put their fingers on what's wrong. But they err in their prescription, urging instead what will only make matters worse."

"Like that brilliant doctor I had once," Giannina said. "He prescribed a regimen that should have worked but ignored that my body was different from that of the usual person, and his prescription was not working. I changed doctors fast. Oh, here's your coffee. Actually, it looks good."

"Will you have some, Miss?" the waiter asked. "We do have decaf."

"Okay. I'll have a decaf latte, if you have it."

"We can make it," the waiter said and departed.

"He's like a good lawyer," we all three said at once. "He didn't stick to the menu," said Giannina.

Rodrigo's Third Connection: Formalism and Doctrinal Pedagogy Deflect Us from Things That Matter

After the waiter walked away, Rodrigo continued as follows: "Giannina, do you remember how you said that formalism is a type of massive denial? [Giannina nodded yes]. "Well, my third critique builds on that. I think formalism, whether in legal scholarship, teaching, or anywhere else in the law, is bad for its practitioners' souls. It deforms their ethics, inhibits their political options, and predisposes them to develop the bad characters that some of the public accuse us of having."

"Oh, dear," Giannina sighed. "I knew I should have stayed with writing. I made less than three thousand dollars a year but if you're right, I at least was able to preserve my immortal soul."

Rodrigo shot her a defensive look. "I expect this to be the most controversial part of my thesis. Nobody likes being told that their soul is in danger."

"Get on with it," I said. "Don't worry about our feelings. The public already thinks we're a bunch of unscrupulous sharks. If you think you can draw a connection between their low opinion and the way we think and write about law, come right out and say so. It can't hurt and might do some good."

"Let's take the least controversial part first," Rodrigo said, stirring sugar into his cup. "Formalism is a deflection. It points you neatly away from the things that matter. And this is bad for your soul and, in the long run, your reputation."

"By deflection, I assume you mean from politics," Giannina ventured. "I've been reading *The Politics of Law* in my reading group. So if that's your point, it's not exactly new."

Rodrigo shot her a quick look. "I think the crits are right, but I had something a little different in mind. Have you gotten to *Erie v. Tompkins*[47] in civil procedure yet?

"We're starting it next week. I've read it once already, though. I often skip around in the casebook if I find something interesting."

"Then you know *Erie* is about the distribution of judicial power between the federal and state judiciaries. Many consider it one of the handful of most important cases in American law—the fulcrum that separates the state judiciary from the federal version, that allocates power as between the two branches of government. It's said to be the cornerstone of our federalist system.[48] Practically a mystique surrounds it."[49]

"My goodness," Giannina exclaimed. "At first glance it just looked like an interesting case about somebody who happened to be walking along a railroad."

"For many, it's much more than that," Rodrigo elaborated. "It tells when a state versus a federal judge has the right to proclaim the law. In diversity-of-citizenship cases, it says that federal courts must look to state substantive law rules but may apply their own procedure. In federal-question cases, more or less the opposite prevails."

"Nice and neat," Giannina commented. "But why is the case considered so important? It just seems to say that an earlier decision, *Swift v. Tyson*,[50] was wrong in its application of the Federal Rules of Decision Act."

"Supposedly it's the cornerstone of federalism, setting up the limits of federal judicial power and carving out a region of state autonomy. It may well even be rightly decided. What I think curious, though, is the slavish devotion to it by a large number of very bright people. There's practically a cult following, going back to Judge Frankfurter and the Harvard School of institutional analysis, which holds that the most important questions have to do with determining which person, authority, or branch of government is the most appropriate decisionmaker for a particular question."

"A kind of latter-day formalism," Giannina chimed in.

"Exactly," Rodrigo replied. "A way of avoiding hard substantive questions. It *is* important to know whether a federal or a state judge has the right to declare the law, for example on tort duties toward trespassers who walk along railroad tracks at night and get hurt. But in another sense, *Erie* is a trivial case. I hope I'm not poisoning your mind."

"Thank you very much, Professor," Giannina said, with a smile. "Now, I'd love to know why you think it isn't such a big deal."

"Well, consider the profile of the typical federal judge. How old? Say, fifty-five. Which color? White. Male. Socially moderate to conservative. Lives in a nice suburban community. Went to a good but probably not great law school. Plays golf on Sundays. Has two or three kids."

"I suppose you're going to say we need to do better than that," Giannina replied.

"Yes, although that's not my point exactly."

"Oh?"

"Well, consider now the profile of the average *state* judge. Fifty-five years old. Also moderate in his social views. White. Male. Went to a good but not great law school. Plays golf on Sundays. My point is that the two sets of judges look pretty much the same. Not exactly the same, of course; the federal judiciary is sometimes more highly trained. But the similarities overwhelm the differences. Yet *Erie* creates a huge fuss over which white, male, moderate Republican, fifty-five-year-old judge gets to pronounce the law. Now, I'm not saying it makes *no* difference who gets to do so; it does. But there are very few female, black, working-class, or gay and lesbian judges. Few with disabilities. Few younger than thirty-five. Few single mothers. Few with working-class roots."[51]

"Now *that* question is one that really matters," I said.

"Yet the *Erie* line of cases neatly blinds us to it, focusing instead on whether Tweedle Dee or Tweedle Dum gets to announce the law. Doctrinalism—worship of the conventionally framed question—blinds us to ones that really matter."

"Now that's a serious critique," I conceded. "But is it limited to a few big cases like *Erie*? If so, the cure for doctrinalism would be simply to warn the students, and ourselves, that the case is not the be all and end all, that many important questions remain even after this one is addressed."

"I think the risk is broader than that," Rodrigo replied. "Vast reaches of law are shot through with contradiction and indeterminacy.[52] A judge deciding a case can invoke different principles and precedents and come to diametrically opposite conclusions. Legal discourse and all the elements of legal culture—legal education, the bar exam, the rituals, robes, and esoteric jargon—all serve to conceal what is really going on—a series of result-oriented replications of the status quo. Why do we put up with this? The myth of law's objectivity and rationality compel our loyalty."

"In short, we are persuaded by law's veneer of fairness to believe it actually serves our interests when it does not," Giannina interjected.

"Our main chains are mental," Rodrigo continued. "Because of the mystifying ideology we are all imbued with, we cannot conceive of a better world, one based on love and cooperation. We are taught that the rule of law in its majesty must be preserved even though it does injustice in our case. The crits' solution is to think and teach, to move methodically from one area of the law to the next showing how doctrine in each area is contingent, mystifying, and calculated to advance the interests of the powerful."[53]

"I think I see where you are going," I interjected, snapping erect. "You are saying that critical legal studies stands liberalism on its head. Liberal legal theory focuses on the difficult, or controverted, case—the *Brown v. Board of Education* or *Erie v. Tomkins*. It devotes a lavish amount of attention to it. Critical legal studies, by contrast, says we must be most on our guard as to matters and issues that seem routine. Ones that seem comfortable and familiar, that have been relegated to 'rules.' The familiarity and comfort these rules give us—their 'naturalness'—mean they are most likely to form part of the ideology by which we submit to illegitimate domination. Doctrine itself is the source of the jeopardy. And it is precisely liberal culture, the legacy of Locke, Hobbes, Hume, and Bentham, that entraps us and makes us complicit in our own oppression."

"Exactly," Rodrigo replied. "The tyranny of the ordinary. The practical scholarship Judge Edwards advocates suffers from the same vice. It greases the wheels; helps judges accomplish more easily and smoothly what they are already doing. But the point of scholarship ought to be to make judging harder, not easier. Even conservative Judge Posner says the best legal scholarship is that which induces 'a ferment of thought, some good and some bad.'[54] The increase in the new modes of scholarship is almost surely symptomatic of the crisis in the profession, rather than any sort of contributing cause. Outsider scholarship and other forms of impractical, or interdisciplinary, writing may be providing the profession with the means for a much needed rehumanization of the law."

We fell silent for a moment, absorbing what Rodrigo had said. Then I said: "To summarize, Rodrigo, you believe that the current counterrevolution is fundamentally misdirected. Edwards and Carrington ignore that in times of change, like now, the familiar is where the greatest danger lies; reform may be the most practical thing. Thus, in periods like ours, outsider and critical scholarship, which seems to have no immediate practical value, may be what society most needs. The call for a return to doctrine is a form of collective denial of the current inadequacies in our form of social organization."

"Many of my most doctrinal classes," Giannina began, "seem to have had the least practical effect. For example, doctrinal approaches to criminal law have done little to reduce the crime rate or help us understand the forces that lead to crime. Judge Edwards's insistence on a return to practical doctrinal scholarship ignores that doctrine itself may be impractical—drifting and poorly calculated to advance its own ends."

"Speaking of ends," Rodrigo interjected tactfully. "It's getting late and the Professor may be tired. Do we need to think of calling it quits soon?"

"I'm going strong," I insisted. "I'd love to hear your two final connections. If it gets too late I'll just call and ask them to leave a key under the mat. This is all very stimulating. Did I tell you I'm speaking at Mexico's national law school next month? They're thinking of reorganizing legal education more along the American line. They may have in mind the case method, Socratic teaching, and the like. If so, I'd like to be able to report the good as well as the bad. So, please, go ahead."

Rodrigo's Fourth Reason: Doctrinalism Dulls the Moral Senses and Injures Minorities and Women

"I'm glad you find this useful. So do I. You're a great sounding board, Professor. Giannina and I are both in your debt. We hope you have a lot of grandchildren and spend as much time up here as possible."

"You two can always come down to see *me*," I pointed out. "Other than that one brief visit, you've not been down to see me in Mexico at all. My art collection has grown considerably since you were last there. I'd love to show you my new pieces."

"And we'd love to see them," said Giannina with alacrity. "And you promised to introduce me to your friends in that writers' colony. Now, what's your theory about formalism's ethical deficiencies?"

"Conventional teaching," Rodrigo began, "relies on appellate cases. It must—that's where the law is. These cases have relatively few facts and a great deal of doctrine and case-shuffling. No party stands before the court—that happened below; no witnesses, police officers, documents, or expert scientist or medical testimony. All of this is presented in a sterile, highly summarized 'record of the case.' The actors are stick figures—'the plaintiff,' 'the appellee,' and so on. The concrete details, the drama of the trial, are missing. There is very little to get excited about, little to engage the imagination or inflame one's sense of justice."

"I think we spoke about something similar once before. We agreed it is only concreteness, not abstraction, that triggers conscience, engages one's sense of moral outrage. It's as though medical students never studied using actual sick patients but only reviewed hospital records of deaths, accidents, medical dosages, erroneous diagnoses, and so on."

"We did," Rodrigo agreed. "I think it was the fourth or fifth time we met. Seen in this light, the Langdellian case method and Socratic teaching breed reductionism and a rather bloodless attitude. For idealistic students with progressive social aspirations, this approach is soul-sapping, leading to fatalistic acceptance of inadequate regimes of law and politics. With less idealistic students, it can breed crooks. Doctrinalism, much more so than its critique, may be responsible for a pessimistic sense in students and young lawyers that the legal system is hopelessly confining, unfair, and will always be that way."

Giannina added, "I see it all the time. My feminist classmates understand that truth is situated, that the struggle over it is a political negotiation—a power play, really—that seeks a broader (or at least different) equalization of legal benefits and protections.[55] This is not nihilistic—Carrington's charge—at all. Rather, we see law as a sort of orchestral power play, fluid and always ongoing. As such, lawyers must be ever vigilant, never resting on their laurels or content to say, 'Well, that's the doctrine.' Each victory signals another battle to come. Good doctrine always slips away. As legal professionals, we have the duty to be constantly skeptical, watchdogs of the oppressed and disadvantaged, catalysts of social change."[56]

"I wish I had more students like you," Rodrigo exclaimed. "Are you sure you and your friends don't want to transfer?"

"I'm very happy where I am," Giannina answered. "But go on. You said that particularity enhances empathy and moral instincts. But you also hinted that an emphasis on doctrine was especially hard on minorities and women. Do you mean as learners, as consumers of the legal system, or what?"

"Both," Rodrigo said. "You mentioned earlier the Guinier study, which found that women were apt to be more turned off than men by the Socratic classroom, by the verbal aggression, showmanship, bluffing, sparring, and demand for performance. But I was also thinking more of minorities and women as consumers."

"Hold on a second," I said. "The greatest civil rights advocate of recent times, Justice Thurgood Marshall, was a stickler for civil procedure.[57] He had little sympathy for civil rights advocates and others who hadn't bothered to learn the rules of procedure and evidence or how to file a motion properly. Don't civil rights attorneys need to know these things even better than the average attorney because their papers and motions will be scrutinized even more searchingly than those of the average corporate lawyer or drafter of wills?"

"Of course lawyers must know their craft," Rodrigo conceded. "But we also must understand how the rules are stacked against us. Consider the demand for neutral principles of civil rights law.[58] Neutrality—the idea that any rule operates the same way in different settings and for different litigants—very much advantages those who currently enjoy a privileged position in society; whites vis-à-vis blacks, for example. This approach sees affirmative action as reverse discrimination: It disadvantages 'innocent' whites who have done nothing wrong for the benefit of blacks who, for all we know, may never have suffered discrimination during their lifetimes.[59] Our system is color-blind.[60] In one grotesque case, the Supreme Court held that women who could not obtain a pregnancy benefit were not discriminated against, because men could not obtain the benefit, either. The law denied insurance benefits to all 'pregnant persons,' male or female."[61]

Giannina rolled her eyes. "Doctrinalism justifies a current action or rule by virtue of an earlier one. Yet that earlier rule, laid down in an age when women and people of color were less significant factors, will likely disadvantage them. Law's rules and narratives incorporate the sense of the ruling group, in most cases elite white males. Doctrinalism simply passes that invisible advantage down to succeeding generations. Practical scholarship ratifies and renders more efficient the operation of class advantage."

"So," continued Rodrigo, "doctrinalism replicates the status quo. In the classroom, it rewards posturing, self-assurance, and a conventional sort of quick-witted cleverness that relies on a few formulaic maneuvers and axioms. In legal scholarship, it greases the wheels of industry. And in real life, it perpetuates past inequalities."

"The objectively reasonable prudent man standard, for example," Giannina posited. "Consider how it silently advantages men and disadvantages women in tort law and a host of other areas. I was reading of a date-rape case on my campus the other day. Two undergraduates had been talking and walking after a campus party. Both had been drinking. Later they had sex, which the woman said was pressured and unconsented to. The man said she led *him* on. The campus committee adopted his story, holding that a reasonable male could interpret her lack of resistance, the way she was dressed, and her willingness to kiss and cuddle as evidence of her readiness to have intercourse. All this she, of course, strenuously denied. In many such cases, the man believes he is merely being commanding, she coy. The woman, however, experiences the whole episode as degrading and pressured. A legal standard predicated on what a reasonable male date would see as consent simply buys into one story—the man's. And it does this under the guise of neutral rules regarding what a reasonable, average person would understand about the situation."

"Formalism always narrows the range of considerations a rule takes into account," I said. "That's its nature. And in a way it has to. The decisionmaker could take into account potentially an infinitude of details. Yet I gather you are not complaining about that, but rather the way legal doctrine submerges the interest of the weaker party?"

"I am," Rodrigo replied. "Nonstandard cases and people, such as minorities, are neatly excluded by the law's cookie-cutter approach. We use nonformal rules when we want to do *real* justice, for example, to corporations. Consider long-arm jurisdiction and the multifaceted minimum-contacts test we employ there.[62] Or recall the large number of defenses antidiscrimination law makes available to defendants—business necessity, lack of intent, no causal connection, and so on."[63]

"Are you saying that predictability and the rule of law are not goods?" I asked, determined to challenge Rodrigo as long as possible.

"Not at all," he replied. "But legal process and formalism do not deliver them. They allow result-oriented decisions that favor the empowered party or his class. Only in that sense is formalism predictable. The right to property, for example, would protect everyone equally if everyone had approximately the same amount of it. But, of course, they don't. So the way things are now, the right to hold property increases inequality, exacerbating the gap between the haves and the have-nots. Similarly, in a society like ours, a neutral rule that says 'race doesn't count' tends to advantage whites. Since they are members of the more advantaged race, the one that controls most of the assets, and the one whose history, traditions, and narratives are reflected in the law, customs, and form of government, the right to be any race—white, brown, or black—will tend to advantage them at the expense of all the others. All this while everyone loudly proclaims, 'Race is not important; we are all equal; we are all the same race: American.'"

"I agree," I said. "Formalism is not much of a friend of minorities. But what about the formalism that most conservatives love most dearly—ethical formalism or, in a word, merit? Can anyone object to using *that* principle—the most neutral of all—as a basis for distributing benefits and goods, like places in a law school class? You and I are teachers, Rodrigo. We see differences among students every day. Some answers in class are better than others. Some bluebooks are better than others. This you cannot deny."

"I don't," Rodrigo said. "But merit is only relative to some set of conditions and objectives. Move the hoop in a basketball game up or down six inches and you radically change the distribution of who has merit. The LSAT, for example, predicts first-year grades, but only because the curriculum is the way it is. It predicts success as a lawyer much less well, because lawyering requires many skills—empathy, communication, perseverance, cooperation—that neither the test nor the first-year curriculum emphasize."

"Your friends Farber and Sherry have written about that,"[64] Giannina said. "One of my professors held their book up in class as a model of doctrinal clarity and scholarly precision. She urged all of us to read it. In it, as you recall, the two Minnesotans point out that when crits trash conventional merit they neglect the impact upon Jews and Asians. Those two groups have climbed the ladder of conventional merit. So when the crits criticize conventional merit, they are being unwittingly anti-Semitic and anti-Asian."

"A perfect standoff," I said. "Conventional merit hurts minorities but helps Jews. They turn things around, just like you like to do, Rodrigo."

"It's not a standoff at all," Rodrigo replied. "The SAT has a thoroughly disreputable history of racism and Aryan supremacy.[65] Except for Paul de Man, critical thought does not. Nor do civil rights activists, crits, and other progressive people have any comparable history of anti-Semitic or anti-Asian sentiment. Quite the opposite—minority soldiers fought to liberate the Jews in Germany and have opposed domestic anti-Semitism throughout our history. The traditional civil rights alliance includes Jews and blacks marching side by side. Only extreme formalism, ignoring history and context, could make Farber and Sherry's two propositions look similar. A huge difference separates attacking implicit racism in standard testing and attacking Jews and Asians. It's like looking at the World Trade Center and a nomad's tent through blinders and pronouncing them the same because both are gray."

"So you are saying that even the very choice of an ethical principle to justify, or attack, affirmative action is itself nonneutral."

"Exactly," Rodrigo replied. "Ethical formalism, a cousin of the legal variety, obscures the power dimension of the choice."

"Earlier, Rodrigo, you mentioned that formalism was bad not only for minorities but also for lawyers at large. You said something about souls. I'd love to hear why. The older I get, the more interest I take in souls," I quipped.

"It is the last piece of the puzzle," Rodrigo agreed. "But," looking at his watch, "it's five minutes to ten. Do you need to call?"

"Oh my goodness!" I exclaimed. "I'd better or I'll be non grata in my own daughter's household."

"That I doubt," said Giannina, indicating the corner of the restaurant where the pay phones were located. After a brief conversation with my daughter ("Don't worry, Dad, we decided to watch *McNeil-Lehrer*. If we're not up, we'll leave a key under the doormat"), I returned to the table, where my two young friends were conversing animatedly.

"No problem. So long as I can keep my eyes open," I said.

"Giannina was saying she hates psychological critiques. She thinks they're unfair to one's adversary. I think it's curious for a playwright not to be interested in motivation. We just agreed that it's okay to dissect habits of mind so long as you do so in general terms, not as applied to particular people."

"A sensible-sounding compromise," I said. "But is it a neutral principle?"

Both my companions smiled, then Rodrigo continued:

Rodrigo's Fifth Connection: Extreme Doctrinalism Promotes Schizophrenia, Dishonesty, and Similar Traits of Mind on the Part of Its Devotees

"Formalism is a case of legal obsessionism, as Pierre Schlag calls it.[66] One devotes hours to small distinctions between this case and that, looking for minute differences, when they count for very little and when society and the legal system are in tatters. Doctrinalism also makes you lie—profess beliefs, for example, in the majesty of the rule of law, in its internal consistency, and in the underlying coherence of contradictory platitudes. It makes you recite things you know are not true—that racism exists only when it is intended; that everyone knows the law; that all are rational-interest calculators and cost-avoiders; and that judges are capable of balancing incommensurable values. All this amounts to a vast sort of schizophrenia, in which one knows things in ordinary life that one is forced to forget when functioning as a lawyer. This allows the ACLU, for example, to assert that vicious hate speech ought to go unregulated and also that it is in the best interest of minorities that this be so.[67] It allows lawyers solemnly to proclaim that our system of criminal law is the best in the world, when more than 90 percent of defendants plead guilty and get no trial whatsoever. Doctrinal fascination, as Schlag calls it [Rodrigo read from a sheet he pulled out from his briefcase] 'breeds a mentality prone to wheedling, coercion, needling, harassment, and other rude, crude practice.'[68] It also promotes grandiosity. Because no one else thinks that way, one is superior to all the rest—a professional."

"Wouldn't teaching legal ethics help?" I asked. "Carrington and McCrate both think so."

"I doubt it," Rodrigo replied. "For the reasons we discussed earlier. It is concreteness, not abstraction, that triggers the moral impulse. And the usual course in professional responsibility merely takes the students through the rules. In a classic experiment, seminarians stopped to help a man lying groaning on the sidewalk at a rate even *lower* than passersby generally.[69] Some had even just heard the parable of the Good Samaritan in class yet walked right on by. By the same token, most students in professional responsibility classes mainly internalize rules—don't do this or you'll be caught and this is what will happen."

"Well, if not classes and teaching, then what?" I asked.

Rodrigo said, "Get the students out into the world. Give them hands-on experience with real clients, with poverty, crime, and neglect. A main use of language is to lie. Law, as one of the most word-based professions, is apt to be the most debased. David Skover and Ronald Collins, in a fine book,[70] show how junk discourse edges out the tempered, rational kind that is the model for the First Amendment. Like bad money driving out good, small-minded, angling, wheedling habits of legal practice drive out the more civilized, temperate kind. Doctrinalism—too much law, too many formulas—is the main, dominant cause of our sad estate."

"Why do judges like Harry Edwards seem so enthralled with it, then?" Giannina asked. "Is it merely professional self-interest, the natural hope to find a law review article on point that will make it easier to write that opinion?"

"That may be part of it," Rodrigo agreed. "But it may also be like that of a schizophrenic who looks for others to share his or her delusion. There may also be an element of narcissism. Judges are like construction workers. They want the physics department to write about *them* and complain that the theoretical physicists in the ivory tower never print anything they can use. In a way, they are correct. Their own work *is* vitally important. They are on the frontlines. If the rivets aren't put in right, the building will fall down. But the physicist may be researching an altogether new principle of building. Judges are in some respects like the riveters, uninterested in what is going on over in the physics department and wishing they would do something for *me*."

"I'm not sure I'd go that far, Rodrigo," I interjected. "I've known many fine judges who are interested in justice and willing to innovate, if necessary, to find it. Maybe it's that legal scholarship speaks to many different audiences, something my friend Harry Edwards hasn't realized yet. Sometimes we write for the courts; at other times for each other, our communities, or the legislature."

"Can I bring you folks something else?" our waiter asked. I looked at my companions and shook my head. "Not for me."

"Could you bring us the bill?" Rodrigo asked.

"Let me take care of it," I asked. "I *am* on tour, and you two have helped bring me up to date. It's hard for an old guy in semiretirement to keep up, spending as I do half my days outside the United States and without a comprehensive law library except the tiny one at the embassy."

"No, it's on us," Rodrigo said quietly but firmly. "You are always an honored guest."

Resolving to let things lie for now but to make a lightning move when the check arrived, I asked Rodrigo (partly in hopes of distracting him): "But Rodrigo, what use is it to know that doctrinalism in the law schools and as a judicial and scholarly philosophy promotes all these ills we spoke of before? Doctrinalism is law on the cheap. It is easy, lazy, bureaucratic. It deflects you away from things that would make you have to think hard, to take responsibility. By the same token, the Langdellian classroom is legal education on the discount plan: One professor holds sway over a hundred students, dazzling them with imponderable questions and trick riddles. The system has a big stake in formalism. How can we change that without changing the material conditions of our work— that is to say, virtually everything else?"

"Ouch," said Rodrigo, whether because I swiftly and sneakily seized the check the waiter had deposited next to me, probably as the most senior-looking diner at the table, or because of the pungency of the question itself, I could not tell. "You seem to have got me, Professor. As you know, I'm highly sympathetic to the neo-Marxist approach. And now I see that I may have fallen prey to idealism, to thinking that if one simply names and recognizes an evil, it will go away by itself. It obviously won't. The profit motive causes law firms to take on a certain structure, including hiring dozens of young associates they have no intention of making partner and dispatching them to the library to write endless formalistic briefs, for which in turn they charge the client a great deal of money, necessitating that the lawyer on the other side write yet another massive case-cruncher, and so on forever. If the modes of production, the system of incentives, stay the same, tinkering with legal education or scholarship won't help. Law practice gets more and more arcane just as the student pool becomes more and more talented, with LSATs, grades, and numbers of applicants soaring. Competition becomes ever more fierce for seats in law schools. Students become more cutthroat and less collegial than before, then go out into practice, where they become even more that way. And the law schools cater to the large-firm mentality that now defines law practice. The cost of legal education skyrockets; students leave with huge debts; so they must practice in the large firms, which pay the best salaries. The young associates lead lives of overwork, stress, competition, and early burnout."

"Not a very appealing prospect," said Giannina wryly, "for someone who is just starting out. But maybe we can say that identifying an evil is the first step. And discovering its source the second. If so, we've made some progress. At least I've decided to focus on issues that really matter."

"I'm betting your grades won't go down, if you do," I said.

"I hope you're right," said Rodrigo with a laugh. "Our family income rides on it."

After a pause, I said: "I wonder if the profession's dissatisfactions and pathology will eventually stimulate change."

"Women *have* been getting some firms to adopt measures like maternity or family leave, part-time tracks, and childcare support," Giannina pointed out.

"And those are all to the good," Rodrigo agreed. "But I think the Professor is saying that the public's discontent may prove to be a more vital stimulus."

"I wouldn't be surprised," I said. "As my old friend Derrick Bell has pointed out more than once, interest convergence is almost everything. If the public, including the big corporate clients, decide that lawyers are an expensive, nettlesome luxury, prone to tie a case up in knots, perform endless research, and postpone or interfere with an eventual resolution—"

"Nothing like a reality check for a person with a slight case of schizophrenia," Rodrigo echoed.

"Minorities and the poor have long known that the legal system is stacked against them," Giannina observed. "As the economy increases the disparity between high- and low-wage earners, the middle class continues to grow. Unless these consumers fall below the absurdly low cutoff for publicly funded legal aid, they won't qualify for any form of legal assistance. And the regular kind is simply too costly and intimidating. The big law firms, anxious to perpetuate profits, seek out big and wealthy clients, usually corporate ones, leaving middle Americans without affordable legal services."

"Something has to give," Rodrigo summarized. "Costly, nitpicking, formalistic lawyering, as we've said, is not the solution. It's not craft, despite what our three authorities think. In fact, it's the very contrary and what is causing all the trouble."

I signed the credit-card bill the waiter had brought. "Would the two of you like to meet my other daughter and see the baby sometime?"

Giannina looked at Rodrigo. "We'd love to," she said. "How about this weekend? We'll all be back home by then. My moot court reply brief is due Friday, so I'll be feeling less pressured."

I told them I'd check with my daughter and son-in-law and jotted down the address for them on a napkin. "She's been hoping to meet you. She's thinking of going to graduate school when the baby gets a little older, and, would you believe, one of the options she's thinking about is law school. I'm sure she'll have a lot of questions."

We soon parted, Rodrigo and Giannina back to their hotel, me to my daughter's home across town. As I rather sleepily rode the taxi through the darkened streets, I reflected on what we had said. The public is certainly disenchanted with law. Lawyers, too. But was legal formalism the cause, as Rodrigo had argued? Or was it a type of refuge sought by a beleaguered profession? Was it *both* cause and effect? Would outsider jurisprudence, with its emphasis on narrative and creativity, provide a solution? Rodrigo had argued once before that only outsider thought could release a deadlocked West from decline and stasis.[71] Could legal storytelling and the fresh, pungent insights of writers like Derrick Bell, Mari Matsuda, Margaret Montoya, and, indeed, Rodrigo, lead the way to a humanized law and better relations with our various publics?

All this had a personal dimension as well, in light of my own daughter's plans. I looked forward to her meeting in a few days with Rodrigo and Giannina—what fortune to have them as role models!—and wondered, idly, about the wisdom of my own partial self-exile from my native country, where so many intriguing currents were playing themselves out, ideas being tested, new approaches to scholarship surging forward almost daily.

"That's the street," I told the cabbie. "Turn here please."

The key was under the mat, just where my daughter had told me it would be. I resolved to take a look at my visa and ask the dean a few questions when I got back home.

Notes

1. Drafted by a prestigious committee of lawyers, judges, and academicians, REPORT OF THE TASK FORCE ON LAW SCHOOLS AND THE PROFESSION: NARROWING THE GAP, LEGAL EDUCATION, AND PROFESSIONAL DEVELOPMENT (1992) (the "McCrate Report"), recommends a series of changes aimed at making legal education more practical by emphasizing the teaching of skills and values.

2. Harry T. Edwards, *The Growing Disjunction Between Legal Education and the Legal Profession*, 91 MICH. L. REV. 34 (1992).

3. Paul D. Carrington, *Of Law and the River*, 34 J. LEGAL ED. 222 (1984).

4. Associated with Christopher Columbus Langdell and the early Harvard School, legal formalism holds that law is a science; that the principles of this science are to be found through the study of case decisions; that these principles form a vast, comprehensive set; that each legal problem has one right answer; and that the purpose of legal education is to instill the principles of inductive and deductive science through a case-centered, Socratic dialog. Formalism went into decline with the advent of Realism during the 1920s but has been making a comeback. *See* Pierre Schlag, *Normative and Nowhere to Go*, 43 STAN. L. REV. 167, 180 (1990).

5. John Dart, *Public's Esteem of Clergy Slipping, Gallup Poll*, L.A. TIMES, Oct. 2, 1993, at 11; Alan M. Slobodin, *Pro Bono Should Be Free Choice*, NAT. L.J., May 25, 1992, at 13; see also Marilyn Kalfus, *Public Perception of Lawyers Declines in Two Opinion Polls*, ORANGE COUNTY REGISTER, Dec. 12, 1988, at A-1; The Gallup Poll, International Social Statistics, Feb. 1994; U. Connecticut, Roper Center Public Opinion On-Line (1992, available on LEXIS-NEXIS). *See id.* (1996), reporting lawyers trusted least of eight professions included in poll; Gordon Black, USA Today (on WESTLAW POLL database) (1996 Roper Center for Pub. Op. Res.).

6. Rep. of Comm. on Professionalism to the Board of Governors and the House of Deleg. of the ABA, "In the Spirit of Public Service." A Blueprint for the Rekindling of Lawyer Professionalism (1986); Barbara Sheehan, *Lawyers Urged to Address Criticisms of Profession*, N.J. LAWYER, Dec. 26, 1994, at 9.

7. *Anti-Lawyer Attitude, supra.*

8. *Id.*

9. *Id.*

10. *Free Choice, supra.*

11. *Id.*

12. *Id.*

13. Andrea Sachs, *Have Degree, Will Travel: Fed Up with Thankless Conditions, Many Lawyers Are Taking a Hike,* TIME, Dec. 11, 1989.

14. *Id. See* MARY ANN GLENDON, A NATION OF LAWYERS 29–31, 69 (1994); SOL LINOWITZ, THE BETRAYED PROFESSION 22, 31, 128 (1994).

15. *Fed Up, supra.*

16. FULL DISCLOSURE: DO YOU REALLY WANT TO BE A LAWYER? (Susan Bell ed., 1992).

17. DEBORAH ARRON, RUNNING FROM THE LAW (1989).

18. Steven Keeva, *Opening the Mind's Eye,* A.B.A.J., June 1996, at 49. NATION OF LAWYERS, *supra* at 37; BETRAYED, *supra* at 2, 24; Richard Delgado & Jean Stefancic, *Panthers and Pinstripes: The Case of Ezra Pound and Archibald MacLeish,* 63 S. CAL. L. REV. 907, 920–21, 929–31, 936 n. 228 (1990).

19. Sheila Neilson, *What Firms Do to Alleviate Attorney Dissatisfaction; Drastic Times Call for Drastic Measures,* ILL. LEGAL TIMES, Oct. 1995, at 6; Lynne Pregenzer, *Substance Abuse Within the Legal Profession,* 7 NOTRE DAME J.L. ETHICS & PUB. POL'Y 305, 306, 351 (1993); Timothy Harper, *The Best and the Brightest, Bored and Burned Out,* A.B.A.J., May 15, 1987.

20. *Drastic Measures, supra.*

21. *Best and Brightest, supra.*

22. *Id.; Nation of Lawyers, supra* at 29.

23. *Best and Brightest, supra.*

24. *Id.*

25. Richard L. Fricker, *Frankly Speaking: Conversations with Seven Lawyers,* A.B.A.J., Dec. 1992, at 69.

26. *Taking a Hike, supra;* Martin Wald, *Why a Law Firm Is Not a Business,* LEGAL INTELLIGENCER, Nov. 27, 1995, at 3.

27. *Best and Brightest, supra; Quality Time, supra; Running from the Law, supra.*

28. NATION OF LAWYERS, *supra* at 37–51; BETRAYED, *supra* at 29; *Best and Brightest, supra; Blue-Collar Law,* CONN. L. TRIB., Nov. 20, 1995, at 39.

29. *Uncivil Lawyers: Or Just Bad Image,* N.J. LAWYER, Jul. 24, 1995, at 1; interview with Andy Taslitz, Professor of Law, Aug. 18, 1996 (member of task force addressing this problem).

30. *Not a Business, supra; Bad Image? supra;* BETRAYED, *supra,* at 10, 14, 18, 104.

31. Rocco Cammarere, *How Lawyers See Their Image: From Bad to Worse,* N.J. LAWYER, Apr. 29, 1996, at 1.

32. *Id.*

33. *Justice Laments Legal "Capitalism,"* DENVER POST, May 26, 1996, at 17-A.

34. A NATION OF LAWYERS (1994).

35. THE TRANSCRIPT, Spring 1996, at 5.

36. BETRAYED, *supra* at 10, 67, 88, 134; *Quality Time, supra; Mind's Eye, supra.*

37. On Legal Realism, see sources cited *supra*. An approach to law that developed during the 1920s as a reaction to the crude scientism of Langdellian thought, Realism argued that law's essence is not science or any other form of mechanical precision, but experience. According to the early Realists, judges decide cases on the basis not of precedent, blindly and mechanically followed, but of politics, practicality, instinct, experience, and wise social policy. Realism later spun off critical legal studies, feminism, critical race theory, and other such approaches. *See generally* THE POLITICS OF LAW (David Kairys ed., 3d ed. 1998).

38. *See Rodrigo's Tenth Chronicle: Merit and Affirmative Action*, 83 GEO. L.J. 1711 (1995), introducing "Laz," Rodrigo's young colleague and best friend at the law school. A conservative, Laz serves as the faculty adviser to the local Federalist Society and engages in spirited and freewheeling discussions with Rodrigo over faculty politics, race, and affirmative action. *Id. See also Rodrigo's Fourteenth Chronicle: American Apocalypse*, 32 HARV. C.R.-C.L. L. REV. 275 (1997) (Rodrigo and Laz discuss America's racial future).

39. 5 U.S. 137 (1803) (holding that courts have the power to review and overturn legislation).

40. *Of Law, supra* at 224, 226.

41. BETRAYED, *supra* at 88.

42. *See* Lani Guinier, Michelle Fine, Jane Balin, Ann Bartow, & Deborah Lee Stachel, *Becoming Gentlemen: Women's Experiences at One Ivy League Law School*, 143 U. PA. L. REV. 1 (1994).

43. Guinier, *supra.*

44. ANARCHY AND ELEGANCE: CONFESSIONS OF A JOURNALIST AT YALE LAW SCHOOL (1991).

45. *See* Duncan Kennedy & Peter Gabel, *Roll Over Beethoven*, 36 STAN. L. REV. 1, 10 (1984).

46. *E.g.*, MICHEL FOUCAULT, POWER-KNOWLEDGE: SELECTED INTERVIEWS & OTHER WRITINGS 1972–1977 (1980); P. BERGER & T. LUCKMAN, THE SOCIAL CONSTRUCTION OF REALITY (1967). *See also* Derrick Bell & Erin Edmonds, *Students as Teachers, Teachers as Learners*, 91 MICH. L. REV. 2025, 2038 (1993) (Judge Edwards's article a throwback to positivism).

47. 304 U.S. 64 (1938).

48. *Id. See also* CHARLES A. WRIGHT, FEDERAL COURTS 374, 377 (5th ed. 1994) (on *Erie's* prominence and importance in American law).

49. My colleague Leon Letwin first pointed out this mystifying quality of the famous case to me.

50. 41 U.S. 1 (1842).

51. For information on the makeup of the state and federal judiciaries, see generally ALMANAC OF THE FEDERAL JUDICIARY (Christine Housen et al. eds., 1996)

(two-volume set containing profiles and evaluations of all judges of the United States district and circuit courts); 1995 JUDICIAL STAFF DIRECTORY (Ann L. Brownson ed., 1995) (containing 1900 biographies of federal judges); THE AMERICAN BENCH (Marie T. Finn et al. eds., 1995/96) (comprehensive biographical reference to the American judiciary, containing nearly 18,000 biographies of judges from all levels of both the federal and state court systems); see also Susan Maloney Smith, *Diversifying the Judiciary: The Influence of Gender and Race on Judging*, 28 U. RICH. L. REV. 179, 179-81 (1994) (laying out statistics that show the relative lack of women and minority judges in both federal and state courts).

52. *See Symposium: Critical Legal Studies*, 36 STAN. L. REV. 1 (1984).

53. Mark Kelman, *Trashing*, 36 STAN. L. REV. 293 (1984).

54. *Id.* at 1928.

55. *E.g.*, CATHARINE MACKINNON, FEMINISM UNMODIFIED (1987).

56. *E.g.*, Derrick Bell, *Racial Realism*, 24 CONN. L. REV. 363 (1992); Richard Delgado, *Shadowboxing: An Essay on Power*, 77 CORNELL L. REV. 813 (1992).

57. Geoffrey C. Hazard Jr., *Justice Marshall in the Medium of Civil Procedure: Portrait of a Master*, 80 GEO. L.J. 2063 (1992).

58. Herbert Wechsler, *Toward Neutral Principles of Constitutional Law*, 73 HARV. L. REV. 1 (1959).

59. Thomas Ross, *The Rhetorical Tapestry of Race: White Innocence and Black Abstraction*, 32 WM. & MARY L. REV. 1 (1990); Thomas Ross, *Innocence and Affirmative Action*, 43 VAND. L. REV. 297 (1990).

60. Neil Gotanda, *A Critique of "Our Constitution Is Color Blind,"* 44 STAN. L. REV. 1 (1991).

61. Geduldig v. Aiello, 417 U.S. 484 (1974).

62. *E.g.*, International Shoe v. Washington, 326 U.S. 310 (1945).

63. *See, e.g.*, NORMAN VIEIRA, CIVIL RIGHTS 228, 231–33, 238, 252 (1990).

64. *See* Chapter 7, this volume.

65. THE COMING RACE WAR, chapter 3 (on merit and affirmative action).

66. Pierre Schlag, *This Could Be Your Culture—Junk Speech in a Time of Decadence* (Book Review), 109 HARV. L. REV. 1801–1820 (1996).

67. Richard Delgado & David Yun, *Pressure Valves and Bloodied Chickens: An Analysis of Paternalistic Objections to Hate-Speech Regulation*, 82 CAL. L. REV. 871, 881–83 (1994).

68. Pierre Schlag, *Your Culture, supra*, at 1816.

69. Kohn, *Between Good and Bad, Research Shows Believers No More Likely to Love Their Neighbor than Nonbelievers*, S.F. CHRON. & EXAMINER, July 8, 1990, This World, at 15.

70. RONALD K.L. COLLINS & DAVID M. SKOVER, THE DEATH OF DISCOURSE (1996).

71. THE RODRIGO CHRONICLES, *supra*, at chapter 1.

10

Rodrigo's Notebook

Race, Resistance, and the End of Equality

Introduction: In Which Rodrigo and I Meet at His Law School in the Wake of a Somber Event and Ponder the Future of Radical Social Thought

"Professor!" my young friend exclaimed, leaping up from his desk and shaking my hand warmly. "It's great to see you! Come in. I just got your message that you'd be back in town. Did you get mine?"

"I did," I said, easing my body, tired from the crosstown walk, into Rodrigo's comfortable office couch. "Did you say you had student advising today?"

"I do. I'm sure you know the routine," Rodrigo replied. "We're expected to stick around our offices, dispensing advice about careers and class sequences, as if I really knew anything about bills and sales. I had a crowd this morning, but it's been slowing down the last hour or so. Can you talk?"

"I'd love to so long as you're free. I'm happy to just sit here, cool off, and catch up on what's been happening with you and Giannina."

"What brought you to town during your semester off?"

"A funeral, I'm afraid" I replied. "When you're my age, you'll see that these things start to happen with depressing regularity. I just gave the oration in honor of an old friend and colleague at the Legal Defense Fund. We'd known each other for nearly thirty years."

"I'm sorry," said Rodrigo. "Anyone I know?"

"I doubt it," I replied. "An old-time civil rights litigator called Yancey, who labored in the trenches for most of his life. His wife died a few years ago, and his children are fully grown. He'd been retired for some time, but even so, a huge crowd turned out in his honor."

"As well they should," Rodrigo said. "Now I see why the dark suit. You look warm. Can I offer you a drink?" Then with a smile, "Something other than coffee?"

"No, thank you. But I think I'll take my coat off, if you don't mind. If your students come in, I might go get something cold from one of the vending machines downstairs. Can I bring you anything?"

"No, I'm fine. Can you join us later? Giannina and I are having a few friends over, including Laz and his partner."

"I'd love to. How's Laz these days?"

"Very happy. He says that after getting over the initial shock, his parents are taking the news surprisingly well. But how are you? I hope you're not taking your friend's death too hard."

"As well as can be expected. He died peacefully, although the last time we talked—only a month ago—he was questioning his whole life's work. He said the country's mood on civil rights is worse than it was when he started.[1] I tried telling him these things are cyclical, but he didn't seem comforted. He was one of the unsung heroes of his age. It definitely makes me conscious of my own mortality," I mused.

"Oh, Professor. You're going to live forever," Rodrigo replied, with a quick look of alarm.

"I doubt it," I replied. "And when I do depart this vale of tears, I've left instructions to be buried quietly in a simple ceremony. So don't worry that you're going to have to compose a thirty-minute speech."

"That would come easily," Rodrigo replied. "But I hope I don't have to give it for a long time. Do you really think these things are cyclical?"

Just then, a pair of young-looking students materialized at Rodrigo's door. "Excuse us, Rodrigo," one of them said. "Can we drop off these course lists for you to look over? We'll get your comments after class tomorrow, if that's okay."

"Of course," said Rodrigo, and I passed the papers from the youths over to his desk. With a wave of thanks, the two disappeared.

"Nice kids," Rodrigo commented. "They're both in my civil procedure class."

I smiled at Rodrigo's calling anyone kids. *This profession ages you fast*, I thought. "You seem to have good rapport with them," I said. "Mine haven't called me by my first name in thirty years. And I doubt that's cyclical."

Rodrigo waved off the compliment. "They're not above giving me a hard time, on occasion. But you mentioned something earlier that grabbed my attention. Tell me about your sense that civil rights progress is cyclical. Laz and I were talking about this not too long ago. But you've been around longer than both of us put together, and know the big picture."

In Which Rodrigo and I Discuss Laz's Theory
of What Lies Behind the Current Wave of Racial Retrenchment

"Older doesn't necessarily mean wiser," I said. "But I do agree with Derrick Bell and Rudy Acuña that things never seem to get permanently better for blacks and Latinos in this country.[2] Peaks of progress, like *Brown v. Board of Education* or the striking down of Proposition 187 in California,[3] are just followed by another wave of retrenchment."

"Like the current one with English-only laws, restrictive immigration reform, and the virtual dismantling of the welfare net, Head Start, and affirmative action programs that used to enable a few people of color to rise,"[4] said Rodrigo. "Do you remember when the three of us were talking about the potential for a racial cataclysm?"

"I do," I answered. "And it was your conservative friend Laz, if I recall, who suggested that all the pushing, goading, and cutting of programs of importance to minorities—and little cost to elite groups—could be the sign of an impending race war."[5]

"Right," Rodrigo replied. "Otherwise, why would the political right be trying to eliminate affirmative action? I could see railing at it, cutting it back, maybe. But not eliminating it outright, like they're trying to do with referenda in California and other states and through bills in Congress. It's really been a great boon for conservatives, the proverbial goose that laid the golden egg. It enables them to rally support among working-class whites and to depict liberals as unprincipled. It reliably delivers votes, time after time. You would think they would want to preserve affirmative action at all costs."

"So, according to Laz, their campaign to end it, along with the other repressive measures they're spearheading, can only be seen as a throwing down of the gauntlet. With the increase in the population of color, whites soon will cease to be a majority. At that point, political power should, log-ically, shift to minorities. On some level, elite white groups know this and will not allow it to happen. Conservatives in think tanks and elsewhere have decided, perhaps unconsciously, that it's time to take a stand.[6]

"It's the oldest trick in the world," Rodrigo said. "Provoke your enemy into responding, then slap him down."

"Any uprising by blacks and browns will be put down," I said, "just as it was during the sixties. But this time, repressive, not beneficent, legisla-tion will be put in place, penalizing black gatherings, curtailing political rights, and building more prisons, all to prevent a peaceful shift in power."[7]

"That's pretty much where we left off before. But the other day, Kowal-sky and I broadened things somewhat. You see, it's not just conservatives who are spoiling for a fight. Even liberals like Todd Gitlin and Richard Rorty are withdrawing support.[8] Some have even turned far right, estab-lishing conservative think tanks and centers to roll back social pro-grams."[9]

"I can think of a few," I said, shuddering. "And they're very effective. They bankroll thick volumes of impressive-looking pseudoscholarship, produce an unending stream of snappy position papers for members of Congress, dispatch speakers to every corner of the country, and run train-ing camps for young conservatives, judges, and policy analysts. Funded by well-heeled, conservative foundations and philanthropists, they've succeeded in just a few years in shifting the country far to the right.[10] The left has nothing comparable. What do you think it all means?"

"In our very first conversation years ago, when we had just met, we ob-served how northern European culture has produced relatively little fine art, music, and literature. It has, instead, pioneered linear thought, which gave it some initial advantages in inventions and warfare, which in turn enabled northern Europeans to conquer more peace-loving nations."[11] Rodrigo looked at me expectantly.

"Yes, I recall. My memory isn't that bad," I smiled. "And I remember I took serious issue with you. I bet your friend Laz objected strenuously, too?"

"Not at all. His own ancestral country has been overrun several times. But he went on to describe a more general pattern that not only explains our current troubles but also interest convergence and Derrick Bell's con-jecture."[12]

"You mean his theory, set out in an article by that title and a casebook, that the ebb and flow of blacks' fortunes responds not so much to altruism or evolving social conscience as to the material interest of elite groups?"

"Exactly," Rodrigo replied. "Laz put forward a single, simple theory that explains both Bell's conjecture and what we see going on today. It's not exactly what you and I came up with about linear thought, but a sort of corollary."

"Great minds sometimes run in the same gutter," I said. "What did he say?"

"He didn't agree that northern Europeans are naturally, or culturally, linear thinkers and inclined to crank out inventions and weapons endlessly. Like you, he could think of too many exceptions. He thought instead that the West is basically expansionist, territorial, and unable to coexist peaceably with others."

When Rodrigo paused expectantly, I interjected: "You mean they didn't learn to share in kindergarten? This sounds like some kind of touchy-feely, pseudotherapeutic theory, not like Laz at all."

Rodrigo smiled. "There's more," he said quietly. "Engrained in the Western view of our human condition is the idea of unceasing competition. That's why capitalism and free-market approaches and not, say, socialism, resonate so well in this part of the world. Most Western people, and virtually all in northern and central Europe, believe that peaceful coexistence with others is the exception, that wherever two people of radically different kinds meet, one is destined to conquer and subjugate the other."[13]

"Hmmm," I said. "Scandinavia is not particularly capitalist. And as I said to you before, non-Western nations also have been guilty of great cruelty on occasion. But you might have a point. I can think of many examples of Western expansionism and bellicosity: manifest destiny. The relocation and near-extermination of the Indians. The wars with Spain and Mexico, Vietnam. . . ."

In Which Rodrigo and I Apply Laz's Theory to the American Judiciary

"Kowalsky mentioned those examples and many more," Rodrigo continued. "He also pointed out that the notion of constant warfare infects the courts. Our adversary system is much more gladiatorial than that of most other countries, even England, where the common law was born. Some of our greatest judges were Social Darwinists, whose attitudes toward other races included the notion of ceaseless hostility. Oliver Wendell Holmes was a camp follower of the American eugenics movement who saw sterilization of persons afflicted with feeblemindedness as a civic duty, like thinning a herd, necessary to protect society in general. He saw mental defectives as a sort of legion at war with the rest of society." [14]

"Sterilization and eugenics are making comebacks," I added.[15] "And I've read that judicial review of social legislation, going back to Lochner[16] and even before, shows a hostility toward the lower class, which judges often see as engaged in class warfare against their betters, with populist legislation being a prime example."[17]

"And we both know of *Plessy v. Ferguson*, which upheld formal separation of the races on the ground that equality is a pipe dream and that the destiny of the black race is to be permanently inferior to, segregated from, and subjugated by the white," Rodrigo said.

"And before that, *Dred Scott v. Sandford*," I added, "which held that blacks are a race unfit for citizenship because of their innate intellectual and moral inferiority."

"Not to mention certain latter-day cases," Rodrigo pointed out. "In *Croson* the Supreme Court came close to saying blacks in city government cannot be trusted to craft an evenhanded affirmative action program.[18] Apparently, only whites can. And just before you came in I read a commentator who wrote [Rodrigo held up a hand while he rummaged through a well-worn reprint lying on his desk]: "Quote, 'In all of these social relations, from the late nineteenth century well into the . . . twentieth, we can see how the premise of fundamental hostility and the judicial endorsement of that premise led not simply to drawing sharp lines of differentiation . . . [but] also . . . to the escalating brutalization of the vulnerable people on the disfavored side.'"[19]

"That's quite a passage," I said, peering at the article on Rodrigo's desk. "Who's the author?"

"Robert Burt, citing a federal judge named David Bazelon," Rodrigo replied. "My friend Laz has some good company."

"I seem to recall a book on a related theme," I said.

"Right," Rodrigo said. "Entitled *The Constitution in Conflict*[20] and written by that same Robert Burt, it shows that the Supreme Court's experience with war, including our own Civil War, colored its fear of organized labor, which it sees as potentially wild, reckless, and out of control."

"Like a foreign army," I said.

"Exactly," Rodrigo replied. "And it occurs to me that our law of mental commitment, at least until very recently, reflected the same sort of we-they thinking."

"We certainly drew sharp lines between ourselves and the mentally ill," I agreed, "performing lobotomies, electric shock therapy, putting people away under atrocious conditions for long periods of time, long after other countries had abandoned these practices."[21]

"We impose harsh punishment on criminal offenders, as well," Rodrigo added. "Our rates of incarceration and capital punishment are among the highest in the world, especially for black men.[22] We execute juveniles and pregnant women, practically alone in the industrialized world. Here's another quote from that author: 'Today, the dominant voices in our judicial, as well as our political, institutions emphasize human differences more than commonalities . . . based on the premise that social hostility is widespread and incorrigible, that harmonious social relations among differing groups cannot reliably be achieved.'"[23]

At that moment, a somewhat agitated student burst in and told Rodrigo how upset she was that her favorite environmental law class had been cancelled. Rodrigo patiently explained to her the procedure for petitioning to have it restored, then, after she left, commented, "She's certainly ready for battle."

"Although she's doing it through established processes," I said, then felt foolish for having uttered such a platitude.

"The faculty committee will never grant her wish," Rodrigo replied, a little wistfully. "They rarely do so when a student demand costs money. Maybe it is class warfare."

"Originally, students ran the universities, hiring the professors and setting up the curriculum. In other societies, students play a more active role in university affairs," I added.

"Not here," Rodrigo said. "We have exactly one student on each of the faculty committees. Students from the various ethnic associations used to be able to see admission files and interview applicants. No more. We took that power away from them just last year."

"Maybe the school fears reverse-discrimination suits," I hazarded.

"Affirmative action is certainly under attack these days," Rodrigo said. "Conservatives want to end it altogether."

"Not all conservatives," I said. "Laz doesn't, and at the national level, Jack Kemp and a few others want to see it continued, if in a different form."[24]

"Many large businesses, as well," Rodrigo seconded. "But this isn't stopping the hard right, which has the ear of the citizenry right now. For the first time ever, polls show that a majority of white Americans favor abolishing affirmative action. A whole generation of leaders and profes-

sionals of color is about to be obliterated. How unfair! And so unde-
served. People of color have been some of our more peaceful, long-suffer-
ing citizens, have started no wars, amassed few if any weapons, and engaged in little civil disobedience except of the peaceful, prayerful
variety."

The phone rang suddenly. "Hello?" answered Rodrigo. "Yes, he's here!
We'll be leaving shortly. I won't forget." Rodrigo hung up. "That was Giannina, reminding me to pick up something on our way home. Where
were we?"

"The West does not believe in peaceful coexistence, you were saying.
At first, I thought the whole idea was outlandish. But now I'm not
so sure. Laz's theory does explain a great deal. In some eras, people
 of color are no threat to elite whites—during periods of full employment,
or during wartime. Or when foreign relations dictate that we mind our
manners at home. But when none of these is in effect, society returns
to business as usual and minorities suffer. But if the West, as you say, is
inclined to see the world in black-white, militaristic terms, what's to
be done about it?"

In Which Rodrigo and I Discuss Minorities'
Predicament and Whether Current Radical
Thought Offers a Solution

"We didn't have time to talk about that," Rodrigo replied. "Laz had a call
from his parents, who were still trying to come to terms with his announcement. We agreed to talk about it more the next time we met.
Which will be [Rodrigo looked at his watch] less than an hour from now."

"Do we need to get going?" I asked.

"Technically, I'm supposed to sit here for another thirty minutes, although I doubt anyone else will come. Let's talk a little longer, then go.
What do you think progressive people should do?"

"I was hoping to hear what your generation thinks. How about critical
race theory? Do you think it offers a way out?"

"I wish it did," Rodrigo began, slowly. "But I have my doubts. If anything, some of critical race theory's leaders—the blacks, anyway—are
softening their stance, adopting an ingratiating manner toward whites,
writing about racial healing. One sees books like *My First White Friend*.[25]
Others are writing about the spiritual crisis in black leadership.[26] One article calls for a therapeutic race theory, in which everybody would ex-

change stories of oppression.[27] Another urges that the search for interracial justice begin by acknowledging the humanity of the people you have been oppressing and issuing a heartfelt apology. A third scholar, in a much-heralded book about crime, actually called for a "politics of respectability" in which decent, law-abiding black folks would distance themselves from black criminals and gang members and call for more, not less, criminal enforcement and crackdowns.[28] Even Chicanos and Asians are preaching forgiveness and reconciliation."[29]

"All of which I gather you think is exactly the opposite of what's needed?" I asked.

"I do. But first, recall how critical race theory began in the early 1970s, as bright lawyers all across the country realized, more or less simultaneously, that the gains of the heady civil rights era had stalled and, in many cases, were being rolled back. New approaches were necessary to deal with a less sympathetic public and the new forms of institutional, subtle, and unconscious discrimination that were making their appearance. As Alan Freeman once put it, if you are up a tree and a flood is coming, sometimes you need to risk climbing down before seeking shelter in a taller, safer one."

"And so early articles took issue with neutralism, color blindness, the requirement of discriminatory intent, and other mainstays of liberal racial jurisprudence," I added.

"Right," Rodrigo replied. "And for good reason. Liberalism, with all its defects—its incrementalism, perverse neutralism, and lack of staying power—posed the major hurdle to racial reform. Thus, early works questioned whether liberalism promotes the cause of social reform more than it hinders it or urged the legal system to address unconscious or institutional discrimination."

"I agree that is the course the early movement took," I said. "Although today scholars are writing about perspective, multiple consciousness, essentialism and antiessentialism, and many other ideas imported from philosophy and critical social science."

"All of which are interesting but nevertheless an evasion. The primary obstacle to racial reform today is not liberalism, much less an inadequate account of the self, but rather out-of-control, rampant, in-your-face conservatism. And the principal challenge for racial reformers—in my opinion, at least—is not to write yet another article on the phenomenology of multiple consciousness or the need for universal love but to resist the conservative juggernaut that is rapidly revising the American landscape, appointing conservative judges, enshrining antiminority attitudes and measures into the law, repealing welfare, and rolling back three decades of civil rights progress."[30]

"So critical race theory, because it began with a quarrel with liberalism and has not changed with the times, is missing the boat?"

"I'm afraid so," Rodrigo said sadly. "I just got back from one of the group's annual meetings. The panels and plenary sessions sounded the softest, most conciliatory notes imaginable. Others dealt with multiracialism and the new census category. Only a few concerned such survival issues as the role of the criminal justice system in the black community, jury nullification, or restoring welfare rights."

"Maybe that's a problem inherent with academics. Removed from reality, we're always looking for interesting problems to solve and theories to critique, rather than coming to grips with the real-world problems of the community of color. Perhaps the action is in the courts, with the unfinished program of the various legal defense funds and people like my friend Yancey?"

In Which Rodrigo and I Discuss Whether Litigation and Law Reform Offer Promise for Beleaguered Communities

"I don't think the solution lies there, either," Rodrigo replied, shaking his head. "As we said earlier, judges, including Supreme Court justices, believe in eternal conflict, too. The Court interprets any antidiscrimination measure as an assault on whites.[31] Consider how it has limited equal protection doctrine and interpreted civil rights statutes so as to make it harder for one of us to sue under them."

"I know what you mean," I said. "Cases requiring proof of intent, tight chains of causation, expanding defenses such as business necessity, and limiting the relief a court may order. Any measure aimed at making things better for minorities, such as voting districts drawn to increase the chance of a black or brown representative, will be struck down unless it passes the test of strict scrutiny. Maybe Yancey was right after all."

"Giannina and I were talking about this the other day. The Supreme Court has made it much more difficult to prove a case of discrimination than one for, say, breach of contract, tort, or fraudulent conveyance. In virtually every area of civil litigation, the plaintiff must prove only by a preponderance of the evidence that a certain type of legally redressable harm occurred. With discrimination, the plaintiff's task is much harder.

Burdens of proof, evidentiary rules, res judicata principles, and presumptions are all stacked against you. You must prove everything virtually by a criminal standard. Sometimes the new tests make it even harder than that."[32]

"It sounds like equal protection doctrine is unconstitutional under itself!" I exclaimed. "When you think about it, this handicapping of one area bespeaks discrimination, pure and simple. It seems that courts simply don't want blacks and others winning their cases. When a nice, white suburban family is injured in a car accident or cheated in a consumer transaction, they do. It's as simple as that."

We were both silent for a moment, absorbing the quandary our analysis had left us in. Then I continued: "So, if neither critical race theory nor litigation is the solution, what is? One time, you suggested terrorism and forceful disruption."

"That was years ago," Rodrigo said. "Today, I think one has to be more guarded. The right is spoiling for a fight. One doesn't want to play into their hands."

"Then what?"

In Which Rodrigo Outlines a New
Program of Resistance and Social Reform,
Then Goes Off to an Uncertain Fate

"I think the answer may be resistance, but of a somewhat less frontal sort than we discussed before. I've been rereading W.E.B. DuBois, Martin Luther King, and Mahatma Gandhi. I think we may have to go back to these sources. Antonio Gramsci's prison writings, too.[33] And have you read the work of Oscar 'Zeta' Acosta, the radical lawyer-novelist,[34] and of Cesar Chavez?"[35]

"Chavez, yes. Architect of the farmworkers' movement and organizer of a series of successful grape boycotts in California and elsewhere, he's a prime champion of grassroots organizing and resistance. Acosta's work I'm less familiar with."

"I can lend you a book of his, if you like. Giannina and I have been taking turns reading it. Entitled *Uncollected Essays,* it describes the career and life of a legendary Chicano lawyer activist. Raised in California, Acosta attended law school in San Francisco, after which he immersed himself in 1960s counterculture, taking drugs, meeting famous rebels, and trying to decide on a direction in life. After a short but unsatisfying period as a Legal Services lawyer, he decided to become a solo practitioner, concentrating on political cases. He represented Chicano activists charged with crimes in connection with high school walkouts, and one time he sued all the judges of the Los Angeles superior court to show their class biases in selecting members of the grand jury. He ran unsuccessfully for Los Angeles County Sheriff. A charismatic figure, he disappeared suddenly off the coast of Baja California in 1972 and is presumed dead."[36]

"Quite a story," I said. "If he were alive today, I imagine he would have much to say about what we should do."

"I suspect he would, although I'm not sure how much sympathy he would have with critical race theory. He'd be out in the trenches, like your friend Yancey, or splitting his time between bringing cases and street organizing."

"What about the legal storytelling strand of critical race theory? Acosta was a great storyteller, himself. Maybe he'd approve of what writers like Derrick Bell and Patricia Williams are doing."

"Possibly, although I suspect he would say things are so bad we don't really need stories anymore. All we need to do is tell the truth."

"Some friends I know are actually doing that," I replied. "Did you read the news stories the other day about how the U.S. Justice Department is beginning to collect documentation on past discrimination in various industries? They hope to show that affirmative action measures in those areas meet the compelling state interest test the Supreme Court now requires."[37]

"I did," Rodrigo replied. "And are your friends doing something similar?"

"Yes. In hopes of preserving diversity programs in higher education, they are collecting archival evidence and oral histories of racial discrimination in three states. After *Hopwood*[38] and *Podberetsky*,[39] colleges and universities may not consider race in admission and scholarship programs. The Supreme Court is expected to hand down a similar ruling in one of two cases making their way up to it.[40] If the Court strikes down the diversity rationale for affirmative action—"

"Which everyone thought *Bakke*[41] stood for," Rodrigo interjected. "But the Fifth Circuit in *Hopwood* rejected."

"Yes. Then the only basis left will be reparations, that is, making amends for past discrimination. Under this approach, institutions can be required to admit minorities from groups they have excluded in the past."[42]

"An odd situation for a conservative judiciary to leave things in," Rodrigo mused. "It will require digging up dirt on every single institution.

Instead of leaving the past buried, as the more forward-looking diversity rationale does, it entails researching the sordid history of Jewish quotas, tacit or explicit rules against admitting Negroes, whites-only fraternities, and more."

"Exactly," I replied. "In Colorado, for example, the government was controlled by the Ku Klux Klan as late as the 1920s.[43] Texas universities maintained an explicit color line until the early 1970s.[44] In many states, high school counselors and university recruiters worked together to see that the children of respectable, middle-class, suburban families got in while the unwashed went to community colleges if they went anywhere at all.[45] In others, university planners located new campuses in white towns in order to cater to a certain kind of constituency.[46] In towns such as Boulder, Colorado, land use controls and zoning, abetted by a powerful environmental movement and fueled by university interests and investment, kept housing prices so high that the town has a negligible minority population."[47]

"And your friends are bringing all of that out?"

"That and more. Just as the Justice Department is doing with workplaces and industries," I replied.

"And researchers in Mississippi recently brought out that the state had maintained an official, but secret, department aimed at resisting desegregation and discrediting civil rights workers and organizations," said Rodrigo.[48] "But do you think any of this will work?"

"It's hard to say," I replied. "The courts are not above changing the rules as plaintiffs start deploying empirical proof with telling effect. We've seen that happen in employment discrimination.[49] And in *McClesky v. Kemp*,[50] the Supreme Court rejected an almost overpowering case, based on statistical disparities, that the state of Georgia was executing blacks disproportionately compared to whites, especially when the victim was white."

"And you think they would do it with higher education, too?" Rodrigo asked.

"It would be all too easy. They could start by holding that collusion between universities and other bodies, such as local chambers of commerce, town councils, high school counselors, or campus planners, was irrelevant or mere societal discrimination of a form that law does not recognize.[51] They could shrink the time window so that a university that discriminated blatantly until recently and enjoyed a justifiably bad image in the minority community and drew few applicants would be let off the hook.[52] They could even hold that the requisite unit is the individual department, so that an English department could not engage in affirmative action merely because a hundred other departments in the university discriminated."

"Theoretically, they could require a showing of proof with respect to every single chair or professorship!" Rodrigo exclaimed. "And that the university discriminated five minutes ago and with respect to this very same applicant or one almost identical to him or her. Nobody will be able to meet burdens like that."

We both started as a middle-aged man carrying a briefcase materialized in Rodrigo's doorway. "If they don't know it by now. . . ." he said with a smile.

"Oh, we're heading off soon," Rodrigo said, half standing as though to introduce us. But Rodrigo's visitor disappeared with a wave and a quick smile at me.

"That was Jurnegan," Rodrigo explained. "My best friend on the faculty after Laz and easily the most liberal. He volunteered to chair the admissions committee, even though we're likely to be sued this year and he'll be a defendant."

"My," I said. "That's putting your body on the line. I've been sued one time in my life and hated it. Even though I was a litigator before entering teaching, it's always different when it's you being sued. I think I could never get used to it, no matter how often it happened."

"Speaking of putting your body on the line," Rodrigo said, "we'll have to be moving along fairly soon. My office hours end in five minutes, and we don't want to be late for dinner. We're picking up some takeout at a place Giannina and I like. By the way, I hope you still like Italian?"

"Of course," I said, nodding enthusiastically.

"Giannina is making a few things, including a cold soup that's to die for. We don't want to be late."

"Sounds good to me," I said, picking my coat up off Rodrigo's couch. "I'm ready when you are."

Rodrigo turned off the light and locked his office door. As we rode the elevator down to the parking structure in the basement of his law building, Rodrigo said, "I hope we get some time over dinner to talk about some ideas Giannina and I have been tossing around for a program of social change and resistance."

"I'd like nothing better," I said.

Rodrigo quickly perused a notepad he pulled out of his breast pocket, then fished out his car keys. Later, in reconstructing the afternoon, I returned to this small action on Rodrigo's part, which struck me as odd at the time. The quick-witted Rodrigo had never been at a loss for words or ideas. Yet there he was, consulting some sort of list he had made. I resolved to ask him about this later, if I got the chance. As it turned out, I did not.

The evening was warm and convivial. After a quick stop to pick up food, Rodrigo and I arrived at his and Giannina's apartment just as Laz and his friend were driving up. Although I had hoped Rodrigo would tell me more about his plan, this was not to be. Laz's new friend, Enrique, turned out to be a documentary filmmaker, some of whose films I had seen and admired. The three of us immediately zeroed in on Enrique, whose work seemed so much more interesting than our own, and the rest of the evening was consumed in learning about the film industry. I recall another incident from that night—learning, from a slightly embarrassed Rodrigo, that Giannina was pregnant. *So that accounts for her radiant beauty*, I thought, for his companion looked even more strikingly beautiful than usual that night. I immediately went to the kitchen, where she was ladling out the cold cherry soup, and congratulated her.

The evening ended with warm embraces and vows all around to get together soon. Still curious about the content of Rodrigo's notebook, I called him a few days after I arrived home. When I got no answer, I assumed it was because Rodrigo was caught up in the usual end-of-semester exam-writing, grading, and graduation exercises. Days stretched into weeks. In the meantime, the news contained reports of several events that made me wonder if Rodrigo might be behind them, including a street demonstration, some op-ed columns that seemed to mirror his thought, and an outbreak of student activism on several campuses. Then, in late summer I received a six-page letter from him, postmarked from an unfamiliar city, that began with apologies for the long gap in communication and continued:

And so, Professor, I hope you'll forgive me for not being a better correspondent. At our dinner, I was hoping to share with you some news of Giannina's and my plans. As you know, I've been up for a sabbatical for sometime. Well, it finally came through, along with a modest grant that Giannina and I had applied for to a small, liberal foundation. As you can tell from the postmark, we've set up a small nonprofit organization with seed money from the grant, in a storefront in a decaying midwestern industrial city not too far from where we used to live. Part think tank and part activist center, it combines scholarly activity and grassroots activism. Giannina, whose pregnancy is going very well—she's feeling fine, now that a short bout of morning sickness is behind her—is the center's director. I'm in charge of development (which means fundraising—a new role for me!) and research. Laz plays a small role, as well. The enclosed booklet describes our three-part program, which, as you'll see, includes policy analysis, community organizing, and youth training in a unified effort aimed at counteracting the right-wing juggernaut and, we hope, serving as a model for similar centers around the country. I see no reason why the left should meekly give in, when we have just as much brainpower, ideas, and will as the right and, in addition, are better positioned to appeal to students, workers, and the community of color. Our general approach is resistance—the very theme you and I were discussing that day in my office. In fact, you'll see from the booklet that we've stolen an idea or two from you. Currently, we have five scholars on full-time fellowships, including some whose names I'm sure you will recognize, at least the ones in law. In addition, we have up to eight others who bring their own funding or are on sabbatical, their salaries paid by their schools. We're about halfway through raising money for a senior megachair for you. I realize I should have asked you about this, but I assumed you'd be interested and that your institution wouldn't mind lending you to us for a couple of years. If the timing's bad, I'm sure we can get a lesser figure to keep the chair warm for you until you're ready.

You may have seen coverage of some of our efforts, although the reporters are not always good about attribution, which, as a fundraiser, bothers me. I've included press clippings, stuck inside the booklet, showing what we've been up to. We've had a few threats, which we hope will settle down by the time you get here. One anonymous letter took issue with something one of our fellows proposed in an op-ed column, not too subtly pointing out what happened to those black churches and abortion clinics. I don't take these threats too seriously, but I have arranged for a security guard, especially when I've been away. Laz's brother actually runs a private security agency. Giannina thought it a waste of money, but I thought it a wise investment, especially since sometimes the scholars prefer to work at home or go off to the library, and she's there alone. We hope to get away to Baja for a few days next month, before she gets too uncomfortable to travel, for a few days of rest and recreation. You know how much she loves desert plants and scenery.

Well, that's all the news for now. Please let me know what you think of our agenda and whether you'd consider a one- or two-year fellowship sometime soon. We'd be honored to have you—you could work on any of a number of things within our broad areas of interest—and despite the plain, storefront appearance of the place, we have pretty good support inside. You'll find an office manager, a secretary (maybe we'll have a second one by the time you get here), copy machines, and some new computers, although I know you're not much into technology yet. We can also help you find nice but inexpensive housing nearby. If you come the year after next, Giannina and I will be back at our schools, but Laz, who is up for a sabbatical, has agreed to run things that year and will be sure you're comfortable and have what you need. After that, we'll reevaluate where we are. If one or two big grants come through, we'll hire a full-time director (are you possibly interested?)—and maybe install a sprinkler system, just in case that character who wrote to us is actually serious.

Best regards,

The letter was signed by Rodrigo and initialed by Giannina, who added a short postscript about the baby, a book she was finishing, and how much they hoped I'd say yes.

The letter arrived at my mailbox at work, so that it wasn't until that evening that I was able to take a closer look at the brochure Rodrigo had enclosed. Full-color photographs showed clean, spacious, but unpretentious offices, computers, a conference room, and a small library. The roster of fellows did indeed include some well known figures in civil rights, labor, and political science, and one novelist. But what riveted my attention was the itinerary of action and research the institute sponsored and already was well on the way toward accomplishing, judging from the list of activities and news clippings reproduced in the back pages.

A dizzying array of programs ranging from a speaker's bureau, book-length scholarship, writing aimed at the mass media, and grassroots activism jumped off the page. Many of the activities reminded me of news stories I had read earlier, perhaps discussions Rodrigo and I had had. One section of the brochure outlined a program of resistance for laypeople, including teaching courses on the notion, which Rodrigo and I had discussed before, of the 'race traitor,'[53] and training sessions aimed at showing community and college activists how to challenge standardized testing that disadvantages not just blacks and Latinos but working-class whites and anyone else who attended poorly funded schools or could not afford an expensive test-prep course. Another project, directed by a well-respected professor of pharmacology, took aim at drug laws, one prong mobilizing citizens in favor of legalizing relatively harmless substances like marijuana, the other at challenging racially discriminatory enforcement and legal classifications, such as ones punishing crack cocaine use and possession much more seriously than the powdered drug. Another, which I had read about in the newspapers, used animal analogies, drawn from the South African antiapartheid literature,[54] to deride conservatives who opposed affirmative action, misappropriated and distorted Martin Luther King's language,[55] and cut welfare and educational programs for the poor.[56] (My favorite animal analogy was *The Ostrich*, for reasons you might imagine.) Another aimed at integrating trade unions and teaching white workers how to make common cause with blacks and browns against the corporations and capitalists that oppressed them both;[57] a final project offered research support for black activists urging reopening of the case for black reparations in light of recent payments to Asians, Indians, and Jews.

Another section outlined programs for students. It included advice on how to establish a liberal campus newspaper to counter the host of lavishly funded conservative ones that had been springing up around the country[58] and announced an upcoming summer training course for editors. Another program sponsored the writing of short pamphlets for aspiring campus leftists, providing them with ammunition to counter professors from the National Association of Scholars and showing them how to hold their own in debates with members of the Federalist Society.[59] One program, which struck me as quite daring, showed how students incensed by campus cutbacks in affirmative action could throw their support behind right-wing legislators and governors urging cutbacks in higher education and the elimination of public law schools—a call that I remember had been sounded by a Republican governor in California.[60] *That should get the attention of sluggish campus liberals!* I thought. A final project funded student law review notes and comments supporting measures for legislative reform. One that struck my eye proposed a scheme for imposing state and federal income tax on the main forms of socially constructed privilege, such as the one that allows men to earn one dollar for about every 70 cents that women earn for similar work. *Now that's an equalizer!* I thought, then immediately wondered how it would affect me. As a man, my salary is higher than that of many women law professors I knew of similar seniority and much greater talent than mine. Yet as a man of color, I could remember many times when I had been passed over for a promotion, appointment, chair, or other reward that went to a less deserving (in my opinion) white male who pursued a more mainstream course of scholarship. *Overpaid by one measure, shortchanged by another,* I thought.

But the section I examined most closely was labeled "Faculty Activism and Scholarship." It set out a program of sabbaticals and one- and two-year fellowships, at full pay, under which scholars like me could spend time at the center pursuing work of their own choosing. The brochure mentioned, as possibilities, several projects that immediately appealed to me. One was a litigation internship, in which senior and midlevel law faculty members could brush up on practice skills under the direction of an appellate lawyer-supervisor, after which they would undertake their own cases or affiliate with one of several litigation centers located in the region dedicated to combating environmental racism, reforming poverty law, and pressing for workplace equity. A second project looked to exposing hypocrisy and elite self-interest in legal theory and bringing this to the attention of laypeople. The brochure mentioned a study, under the direction of a young scholar whose work I admired, that examined the doctrinal presuppositions of the absolutist wing in the hate-speech debate. Among other things, the scholar expected to demonstrate, in a report she planned to distribute to minority leaders and campus administrators, the economic-elitist underpinnings of *New York Times v. Sullivan*,[61] a central case relied on by the free-speech camp. The scholar was documenting the way this cardinal case, which announced a ringing victory for freedom of the press and free speech, really was rooted in the economic self-interest of elite whites. When *Sullivan* laid down near-absolute protection for libelous speech (at the same time making it very difficult for colleges to enact reasonable hate-speech curbs), the computer chip had just been invented. Business leaders could foresee a technological revolution and an economy based on information. When *Sullivan* protected the printed word, then, it was not safeguarding individual speakers so much as the captains of industry and business, who needed a judicial security blanket to protect their profit lines in the upcoming Information Age.

Other professors were at work showing sympathetic judges how to get around harmful precedent in cases dealing with race, workplace equity, and individual rights. One was producing a book showing how Northern judges, before the Civil War, used various dodges to avoid enforcing runaway slave laws.[62] A Latino scholar was writing a manual countering the premises of the turn toward reconciliation among portions of the left. A passage that leapt out at me asked, "How can you forgive someone who refuses to say they are sorry and denies any responsibility for your misfortune and his or her own privilege?" Another was building on the astonishing work of Paul Butler in jury nullification,[63] expanding it to other areas in which ordinary people could turn established legal rules to the advantage of their communities. Some of the examples possessed the blindingly simple, always-there quality of Butler's nullification proposal, making me exclaim, "Of course!" The scholar planned to bring these opportunities to the attention of the minority and poor communities by going on talk radio and publishing columns in black and Latino newspapers, much as Butler had done with his jury nullification proposal. A final scholar was working to find convergences of interest between the principled right and the left and for ways to bring old-time conservatives, like Nathan Glazer, who recently changed his position on affirmative action, into rapprochement with the forces of progressivism.[64]

Shortly after receiving Rodrigo's letter, I began work on my own proposal in hopes that Rodrigo would indeed raise the money for the position he had mentioned. I also made an appointment with my dean to explore her receptiveness to my taking a full year off in the event I was selected. As luck would have it, the dean was on a two-week trip with an accrediting committee to evaluate three new law schools, and so I could not get an appointment until later that month. The day before my appointment, a letter arrived from Giannina. Handwritten, it spoke in urgent but anguished phrases:

Dear Professor,

I have hesitated to write to you until I was more certain of what has happened. It seems Rodrigo has disappeared. We do not know whether foul play was at work or not. As you may know, our center had come under withering attack by the right. At least two conservative congressmen called for an investigation of our tax-exempt status, and a dean summoned one of our fellows home in midyear, charging that the professor had received his sabbatical under false pretenses and that the work of the center had nothing to do with serious scholarship. One of our grantors got cold feet and backed out. And as Rodrigo may have mentioned, we received all those threatening phone calls and letters. One morning, we came to work to find that someone had forced open the back door and started going through our files. Apparently, they didn't count on leftists having a work ethic similar to theirs, for when we arrived a little before 7:30, they took off, not having gotten very far in their dirty work. It cost us several days, photocopying everything to guard against loss.

Then the most terrible thing of all. One afternoon, during our vacation, while I was resting in our hotel, Rodrigo simply disappeared. When he didn't return for supper or his evening run, I became worried and went searching for him with the hotel security chief. It seems Rodrigo may have rented a small boat. The operator of a charter business reported someone who looked like him setting off in a launch, piloted by a competitor, in the direction of some nearby offshore islands. Usually tours like this last only an hour or so, but even so, Rodrigo ordinarily would have let me know before setting off on something like this. Then again, he knew I was feeling slightly ill and planned to sleep a little.

At any rate, a storm sprang up, and no one knows what happened. The skipper of the boat that might have taken Rodrigo out did not return that afternoon, although another operator reportedly saw him a few days later, packing his belongings into a trailer hauling his boat somewhere. I called you frantically several times, but you were out. I don't know whether Rodrigo is alive or dead. I stayed in Mexico for three solid weeks in hopes he would show up, contacted the embassy, the local police, and even the FBI, which was not at all helpful, insisting he must have run off with a local woman or to escape a gambling debt, which we both know is of course ridiculous. They even asked if he used drugs!

I'm back at my law school, planning to take my final exams early in case the baby arrives ahead of schedule or I hear something about Rodrigo. I have a full-time detective working on the case and plan to go to Baja as soon as I graduate next month and the baby is born. My parents have agreed to look after the baby, and I'll let you know immediately if I find out something. In the meantime, I'm afraid we must both expect the worst. It's a bitter irony. As you know, another well-known Latino activist disappeared in much the same way. Send your prayers that this disappearance will have a happier ending.

I cancelled my appointment with the dean and waited, hoping fervently for the best. Unfortunately, it was not to be. When Giannina's trip and her detective's efforts produced nothing, I rescheduled my appointment with the dean, asked for two years of unpaid leave, arranged to transfer certain funds I had set aside for retirement, and wrote a long letter to Giannina offering to take over the work of the center where Rodrigo had left off.

Notes

1. On this downturn, see, e.g., JEAN STEFANCIC & RICHARD DELGADO, NO MERCY: HOW CONSERVATIVE THINK TANKS AND FOUNDATIONS CHANGED AMERICA'S SOCIAL AGENDA (1996). *See also* Derrick Bell, *Racial Realism*, 24 CONN. L. REV. 363 (1992); DERRICK BELL, RACE RACISM AND AMERICAN LAW 1–72 (3d ed. 1990) (on "interest convergence" theory of African Americans' shifting legal fortunes); ANDREW HACKER, TWO NATIONS: BLACK, WHITE, HOSTILE, UNEQUAL (1995).

2. Compare Bell, RACE, RACISM, AND AMERICAN LAW, *supra*, with RODOLFO ACUÑA, OCCUPIED AMERICA (1972) (economic-determinist views of black and Latino progress in the United States).

3. Patrick J. McDonnell, *Judge's Final Order Kills Key Points of Prop. 187*, L.A. TIMES, Mar. 19, 1998, at A-3.

4. *See* NO MERCY, *supra*; RICHARD DELGADO, THE COMING RACE WAR? AND OTHER APOCALYPTIC TALES OF AMERICA AFTER AFFIRMATIVE ACTION AND WELFARE (1996).

5. RACE WAR? *supra.*

6. *Id.*

7. *Id.*

8. TODD GITLIN, THE TWILIGHT OF COMMON DREAMS: WHY AMERICA IS WRACKED BY CULTURE WARS (1994); Richard Rorty, *The Dark Side of the Academic Left*, CHRON. HIGHER ED., Apr. 3, 1998, at B-4.

9. NO MERCY, *supra*, at 131–35 (describing former liberals who turned to the right and established centers and think tanks to advance conservative causes).

10. *Id.*

11. RICHARD DELGADO, THE RODRIGO CHRONICLES, chapter 1 (1995).

12. *See* Derrick Bell, Brown v. Board of Education *and the Interest-Convergence Dilemma*, 93 HARV. L. REV. 518 (1980) (civil rights advances correlate more with white self-interest than anything else).

13. *See, e.g.*, Robert A. Burt, *Judges, Behavioral Scientists, and the Demands of Humanity*, 143 U. PA. L. REV. 179, 183–85, 187, 189, 191 (1994).

14. Richard Delgado & Jean Stefancic, *Norms and Narratives: Can Judges Avoid Serious Moral Error?* 69 TEX. L. REV. 1929 (1991) (discussing Holmes's role in eugenics and sterilization movements). *See* Sheldon Novick, *Justice Holmes' Philosophy*, 70 WASH. U. L. Q. 703, 729 (1929) (Holmes urged "putting to death the inadequate" in order to speed up natural selection).

15. NO MERCY, *supra* at 13, 35–44. *See* RICHARD HERRNSTEIN & CHARLES MURRAY, THE BELL CURVE (1995) (exemplifying upsurge of interest in eugenics and race-IQ theories).

16. Lochner v. New York, 198 U.S. 45 (1905).

17. Burt, *supra*, at 189. On the Social Darwinism of Justice Holmes and other American judges, see Louise Weinberg, *Holmes' Failure*, 96 MICH. L. REV. 691 (1997); Letter from Oliver Wendell Holmes to Lord & Lady Pollock (Sept. 20, 1928) in THE CORRESPONDENCE OF MR. JUSTICE HOLMES AND SIR FREDERICK POLLOCK 1874–1932, at 230 (Mark Howe ed., 1941) (on his belief that life is a kind of ceaseless war for survival).

18. City of Richmond v. J.A. Croson Co., 488 U.S. 469 (1989) (striking down Richmond's set-aside program for minority contractors as impinging on rights of non-minorities).

19. Burt, *supra*, at 189.

20. ROBERT BURT, THE CONSTITUTION IN CONFLICT (1992).

21. *See* Ennis & Litwick, *Psychiatry and the Presumption of Expertise: Flipping Coins in the Courtroom*, 62 CALIF. L. REV. 693 (1974) (detailing abuses of therapeutic justice and questioning legal faith in science of psychiatry).

22. MARC MAUER & TRACY HULING, YOUNG BLACK AMERICANS AND THE CRIMINAL JUSTICE SYSTEM: FIVE YEARS LATER (1995); SENTENCING PROJECT, INTENDED AND UNINTENDED CONSEQUENCES 12 (1997); Pierre Thomas, *3 Young Black Men in Justice System*, WASH. POST, Oct. 5, 1995 at A-1.

23. Burt, *supra*, at 191.

24. Frederick R. Lynde, *Managing Diversity*, NAT. REV., Oct. 13, 1997, at 56.

25. PATRICIA RAEBON, MY FIRST WHITE FRIEND (1996) (describing how faith and a change of attitude enabled author to overcome distrust of whites).

26. CORNEL WEST, RACE MATTERS (1995).

27. Angela Harris & Leslie Espinoza, *Afterword: Embracing the Tar Baby*, 85 CALIF. L. REV. 499, 557 (1998).

28. RANDALL KENNEDY, RACE, CRIME, AND THE LAW 12–28 ("The New Politics of Respectability") (1997).

29. Eric Yamamoto, *Rethinking Alliances: Agency, Responsibility, and Interracial Justice*, 3 UCLA ASIAN PAC. L.J. 33, 59 (1995); Jerry Kang, *Negative Action Against Asian Americans*, 31 HARV. C.R.C.L. L. REV. 1, 14 (1996) (advocating racial tactics "that will garner support from the political middle and a post-Adarand Supreme Court").

30. NO MERCY, *supra*.

31. *E.g.*, Thomas Ross, *Innocence and Affirmative Action*, 43 VAND. L. REV. 297 (1990) (describing rhetoric of the innocent white male in Supreme Court jurisprudence).

32. Adarand Construction, Inc. v. Peña, 515 U.S. 200 (1995); Michael Selmi, *Proving Intentional Discrimination: The Reality of Supreme Court Rhetoric*, 86 GEO L.J. 279 (1997).

33. Antonio Gramsci, SELECTIONS FROM THE PRISON NOTEBOOKS (Quentin Hoare & Geoffrey N. Smith trans. & eds. 1971).

34. OSCAR "ZETA" ACOSTA, UNCOLLECTED ESSAYS (Ilan Stavans ed., 1995); Michael Olivas, *"Breaking the Law on Principle": An Essay on Lawyers' Dilemmas, Unpopular Cases, and Legal Regimes*, 52 U. PITT. L. REV. 815 (1991) (on life and career of Acosta as exemplifying dilemma of the activist lawyer).

35. On Cesar Chavez's life and thought, see PETER MATTHIESSEN, SAL SI PUEDES: CESAR CHAVEZ AND THE NEW AMERICAN REVOLUTION (1969); GRISWOLD DEL CASTILLO & RICHARD A. GARCIA, CESAR CHAVEZ: A TRIUMPH OF SPIRIT (1995).

36. Olivas, *supra*, at 851.

37. Michael Higgins, *Plan of Action*, ABA J. Apr. 1998, at 68.

38. Hopwood v. Texas, 78 F.3d 932 (5th Cir.), cert. denied, 116 S. Ct. 2581 (1996).

39. Podberetsky v. Kirwan, 38 F.3d 147 (4th Cir. 1994), cert. denied 115 S. Ct. 2001 (1995).

40. *See* Terry Carter, *On a Roll Back*, ABA J., Feb. 1998, at 54.

41. Regents of University of California v. Bakke, 438 U.S. 265 (1978) (college admissions based on racial quotas unconstitutional, but diversity still a permissible educational objective).

42. *See* Hopwood, 78 F.3d 932, at 948–49.

43. *E.g.*, Richard Delgado, *Why Universities Are Morally Obligated to Strive for Diversity: Restoring the Remedial Rationale for Affirmative Action*, 68 COLO. L. REV. 1165, 1168–73 (1997) (describing events in Colorado history).

44. Daria Roithmayr, *Deconstructing the Distinction Between Bias and Merit*, 85 CALIF. L. REV. 1449, 1476–86 (1997) (describing discriminatory origins of standardized testing).

45. On "tracking" in schools, see JEANNIE OAKES, MULTIPLYING INEQUALITIES: THE EFFECTS OF RACE, SOCIAL CLASS, AND TRADING ON OPPORTUNITIES TO LEARN MATHEMATICS AND SCIENCE (Rand Corp. 1990).

46. *For example*, UC-Davis is located there, not in nearby Sacramento or Fresno; UC-Boulder is not in Denver or Pueblo, and so on.

47. Remedial Rationale, *supra*, at 1168–73.

48. Lewis Lord, *Painful Secrets from the Defiant Years*, U.S. NEWS & WORLD REP., Mar. 30, 1998, at 30.

49. Richard Delgado, *On Taking Back Our Civil Rights Promises: When Equality Doesn't Compute*, 1989 WIS. L. REV. 579 (showing how courts retreated from legal rules as civil rights litigants began to satisfy them).

50. 481 U.S. 279 (1987).

51. Hopwood, 78 F.3d 932, at 949–51.

52. *Id*. at 951–54.

53. RACE TRAITOR (John Garvey & Noel Ignatiev eds., 1996) (describing role of "race traitors"—whites who agree to shed the privileges of whiteness and go through life identifying with blacks, insofar as this is possible).

54. *See* Adam Kahane, *Imagining South Africa's Future: How Scenarios Helped Discover Common Ground*, in LEARNING FROM THE FUTURE: COMPETITIVE FORESIGHT SCENARIOS (Liam Fahey & Robert Randall eds. 1998).

55. NO MERCY, *supra*, at 54.

56. *Id*.

57. *See* Anthony Taibi, *Banking, Finance, and Community Economic Empowerment*, 107 HARV. L. REV. 1463 (1994) for a similar program of economic reform.

58. NO MERCY, *supra*, at 111–14, 118.

59. Compare this suggestion with RICHARD LUNTZ, CONSERVATIVELY SPEAKING (1996) offering arguments designed to crush liberals. Published and distributed by the right-wing Center for the Study of Popular Culture, CONSERVATIVELY SPEAKING is just one of several short, snappy pamphlets aimed at assisting young conservatives in articulating their positions.

60. Mark Walsh, *Wilson Wants to Take a Law School Private*, THE RECORDER, Jan. 11, 1993, at 3 (describing California governor's threat to eliminate one of state's four public law schools).

61. 376 U.S. 254 (1964).

62. Compare with Louise Weinberg, *Methodological Interventions and the Slavery Cases; Or Night-Thoughts of a Legal Realist*, 56 MD. L. REV. 1316 (1997) (describing discomfort of Northern judges confronting cases of runaway slaves).

63. Paul Butler, *Racially Based Jury Nullification: Black Power in the Criminal Justice System*, 105 YALE L.J. 677 (1995) (urging that black jurors vote to acquit black de-

fendants charged under unjust laws or who are no threat to the black community).

64. *See* Nathan Glazer, *Why I No Longer Think Affirmative Action is Unjust*, SACRAMENTO BEE, Apr. 12, 1998, at F-1 (reversing longtime opposition to affirmative action because its elimination is likely to devastate search for social equality); Glazer, *supra* note 46 (same).